W9-BKL-486

The Art of Digital Audio Recording

Gulf Coast State College
Library
5230 West US Hwy 98
Panama City, FL 32401

The Art of Digital Audio Recording

A Practical Guide for Home and Studio

Steve Savage

With photos by Robert Johnson
and diagrams by Iain Fergusson

 DISCARDED

 OXFORD
UNIVERSITY PRESS

OXFORD
UNIVERSITY PRESS

Oxford University Press, Inc., publishes works that further
Oxford University's objective of excellence
in research, scholarship, and education.

Oxford   New York
Auckland   Cape Town   Dar es Salaam   Hong Kong   Karachi
Kuala Lumpur   Madrid   Melbourne   Mexico City   Nairobi
New Delhi   Shanghai   Taipei   Toronto

With offices in
Argentina   Austria   Brazil   Chile   Czech Republic   France   Greece
Guatemala   Hungary   Italy   Japan   Poland   Portugal   Singapore
South Korea   Switzerland   Thailand   Turkey   Ukraine   Vietnam

Copyright © 2011 by Steve Savage

Published by Oxford University Press, Inc.
198 Madison Avenue, New York, New York 10016

www.oup.com

Oxford is a registered trademark of Oxford University Press.

All rights reserved. No part of this publication may be reproduced,
stored in a retrieval system, or transmitted, in any form or by any means,
electronic, mechanical, photocopying, recording, or otherwise,
without the prior permission of Oxford University Press.

Library of Congress Cataloging-in-Publication Data

Savage, Steve.
The art of digital audio recording: a practical guide for home and studio /
Steve Savage; with photos by Robert Johnson and diagrams by Iain Fergusson.
    p. cm.
Includes bibliographical references and index.
ISBN 978-0-19-539409-2; 978-0-19-539410-8 (pbk.)
1. Sound studios. 2. Sound—Recording and reproducing—Digital techniques. I. Title.
TK7881.4.S38 2010
621.389'3—dc22   2010032535

9 8 7 6 5 4 3 2 1

Printed in the United States of America
on acid-free paper

For my daughters Sophia and Thalia.
Thanks for all the hours of training!

Acknowledgments

This book was written because Norm Hirschy at Oxford University Press read something else that I had written. He asked me if I was interested in writing a practical guide to recording, and I was very interested. I had been a professional recording engineer for twenty years, and I had been teaching recording for ten years, so I felt ready to tackle a book of this nature. Norm initiated the project and has nurtured it through each stage—thank you! My first mentor was Brian Risner, who mixed a record I had produced with the artist Bonnie Hayes. Brian had worked extensively with the band Weather Report, and over the course of several projects with him I began to learn how creative the art of recording could be. Brian's ability to create a very productive and positive environment in the studio—while effortlessly handling all the technical requirements—has been a model for all of my work. My good fortune to be teaching in the outstanding Recording Arts program at Los Medanos College has provided the proving ground for much of what is contained here, and it was the site used for much of the photography.

I was delighted to discover Iain Fergusson's diagrams on Wikipedia, and I was able to track him down in New Zealand and engage him to do the diagrams for this book. His work exceeded my expectations and is a model of clarity. The diagrams add enormously to the sometimes laborious descriptions of many recording functions. My only regret is that we have yet to meet in person (the joys and vagaries of the Internet)! Robert Johnson is one of the most outstanding students to have come through my recording classes, and just happened to be a very accomplished photographer as well. His photographs capture details of the recording process that can only be suggested in words. I was fortunate to have a long-term working relationship with Fantasy Studios in Berkeley, California, and was able to access their spectacular studios and mic closet for additional photos included here. I was aided in creating many of the screenshots by long-time musical collaborators Curtis Ohlson and Paul Robinson. Curtis runs Digital Performer in his home studio, as well as being a gifted bass player and producer. Paul Robinson is a Logic user, as well as a wonderfully versatile and talented guitar player.

I am indebted to a long list of artists and producers whom I have worked with over the years for all of the wonderful hours we have spent together in the studio. I have attempted to condense something of the breadth of those experiences and the joy of making records into these pages.

Contents

Introduction

About This Book

Making great recordings requires striking the right balance between technical know-how and a practical understanding of recording sessions. Even in the digital age, some of the most important aspects of creating and recording music are completely nontechnical and, as a result, are often ignored by traditional recording manuals. Getting the best audio recording results often requires as much common sense and attention to the recording environment as it does a deep understanding of the technical elements involved. Too many books about recording provide technical information but don't supply the practical context for how and when to apply the tools and techniques described. This can leave the reader without a sense of priority, trying to figure out what is actually important to the recording process in specific situations. *The Art of Digital Audio Recording* can teach readers what they really need to know to make great-sounding recordings with their computers—the essential practical, as well as technical, information, including:

- What to look and listen for in your recording environment
- Straightforward advice on recording almost any instrument
- The essentials of digital audio workstations (DAWs)
- The essentials regarding recording gear: microphones, mixers, and speakers
- The fundamentals of understanding and applying EQ, compression, delay, and reverb
- The secrets to running creative recording sessions
- The practical application of digital editing, mixing, and mastering
- A special section that identifies the most common challenges of the recording studio.
- Addendum:
  - How to walk into a commercial studio and be the engineer
  - Researching and buying gear: Internet vs. brick and mortar.
- Appendix
  - Digital formats, delivery, and storage

The Art of Digital Audio Recording is a reference manual for the home recordist, a textbook for any basic to intermediate DAW training class, and a primer for the musician who is either doing his or her own recordings or simply wishes to be better informed when working in the studio.

About the Author

My personal path into recording and audio production, and from there to this book, began with a career as a drummer. I played in numerous unsuccessful rock bands, learned some jazz without ever coming close to mastering it, studied and performed African music with a master drummer from Ghana, and spent a couple of years actually making a living as a musician, playing in a dance band. After a short but glorious stint in a punk band, my career transitioned into recording and production.

I discovered that the other side of the glass—the control room rather than the recording room—fit me better, and my career slowly built up around recording. I had a 12-track studio in my garage (equipped with the short-lived Akai recording format) and recorded demos for rock bands for dirt-cheap. One of those bands put its resources together to go into a professional studio to record a single and asked me to be the engineer/producer. There, I got my first taste of making commercial recordings and I was hooked. I recorded a variety of fledgling "new wave" artists' singles and albums in the heady early 1980s, and I cut my teeth on 24-track analog recording. After a stint as house producer for a small indie label—where I built and learned to operate a lovely little state-of-the-art SSL studio (Solid State Logic makes some of the best and most expensive consoles and control surfaces)—I became a full-time independent record producer and engineer.

One tends to get work in areas where one has some successes, so it was through my work with the very talented songwriter Bonnie Hayes that I have ended up working on many singer/songwriter music projects, and after three Grammy-nominated CDs with the master blues artist Robert Cray, I have had the pleasure of working on many blues records. I have also recorded jazz, R&B, rap, hip-hop, country, opera, music for musicals, and children's records. I have been the engineer and/or producer on over 100 commercial releases and have served as the primary recording engineer and mixer on seven Grammy-nominated CDs, including records for Robert Cray, John Hammond Jr., Elvin Bishop, and The Gospel Hummingbirds. I have also taught recording in the Recording Arts Department at Los Medanos College in Pittsburg, California, one night a week for the past ten years. This book is a result of those experiences, both in the studio and in the classroom, along with the countless hours reading various books, trade magazines, and (increasingly) Web sites that provide an endless supply of information and opinion about the world of recording. Through it all, it is my love of music that makes me love my work. I am deeply grateful for the opportunity to have participated in the making of recordings with so many talented artists.

www.stevesavage.net

The Art of Digital Audio Recording

Chapter 1

The Starting Point
Sound Meets the Computer

1.1 Why Computers

The title of this book is *The Art of Digital Audio Recording,* but it will be apparent to even the most casual reader that the book covers a wide variety of topics that extend beyond the specifics of computer-based, digital recording. Nonetheless, the title indicates this book's orientation and that all of the information here is presented primarily in the context of the digital audio workstation (DAW). Even the most basic recording practices have been influenced by the migration from analog to digital recording, and this book maintains its focus on computer-based audio production throughout.

While I don't think I need to convince you that audio production is dominated by computer-based systems, analog gear remains an important part of the recording process. After all, sound itself is an analog phenomenon—created by disturbances in the air—and certain elements such as microphones and speakers remain essentially analog. With other primary recording technologies, such as EQ, the debate regarding preferences for analog versus digital gear is not over (and probably never will be), despite the fact that digital dominates almost every recording environment today. But wherever you stand on the aesthetics of analog versus digital, it is valuable to examine why DAWs represent the standard in contemporary audio production. By detailing the primary advantages of DAW recording over its analog predecessors, I set the context for the remainder of this book.

A brief survey of the primary audio practices includes recording, editing, signal processing, mixing, and mastering. In each of these areas, the DAW has introduced revolutionary capabilities. The most fundamental change from analog production has come in the nondestructive capabilities of DAW recording and editing, but signal processing, mixing, and mastering have also seen dramatic changes in the digital world.

Recording

DAWs generally record to hard drives, which allow data to be stored in any available area of the medium. There is no "erase" head on a DAW recorder—which is to say that it is no longer necessary to erase (or destroy) previous recordings when making new recordings. As long as there is drive space available, further recordings can be made. With the enormous capacity and relative low cost of current hard drives, this effectively means that no recordings need ever be eliminated.

Along with doing away with the need to ever erase anything, nondestructive recording has transformed the recording process by allowing for many more recorded elements to be available in any given project. As you will see in more detail in chapter 4, when I explore virtual tracks, nondestructive recording changes the way people work with audio in more ways than just eliminating the problem of running out of analog-tape tracks. Whole new working procedures have evolved within the nondestructive environment of the DAW.

One such example is the way that nondestructive audio has transformed one of the most basic production practices: punching-in. Punching-in typically involves the rerecording of parts of previously recorded elements. A common example is replacing a line from an already recorded vocal performance. On an analog tape recorder, punching-in required erasing what was previously recorded. This sometimes led to difficult decisions about whether it was worth losing the previous performance in the hope of getting something better. Analog punching-in also involved the potential risk of accidentally losing parts of the recording, because the beginning or ending of material around the part to be replaced might get clipped off if the punch-in was not done accurately enough. With nondestructive recording, these problems have been eliminated. Parts of recordings may be replaced without losing (erasing) the part that has been replaced; you never actually have to "record over" any element, as each element remains stored and accessible from the hard drive. Also, accidental "punches" (recordings) don't eliminate previously recorded material for the same reason—the process is nondestructive so nothing is actually lost. *Nondestructive recording has eliminated many of the most basic limitations of the analog recording process.*

Editing

In regard to editing, new capabilities in the DAW are even more significant than the changes DAW brought to recording. The nondestructive quality of DAW-based editing provides vast new opportunities for audio manipulation. With nondestructive DAW editing, you simply create alternative instructions as to how to play back the audio that has been recorded. Because the manipulation of audio in a DAW is separate from the storage of that audio on the hard drive, you can edit without altering the original recording. This is a major improvement over tape-based editing, which required the physical cutting and splicing of tape. Not only do you no longer endanger the storage medium by cutting tape, you are able to edit much faster and in many more flexible ways than ever possible with tape splicing. *Whole new recording and working procedures are now built around these editing capabilities.* I explore this new world of editing capabilities in much greater detail in chapter 4.

Signal processing

Signal processing has also been transformed by the DAW, though that has been a slower process of change than with recording or editing. Digital EQ, dynamics processing (compression, etc.), and ambient effects (reverbs, delays, etc.) operate in much the same way as they did in the analog world. While it has taken a considerable amount of time and development to produce digital equivalents of these signal processors that compare in quality to their analog relatives, they have finally arrived, though whether they are truly a match for the best of the analog versions is a still very much debated. These processors were already used nondestructively in analog production—applied to already recorded signals and easily altered or removed at any time. The big changes in signal processing have come with wholly new capabilities that were not at all available in analog. These include the ability to speed up or slow down audio without changing pitch and the ability to analyze and alter the subtleties of pitch with tools such as Auto-Tune. There are also an increasing number of processing tools that operate based on a detailed analysis of audio content that is available only through computerized technology. I look more thoroughly at some of these developments at the end of chapter 2, when the discussion goes "beyond" the familiar kinds of signal processing.

Mixing

The DAW has advanced the kinds of control over the mixing stage—controls that were begun when automation and recall began to be implemented in analog consoles. Automation allows for the "automatic" replaying of changes in volume and other typical mixing moves, while recall enables the recordist to regain all of the mix settings at a later time—in order to revise mixes. Suffice it to say that even the early implementation of automation and recall in the analog realm required the interfacing of a computer to control these functions. Now that the entire mixing process may be computer based, the implementation of automation and recall have become much more elaborate and also more reliable.

The DAW has also vastly improved the ability to automate mixing moves off-line, using a graphic interface that provides extremely fine control over desired changes. These features and the evolution of mixing in the DAW are covered thoroughly in chapter 6.

Mastering

The final stage of production—mastering—prepares the final mixes for manufacturing. The combination of digital delivery (from CDs to mp3s and beyond) and DAW production has meant that just about anyone can create a master that is usable for CD manufacturing or online delivery. The large lathes required to create vinyl LP masters are still used for that format, but that has become a very small part of the audio marketplace. New tools for mastering to digital formats such as CDs have resulted in what many believe to be both a blessing and a curse—a blessing for the technologies that allow CDs to sound better than ever, and a curse for the ability to overuse some of these technologies at some significant cost to the original musical dynamics. All of these techniques and controversies are covered in chapter 7. It is noteworthy that books such as this one now cover the practical application of mastering techniques for a broad audience, as these technologies have only recently become available outside of what was once a very specialized (and expensive) mastering facility.

Digital versus analog

The overwhelming advantages of DAW production have resulted in the predominance of computer-based audio production in both amateur and professional music recording. Still, this leaves the question: Does digital sound better or worse than analog? The wide range of opinions you find in a typical audio discussion group suggests that there is no one answer to this question, though I would maintain the following: (1) There are so many factors in creating good-sounding audio (and even in defining what is meant by "good-sounding") that the analog/digital divide is a relatively small element in the overall mix of factors pertaining to quality; and (2) like it or not, we live in a digital audio world and most of us will spend most of our time recording, editing, processing, mixing, and mastering audio in a DAW!

1.2 What Does It Sound Like?

While many things in the digital domain are held over from the analog era, at the same time much has been changed by the DAW environment. For all the changes, one thing—the most important thing—remains the same. This is the guiding principle in audio production: *What does it sound like*? These are the words spoken by Ray Charles in the extraordinary documentary *Tom Dowd & the Language of Music,* which traces Dowd's remarkable career in audio production. Ray is summarizing his point of view about recording and expressing his affection for Tom Dowd, who shared his passion for sound. Ray reminds us to keep the focus where it belongs, on the sound, instead of on preconceived or technically drilled notions of what "proper" technique is. After all, it is only the sound of the recording that the listener hears.

So throughout this book, while the bulk of the time is spent on the technicalities of recording, I have tried not to lose sight of this much more subjective and much more important element in audio production: creative listening. There's a saying in jazz that in order to play "outside," you must first learn to play "inside." This means that the important business of pressing the boundaries and breaking the rules works best when the boundaries and rules are well understood. As with playing music, the art of recording music requires that rules be broken, as well as followed; and as with music, the better the rules are understood, the more effective will be the bending and breaking of those rules. So dive into the technique and the theory, but don't forget to come up for some creative breaths of fresh air!

1.3 Signal Path

Technically speaking, the entire job of a recording engineer is summed up in these two words: *signal path*. The engineers are responsible for what is happening to audio from the beginning to the end—from the creation of the sound waves by the musician playing his or her instrument to the recreation of the sound waves by the speakers in the listener's living room. You might pick up and/or leave the audio chain at intermediate points—perhaps starting as samples used in drum loops and ending when you turn the project over to a mixing or mastering engineer—but in any event, when you work on sound you work within the context of a signal path.

One of the first challenges of signal path is simply getting the sound from one place to the next. Getting the sound from the microphone to the recorder and from the recorder to the playback system can be a challenge in itself. Add a lot of processing gear, such as compressors and EQs, and monitoring demands, such as headphone mixes for musicians, and setting up the correct signal path can be complicated. I can't cover all the contingencies here, but there is much more said about signal path in almost every section of this book. Here, at the beginning, I lay out some basics.

Input and output (I/O)

To start with, signal path is controlled by the most essential technical element in audio production: *input and output* (often shortened to I/O). Following the audio's signal path (also referred to as *signal flow*) is the same as following a series of inputs and outputs, and it is often referred to with another essential audio term, *routing*. I/O routing can be pretty straightforward in some cases. For ex-

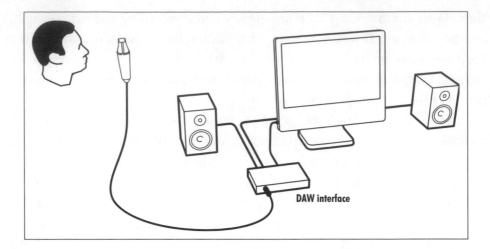

DIAGRAM 1.1

A simple signal path: DAW mic input to speakers

ample, in a system where the DAW interface has a microphone preamp built in, the signal path may be as simple as: sound source inputs to microphone, microphone outputs to the mic input of the DAW audio interface, the interface outputs to the computer software that then handles the signal path until it is output back to the interface, and from there output to the playback system. In this example, assuming the DAW interface is already set up, the only external connection the engineer might have to make is connecting the mic to the mic cable and the other end of the mic cable to the audio interface.

On the other hand, the signal path's I/O routing may be very complicated, involving multiple inserts, patch bays, talkback systems, cue systems, and so on; and each of these may be either hardware of software based (or both)! All of these topics are considered later in this book, with the focus on the software/DAW side, but it is not possible for any book to cover all possible routing schemes. What's more, the internal routing systems within each brand of DAW may differ in both terminology and implementation. You will have to learn the I/O intricacies for your own setup, but it is most helpful to begin with this basic understanding: *every thing you do starts with signal path, and signal path is defined by the input and output routing series.*

The I/O model of signal path is also in operation on a micro scale within each dedicated audio element, from stomp box to DAW. You may have seen schematics for individual pieces of gear or computers; they are complex grids of inputs and outputs. Audio engineers do not necessarily need to be familiar with the internal workings of audio or computer hardware, though sometimes that knowledge can be helpful. In any event, a strong understanding of signal flow between gear and within software is essential for making good recordings.

Troubleshooting

Troubleshooting—an unfortunate but inevitable part of every engineer's job—also starts with signal path. The best way to troubleshoot most technical problems is to investigate each step of the signal path, starting with the sound source, in order to determine where the problem lies. Whether it's poor-sounding audio, noisy audio, or simply no audio at all, the problem lies somewhere along the signal path. A systematic approach that examines the I/Os from the beginning of the chain is the best and most efficient approach to solving almost all technical problems.

Combining the technical and the aesthetic

Recording always entails finding the proper balance between creative and technical demands. Considering the question "What does it sound like?" takes you to the essence of the creative process—ultimately, that is all that matters. Understanding the basis of signal path takes you to the essence of the technical process; these are the nuts and bolts that must serve the aesthetic. With this grounding in both the aesthetic and the technical, you are ready to tackle some much more specific elements in audio production, beginning with the essentials of where and how recordings are made.

Chapter 2

The Essentials
Where and How Recordings Are Made

2.1 Recording Rooms and Control Rooms

This opening section is going to be relatively brief—there are many other resources for delving more deeply into the technicalities of acoustics. For most of us, the idea of constructing a space for recording is not part of our work. We recordists are either stuck with certain spaces because we need to work there or perhaps we live there, or we choose to work at studio spaces based on experience or reputation. Nonetheless, there are some fundamentals about sound and space that every recordist should be familiar with, and some helpful ways of dealing with basic problems. I summarize the issues concerning the physical space that we work in, dividing them into three basic topics: isolation, frequency response, and ambient characteristics.

Isolation

In regard to isolation, there are two main considerations and one basic rule. The things to consider are isolation from outside noise leaking in, and isolation of inside noise leaking out. Either or both may be problematic, but the solution for both—the one basic rule—is the same. That rule is that isolation is created by a combination of mass and density. That is to say, the way sound leakage (in either direction) is prevented is with sufficient mass that is sufficiently dense. What this means in practical terms is that a 12-inch-thick wall of dense concrete will isolate sound much better than a typical wall with two sides of sheetrock and an air cavity in between. Studios in highly problematic environments have been known to resort to sheets of lead as part of the wall structure. This can work well, but can also be very expensive. If you are fortunate to work in an environment with little external noise and without sensitive neighbors, you may have far fewer concerns about isolation. If not, density and mass are your primary allies.

There is sometimes the notion that more absorption inside a room (from acoustic panels, to foam, to rugs, to egg cartons) will help solve leakage problems. Unfortunately, this not the case because materials that absorb sound do so primarily in the higher frequencies and leakage decreases as the frequencies rise. That is why, if you are standing outside a rehearsal studio with a rock band playing inside, what you hear is primarily the bass guitar and the kick drum. It is the low frequencies that permeate walls, mess with recordings, and anger neighbors, no matter how much dampening material you have inside the room. Only mass plus density will do an effective job of decreasing low-frequency transmission.

Isolation does have an effect on the sound in the room, as well. The more low frequencies are prevented from escaping because they are reflected with sufficient density and mass (such as a concrete wall), the more problems with bass buildup within the room itself. Solving transmission problems to and from the outside also engages you in absorption and reflection issues within the room.

There are many other technical elements that will affect transmission, reflection, and absorption; and there are a variety of books that describe common approaches to designing and constructing walls, floors, ceilings, doors, windows, and HVAC (heating/venting/air-conditioning) systems for recording studios. These topics are beyond the scope of this book, but very much worth exploring if you are building or remodeling a space to be used for recording.

Frequency response of a room

The *frequency response* of a room refers to the way different frequencies, from low to high, respond to the absorptive and reflective qualities of room surfaces. Every room has different frequency responses—the room's physical characteristics cause boosts or dips at certain frequencies—and these are variable to a certain degree, depending on where you are in the room. Generally, a room with relatively even frequency response across the spectrum is desirable, and this can be achieved by controlling the absorption and reflection of sound in the room. There are some basic principles in this regard, though the details of designing and controlling room acoustics can get very complex and the results are never thoroughly predictable.

There are two main enemies of a smooth and even frequency response. These are right-angle corners and parallel surfaces. Right angles, such as at most wall-to-wall, floor-to-wall and ceiling-to-wall intersections, will reflect sound back in the same direction as it has come from and will cause the most prominent frequencies of the original sound to build up, disrupting an even frequency

PHOTO 2.1 and 2.2

Various wall treatments

response. Opposing parallel walls (or floor and ceiling) create *standing waves* by reflecting the sound back into its own original path. Standing waves also amplify certain frequencies and disrupt an even frequency response. Unfortunately, most typical room construction uses a lot of right angles and parallel surfaces. Bass frequency buildup and other unwanted room resonances are an especially common problem that may be made worse by right angles and parallel surfaces, but they are not necessarily eliminated by a room with neither of those design characteristics. A whole world of "bass trap" solutions has evolved, and there is some debate as to how effective any or all of these solutions may be. There are companies that specialize in products to aid in improving room acoustics without your having to tear down walls and rebuild. These are definitely worth exploring unless you are working in an already well-designed acoustic environment. Most home and project studios need some acoustic treatment.

Besides creating problems, room reflections can be used to help solve problems. While many room frequency imbalances caused by reflections may be solved using absorptive material, too much absorption can make a room

PHOTO 2.3

Diffuser

sound "dead," and that may not be desirable either. For many recording applications, the recording environment works best when it is enhancing the natural acoustics of the musical instruments. There has been a trend toward using diffusers to balance the frequencies of room reflections. Diffusers are specially built wall treatments that break up frequencies and scatter them to reduce unwanted frequency buildup. The physical dimensions of the wells of the diffuser (width and depth) determine the frequencies that are affected. Diffusers have the advantage over absorption materials in that they don't make rooms excessively dead sounding, but absorption materials can eliminate some problems too severe for diffusers to manage. The best solution for treatment of critical audio spaces usually involves a combination of absorption, bass trapping, and diffusion.

Room ambience (reverberation)

The ambient characteristics of a room refer to the quality and length of the delays created when sound is produced in the room. *Reverberation* is the audio term used to describe these characteristics. It is the reflections of sound off all of the various surfaces in a space, returning with varying degrees of intensity and delay to the listener, which create reverberation. The ambience created by room acoustics is the "natural" reverb, whereas the addition of "artificial," or simulated reverb, will be covered later in this chapter (section 2.7). As noted, room acoustics may create problems for recordings (standing waves, bass buildup, etc.) or may enhance recordings by the addition of a pleasing spatial quality. Using microphones to capture the ambient characteristics of a room is covered later (section 2.3).

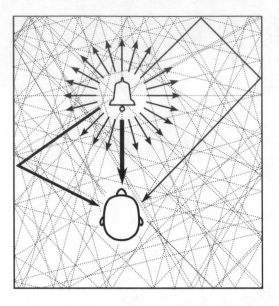

DIAGRAM 2.1

Reflecting sound

The reliance of recordings on room acoustics for ambience varies enormously. Vocals are often recorded in small booths with lots of absorptive material on the floor, walls, and even ceiling. The microphone is close to the singer's mouth, so the minimal room reflections are virtually nonexistent relative to the direct sound of the voice. In contrast, many orchestral recordings are made primarily using microphones at some distance from the orchestra, and the room ambience is a major portion of the sound that is captured along with the direct sound from the instruments. Along this continuum lies the world of aesthetic decisions about how to place the musicians and microphones and how to capture or minimize the effect of room acoustics on recordings. Such decisions begin with your feelings about the particular acoustics of the room you are recording in. In most instances, it is impossible to completely separate decisions about how to record from considerations regarding room acoustics, so the aesthetics of recording are always intertwined with the sound of the recording room.

Control room acoustics

For many home recording environments, there is no difference between the recording room and the control room—that is, they are the same room. This can be a workable recording situation, but it does challenge the acoustic priorities of the two functions—recording and listening. In general terms, it is desirable to minimize the effects of room acoustics in the listening environment (control room), whereas room acoustics are often used to enhance the recording environment (studio room). Those using one-room studios inevitably have to seek some compromise between these two priorities. Certain trends have encouraged a relatively easy mix: using more diffusion in control rooms has made them more "live" sounding without too many frequency irregularities. This increases the aesthetics of listening compared to overly dead rooms and makes the room more suitable for recording, as well.

2.2 Studio Monitors

Studio monitor speaker selection and placement are critical to your work environment. Your primary studio monitors—usually the near-field speakers—are your most consistent and important reference point for what your recordings sound like. There are a variety of factors to consider in achieving a monitoring environment that you can trust as reasonably accurate.

Near-field monitors

Near-field monitors have long been the principal means of limiting the effects of room acoustics on listening. They also provide a better reference to the "real" world of consumer speakers, which will be what is used by most of those who listen to your recordings. That said, it should be remembered that no speakers eliminate the effects of room acoustics, no matter how near to your ears they are, and no speakers can give you a complete picture of what your recordings are going to sound like out in the real world, because of the wide variety of playback systems (and problems).

Studio monitors differ from most consumer speakers in their basic philosophy. Studio monitors seek a balanced sound, whereas consumer speakers often enhance frequency ranges, effectively "hyping" the sound for the listener (most often with high- and low-frequency boosts). Despite the intentions for studio monitors to be "flat" across the frequency range, this ideal is impossible to achieve. Inevitably, speakers have some variation in frequency response across the spectrum, and crossover points (between the woofer and tweeter or other speaker combinations) provide the greatest challenges in speaker design; they are always compromised in some ways. This is why so many studio monitors are two-way speakers—the more crossovers, the more potential problems.

The overall sound of the speaker comprises its timbre characteristics. These can be described in various ways, but typically you might judge speakers on a scale from smooth to harsh. You might think, "The smoother, the better," but not all recordists would agree. Some find that speakers that have very smooth timbre characteristics don't necessarily translate that well to a wide range of other playback systems. Smooth timbre is good for long listening sessions, but a slightly harsher timbre characteristic might be more "real world"—have more in common with the majority of lower cost consumer playback systems—and therefore translate better in more circumstances outside the studio. I find that some of the finest speakers have a tendency to lull me into a false sense of security—everything sounds good!—so I prefer studio monitors that have a bit of a bite to them, though not too much bite so that they can be listened to for long periods of time with minimum ear fatigue.

When making live recordings in a one-room studio, it is usually necessary for everyone to use headphones (no speakers), so as to limit bleed from the speakers back into the recordings and to prevent feedback. This requires quite a bit of switching back and forth between headphone listening (to record) and speaker listening (to get a better sense of the sound of the recording), but it can be a workable situation. It is important to reference your recordings on your speakers, and not to make sonic judgments based solely on monitoring with headphones.

Powered studio monitors

There has been a growing tendency for studio monitors to come in powered versions—that is, the power amp is built right into the speakers (some manufacturers only make powered speakers). The motivation for this is simple: powered speakers ensure that the amplification for the speaker is properly matched to the speaker design and capabilities. In general, this is a very good development; the only real drawbacks are that it makes the speakers more expensive (though they do have to be powered one way or another, anyway), and it makes them heavier (which can be a bit unfortunate if you are traveling between studios and like bringing your speakers with you). I recommend getting powered studio monitors, if possible.

Near-field monitor setup

Positioning of near-field monitors is an important part of getting an accurate representation of the recorded sound. The basic rule is that the speakers should be the same distance from you as they are from each other, creating an equilateral triangle. This arrangement provides the optimal stereo imaging. If the speakers are too close to each other, the stereo field will sound collapsed; if they're too far apart, it will sound unnaturally spread out. The speakers should be angled toward you (though some recordists like them to point slightly behind their head to lessen fatigue). Proper aiming of the speakers affects the perception of the stereo image and reduces frequency smearing.

The speakers should be isolated (decoupled) from whatever they are sitting on. The best way to do this is with speaker pads such as those sold by Auralex. If the speakers are not isolated, the sound will be transmitted through whatever they are sitting on and it will arrive at your ears prior to the direct sound from the speaker (sound travels faster through solid material). Because the sound is arriving at a different time, there will be phase problems.

It is generally recommended that you set up your playback system along the longer wall of your room so as to minimize reflections off the side walls, but if your room is very narrow, the reflections off the back wall might be a bigger problem and you would be better off setting up facing the narrow side. Reflections off of your console, desk, or tabletop might also create phase prob-

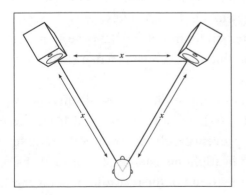

DIAGRAM 2.2

Near-field monitor setup

lems. This can be minimized by angling the speakers up slightly with the tweeters pointing at or just behind your ears. You can also experiment with using extenders to move the speakers closer to you or use stands to move them back if you feel as if you're getting to much reflection from the work surface. Similarly, reflections off the wall behind the speakers or from corners will create phase problems, so it's best to keep the monitors somewhat out in the room and away from walls.

> **WHAT NOT TO DO**
>
> **Do not ignore the basics of speaker placement.** *Do not place near-field speakers up against a wall or in a corner. Be sure that your speakers are isolated from their mounting surface. Take care to have your speakers placed at an equal distance from the listening position.*

Choosing near-field monitors

Probably the most influential element in the effectiveness of near-field monitoring is the familiarity of the recordist with the speakers. Consider the information above and then find speakers you like and stick with them. It's best if you can go to a studio-equipment dealer and audition a bunch at once. Over time you will be able to really trust what you hear from the speakers because you are familiar with them. Eventually you will have heard a lot of different instruments and music through your speakers, and also have had the chance to hear your mixes on a variety of systems. It's important that the speakers and the room have a reasonably flat response, and that they be positioned properly, but beyond that, it is familiarity that will serve you best.

Large monitors

Almost all critical listening is done on the near-field monitors. Large (wall-mounted or soffit-mounted) speakers are nonetheless useful for a variety of other purposes. Large monitors may be used for referencing low frequencies that may not be sufficiently reproduced in the near-field monitor, though subwoofers have become a common alternative for doing this. I generally use large monitors for playback when musicians are recording live in the control room, if they are used to hearing their instruments rather loud, such as with electric guitar players in many rock bands. When there are no problems with leakage or feedback, such as when a guitar player is in the control room but his or her amp is isolated in another room, it can be very convenient to have the musician playing in the control room. This bypasses the use of a talkback system, making communication between you and the musician easier. (I explore this practice more thoroughly in chapter 8, on best practices.) Large monitors are also useful for impressing clients; there's nothing quite like loud playback over big, high-quality speakers, done preferably at the end of the session so as to avoid too much ear fatigue.

Big monitors can be useful for more general listening evaluations if they're accurate across the frequency range, but this is not easy to accomplish. Large monitors are typically farther away from the listening position, so they interact much more with room acoustics than near-field monitors, and this often causes complications in achieving a well-balanced frequency response. Large monitors also usually need to be wall or soffit mounted, and this also can cause problems as the sound interacts with the walls. As a result, it is almost always necessary to EQ the large speakers to fix unbalanced frequency response. To do so properly requires "shooting the room." This is done by broadcasting and measuring various kinds of noise (white noise, pink noise, etc.) through the speakers and capturing it with a well-balanced microphone, reading the results via a spectrum analyzer, and adjusting the frequency balance accordingly, using EQ. It sounds scientific, and it is up to a point, but the variables are enormous: small variations in mic placement can cause different readings, and so on. Shooting a room has become a highly developed craft, with a variety of tools available to aid in the process and with certain practitioners gaining reputations for producing particularly pleasing results. The same set of speakers in the same room can end up with pretty different EQ curve corrections, depending on who "shoots the room."

2.3 Microphones and Mic Placement

Microphones are often at the beginning of the recording chain, and there are an enormous number of microphone brands and types to choose from. There may be no more important element in many recording situations than the selection and placement of microphones. There are complete books about microphones, but here I focus on the practical side of the most common kinds of studio microphones and their uses.

Microphone types

There are two types of microphones used the majority of the time for recording: condenser mics and dynamic mics. *Condenser mics* use a diaphragm that vibrates next to a solid backplate and the mic measures the electrical charge of the movement of the diaphragm relative to the backplate, changing these measurements into an electrical representation of the sound. Condenser mics require external power, called *phantom power*, which is supplied as an option by most mic preamps. *Dynamic mics*, which are also referred to as moving coil mics, capture sound by using a coil attached to the diaphragm that is vibrated in a magnetic field by the movement of the diaphragm. The moving coil creates an electrical current that is a representation of the sound. Here is a list of the primary differences between condenser and dynamic mics:

Condenser Mics:
- Require external (phantom) power
- Provide the greatest detail of frequency response
- Respond quickly to capture leading-edge transients
- May be sensitive to loud sounds
- Are somewhat fragile

Dynamic Mics:
- Do not require external power
- Provide less detail than condenser mics
- Do not respond as quickly to transients
- Are able to withstand loud sounds
- Are quite rugged

There are two primary types of condenser microphones: large-diaphragm condensers and small-diaphragm (pencil) condensers. The primary differences between the two are:

Large-diaphragm Condensers
- Have less self noise and high output
- Have slightly diminished high-frequency response
- May have poor frequency response for off-axis sounds
- May have multipattern switching capabilities

Small-diaphragm Condensers:
- Have slightly more self noise and lower output
- Have a slightly extended high-frequency response
- Tend to have pleasing off-axis capture capabilities
- Most versions require changing capsules to achieve different patterns

On the basis of this information, you can understand why condenser microphones are used most of the time in the studio. The exceptions come primarily when the sound to be recorded is too loud for the sensitive condenser capsule. The most common application for dynamic microphones in the studio is for drums and for miking electric guitar amp speakers. However, this is deceptive, as there are now many new designs of condenser microphones that can withstand high volumes, yet dynamic mics are still most often used for drums and guitar amps. And dynamic mics are sometimes used for almost every other kind of studio recording, including vocals. This is because fidelity—breadth and detail in frequency and transient response—is not the only consideration in choosing microphones. Think back to the "What does it sound like?" criterion

20

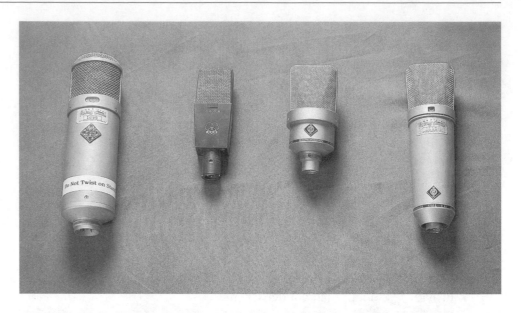

PHOTO 2.4

Some common large-diaphragm condensers, left to right: Telefunken U-47, AKG 414, Neumann TLM-103, Neumann U-87

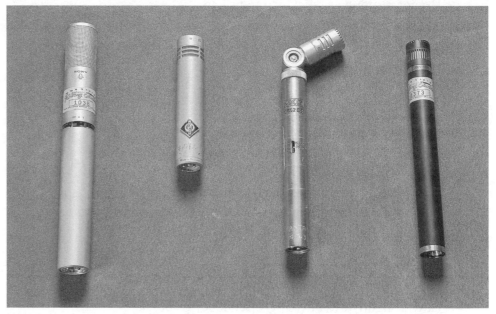

PHOTO 2.5

Some common small-diaphragm condensers, left to right: Sony ECM-22P (electret), Neumann KM-84, AKG C452, Bruel & Kjaer (B&K) 4011

PHOTO 2.6

Some common dynamic mics, clockwise: Electrovoice RE-20, Shure SM-57, Shure SM-58, Shure Beta-58, Shure SM-7, AKG D112, Sennheiser MD-421

from the last chapter; there's a preference for the sound of a less detailed, lower fidelity microphone in certain (sometimes many) studio applications.

There are microphones with technologies other than those used by traditional condenser or dynamic mics, such as ribbon mics, PZM mics (pressure-zone microphones), specialized technologies for miniaturized mics, shotgun mics, and so on. Ribbon microphones, which are a variation on a dynamic mic, have been gaining in popularity and there have been advances made in their ability to withstand higher volume levels and to be more rugged. They have become fairly widely used—especially on guitar amps, as well as for reed and brass instruments—as a result of their balancing the warmth of a dynamic mic and the detail of a condenser mic.

Microphone patterns

There are two primary mic patterns: cardioid and omni-directional. *Cardioid* mics have a directional pickup pattern, meaning they are optimized to pick up sound coming from within the bounds of a directional pattern. These provide excellent fidelity from sounds oriented within the pickup pattern and considerably lesser fidelity for sounds that might be coming off-axis (response to sounds coming from a direction outside the optimal pickup pattern of a directional microphone). *Omni-directional* mics pick up sounds relatively evenly from any direction. Some large-diaphragm condenser mics have variable pattern selection, and some pencil condensers have swappable capsules that provide either cardioid or omni performance.

While microphones operating in omni mode have slightly better frequency response and smoother overall characteristics, they have the disadvantage of picking up a lot of room ambience and limited control over the volume of sounds coming to the mic from different positions. When neither of these things are a problem—such as with orchestral recording, where the idea is to capture the sound of the ensemble and the room acoustics are considered an integral part of the sound—selecting an omni pattern may be a good choice. Orienting omni mics closer or farther from the sound source can also give the recordist a fair amount of control over room acoustics. In most recording instances, however, cardioid (directional) mics are preferred for their ability to capture the maximum direct sound and to minimize room sound and leakage of unwanted, off-axis sounds. Many microphones offer variations on the standard cardioid pattern, providing even tighter directionality, such as with hypercardioid or supercardioid patterns. There are other mic patterns, such as the figure-8 or bi-directional pattern, which provide two opposing pickup patterns, but cardioid and omni-directional patterns are by far the most frequently utilized.

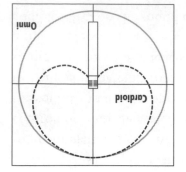

DIAGRAM 2.3

Cardioid and omni-directional pickup patterns

Microphone selection

Remember: *There is no "right" mic for the job, as microphone selection is highly subjective.* Generally speaking, for the greatest detail and fidelity, you would use a condenser. Typically, large-diaphragm condensers are used for vocals, but the sound of the voice, the desired sound, and the available microphones might dictate the use of any of the other types of mics for recording vocals. Where *off-axis* (at an angle to the plane of the element being recorded; *on-axis* means the plane of the microphone diaphragm is parallel to the recorded element) response is a problem, such as with multi-mic setups for ensembles, then pencil condensers might be the best choice. Dynamic mics are often a good choice for loud sounds with a lot of transients, such as drums and guitar amps, and sometimes for horns.

As with speaker selection, familiarity becomes the recordist's greatest asset in choosing and using microphones. Not just familiarity with individual microphones but also developing a familiarity with the quality of sound that different microphone types capture contribute to the recordist's ability to make aesthetic decisions about mics and their effects. (See section 3.3 for more specific information on choosing microphones for individual instruments.)

Microphone placement

After choosing the microphone you are going to use, you have to decide where to place it. The most basic part of that decision is how close to the sound source to place the mic. The proximity to the sound source affects both the detail that the mic is able to capture and the amount of room ambience relative to the direct sound. Studio practices have gravitated toward closer and closer miking techniques in order to capture the most detail from an instrument and to minimize the effects of room ambience—especially now that there are so many alternatives for adding ambience effects later via reverb and delay plug-ins. While close miking is the norm for individual instruments and voices, and it provides excellent results in most cases, it is certainly not the only approach.

Maximum detail is not always desirable. The classic example is in recording stringed instruments. In most cases, you don't want too much detail com-ing from a violin, where close miking may emphasize the scraping bow on the strings. (This is explored more thoroughly in section 3.3.) Similarly, minimizing room ambience is not always desirable. While it gives you the most options for controlling ambience later, sometimes room ambience plays an integral role in the sound and is best captured in the initial recording. Because it is impossible to truly eliminate all room ambience, some decision about balancing direct sound and room ambience is inherent in the microphone placement. When a mic is placed close to the sound source, a difference of 1 inch can have an audible effect on the sound captured. Experience and sensitive listening follow

attention to microphone placement in order to capture the desired results. (Section 3.3 has more specific information on microphone placement for individual instruments, as well as diagrams and photographs.)

As will be emphasized in the discussion on session flow in section 8.1, it is important to keep your priorities straight when it comes to mic placement. Yes, small movements in microphone location will affect the sound captured, but optimal session flow often dictates against taking the time to do a lot of tweaking of mic placement. A musician's state of mind is more critical than small improvements in sound quality. This is why experience is so valuable—it allows you to make good choices quickly, thereby maintaining the creative flow of the session. Sometimes musicians thrive on taking the time for a lot of experimentation with mic placement (and sometimes the budget allows it, as well), but it is up to the recordist to help determine the proper balance between tweaking and keeping the session moving.

Phase and polarity

Phase and polarity are two key elements of concern whenever there are two sources for the same sound. These are central considerations in the stereo miking techniques covered in the sections immediately following this one. Phase issues are also key in the next chapter, which discusses strategies for various instrument recordings, many of which use more than one source and thereby create issues concerning phase relationships. Before I cover stereo mic techniques, though, you need to be clear on how phase and polarity work.

A *phase relationship* in recordings generally refers to the potential time difference between when a single sound source is received by two different microphones (or other signal path). Variations in mic placement or other factors may introduce differing amounts of delay before the signals are recorded. If the peaks and troughs of the waveforms are received at the same time, they are said to be "in phase" and the sound is reinforced by the two sources. If the sound is received at two different times, depending on the relationship of the wave' peaks and troughs, the result may produce phase problems (*phase cancellation*). If the waveforms are somewhat offset, then certain frequencies will be canceled and others reinforced. If the waveforms are off-set completely, then there is the possibility of complete cancellation. The reality is that rarely are two sound sources perfectly in or out of phase, so the degree of phase coher-

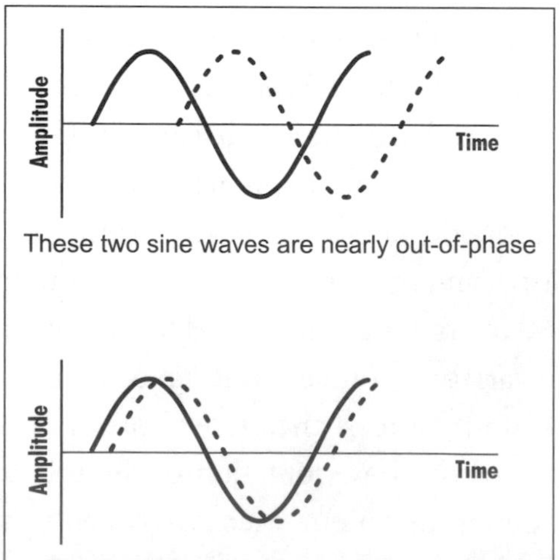

DIAGRAM 2.4
Phase

These two sine waves are nearly out-of-phase

Amplitude / Time

These two sine waves are closer in phase

Amplitude / Time

...ency is the primary concern. In fact, it is the slightly out-of-phase quality that gives stereo recordings their character. If the two signals are perfectly in phase, they would be identical and therefore would be a mono signal. Sometimes phase problems can be detected by careful listening, but there is also a simple test to see if the two signals are generally more or less in phase. You pan the two signals hard left and right, and then switch your monitoring to mono.

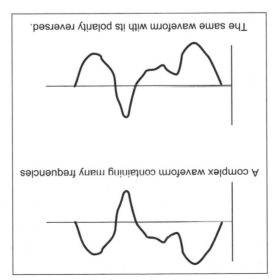

A complex waveform containing many frequencies

The same waveform with its polarity reversed.

DIAGRAM 2.5
Polarity

While monitoring in mono, you reverse the phase or polarity on one of the channels. Whichever setting is louder—the combined signal with one channel's polarity switched or unswitched—is the one in which the signals are more in phase. If more frequencies are reinforcing each other, the sound will be louder.

Polarity is not the same as phase, though the effect is related. Phase is the complex relationships of time between identical sources at their destination; polarity refers to the simple positive and negative voltage values of a signal. Phase differences will vary at different frequencies when the time difference is constant—smaller amounts of phase for low frequencies and larger amounts of phase for high frequencies. Two signals with reversed polarity—caused when the positive and negative voltages are reversed—exhibit the same kind of cancellation effect of signals completely (180 degrees) out of phase. *Switching the polarity is the same as reversing the phase.*

Stereo miking techniques

Stereo miking refers to the practice of using two microphones to create a stereo image. To get the maximum stereo effect, the two tracks that are recorded are panned hard left and hard right (all the way to the left and all the way to the right), but other approaches to panning stereo tracks may also be used. (See the mid/side stereo technique below for an exception to the hard left/hard right rule; and section 6.1 on mixing for more information about panning strategies.) Stereo miking can be used to capture ensembles when the sound is coming from a variety of sources, or it can be used to record a single sound source. With single sound sources, the stereo spread is created by variations in room ambience based on the orientation of the mic to the sound source. Variations in stereo miking techniques generally seek to address two primary concerns: first, the breadth or width of the stereo image versus the desire for a stable, coherent center image; and second, the problems created by out-of-phase information

caused when two microphones pick up the same sounds at different locations. There are four common stereo miking techniques covered below, with information about how they deal with these and other concerns.

The coincident pair or X/Y configuration

The X/Y, or *coincident pair,* technique is one of the most common and most reliable stereo miking techniques. It does a very good job of controlling problems in maintaining a coherent center image and with phase cancellation. Two cardioid microphones are set up with their diaphrams at a 90 degree angle and as close together as possible. Other angles may be used, broadening or narrowing the stereo field, but common practice maintains the 90 degree model. Pencil condensers are frequently used for stereo recordings using the X/Y configuration because of their superior off-axis fidelity.

Matched pairs of the same make and model of microphone are favored, but any pair of mics can be used. Because the two microphone capsules are place so close together, they receive the sound at almost identical times, thus limiting out-of-phase information. Because of their close proximity, they are also receiving enough of the same information to provide for a coherent center image. For the same reason—their proximity— there is a limited degree of stereo image between the two channels, but because the mics are aimed at different parts of the room, there is enough variation in what they pick up to make for a pleasing stereo spread. A broader stereo image will be captured as the coincident pair is moved closer to the sound source. As the mics move farther from the sound source, the differences in sound from one to the other will diminish. For a dramatic stereo effect, with a broad sense of the stereo field, other stereo miking techniques yield superior results (and pose more serious potential problems, as well).

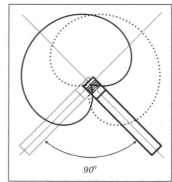

DIAGRAM 2.6

Coincident pair or X/Y configuration

There are also single microphones with stereo microphone capabilities. These mics have two diaphragms and two outputs—they are essentially two mics built into one body and are set to an X/Y configuration (typically at a 90 degree angle, but not always). Some of these mics have the ability to rotate one of the diaphragms from a 90 degree angle into other variations in angle. Stereo mics are convenient, and the two diaphragms are always well matched, but they have the disadvantage of being limited in their approach to stereo mic configuration.

ORTF stereo configuration

The ORTF stereo configuration represents a variation on the coincident pair and is sometimes called *near-coincident pair*. It was developed by the French national public radio and television broadcaster office (acronym ORTF). This technique calls for two cardioid mics placed 17 centimeters apart (about 6.5 inches) and

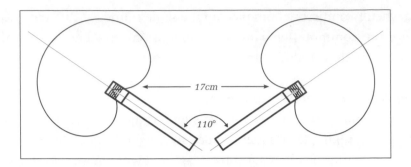

DIAGRAM 2.7

ORTF stereo configuration

at 110 degree angle. The mics should be as similar as possible, preferably the same make and model. Some manufacturers sell frequency-matched pairs that are particularly nice for stereo miking. The ORTF configuration reminds us that the distance and angle between two mics used in a coincident-pair configuration can be adjusted for variation in results.

Considerable research and testing went into the ORTF standard, and it yields reliably good results, but other variations can be used with great success and there are other standards, as well. The advantage of the ORTF technique over the traditional X/Y configuration is that it has a broader stereo field while maintaining good mono compatibility (minimal phase problems) and a relatively stable center image. While strict phase compatibility and center image stability are better with the traditional X/Y, I find that in many cases the more pronounced stereo image is worth the small compromises, and I tend to use the ORTF technique frequently. I've also found that the distance between my thumb and my little finger, with my hands spread wide, is just about the right distance for an ORTF setup. If you can find some easy way such as this to reference this distance, it will speed your setup. Special mic clips that will hold two pencil condensers in either the X/Y or ORTF configuration (as well as other variations) are available and are very handy for this application. (More specific applications of the ORTF configuration can be found in section 3.3.)

Spaced pair (omni-directional or cardioid)

The spaced-pair mic placement is especially good for recording ensembles, from bands to orchestras, because the two mics pick up sound more evenly over a larger area than the coincident pairs. Two matched microphones are generally placed between 2 and 12 feet apart, depending on the size of the ensemble. The mic pickup patterns may be either cardioid or omni, with omni being the preferred pattern (better frequency response) as long as the additional room ambience picked up in the omni position is not a problem. Many engineers employ the 3-to-1 rule, which holds that if the microphones are three times as far from each other as they are from the sound source, there will be minimal phase problems. In practice, this isn't always true, as room acoustics and the nature of the sound source also affect the phase relationship. Trial and error, by moving microphones and listening, is the best way to find the optimal placement for a spaced pair.

Spaced pairs are technically the most problematic of all the commonly used stereo techniques because of the potential phase problems and the possibility of an unstable or "blurred" center image, caused by microphones that are far apart from each other (sometimes referred to as a "hole" in the center of the stereo image). This is why one of the variations on coincident pairs, such as the Decca Tree (see below), may be preferred. However, when the right positioning is found via trial and error, spaced pairs can produce very good and dramatic results. Checking the summed (mono) response of the two mics in a spaced pair is one good way to determine how much of a problem the phase relationship may be. The more the sound is diminished in mono, the greater the phase problems.

Decca Tree

The Decca Tree is a variation on the spaced-pair configuration. The recording engineers at English Decca Records developed it in the 1950s, primarily for orchestral recording. The Decca Tree adds a third mic to the spaced pair in order to provide greater center-image stability. In its basic configuration, the Decca Tree utilizes three omni, large-diaphragm condenser mics with the left and right mic approximately 2 meters (6 feet) apart and the third mic centered about 1.5 meters (4.5 feet) in front of the other two. In practice, many different microphones, including pencil condensers, and either cardioid, supercardioid, or omni patterns maybe selected. Also, the distance between the mics may be adjusted depending on the size of the ensemble, the room acoustics, and the desired effect. Even the standard panning of hard left, hard right, and center may be adjusted. The mics are generally aimed in toward the center; even omni mics exhibit a certain amount of directional bias, especially in the higher frequencies.

Other variations on the Decca Tree include the addition of two more mics, usually farther back from the ensemble and spread more widely, to gain greater stereo width and room ambience. The center mic may be replaced by a pair of mics in the X/Y configuration or other variations on a coincident pair. In whatever configuration that is used, it is the balance between the center and the flanking microphones that will be adjusted to create more or less stereo spread—more flanking mics in the balance for greater stereo spread, more center mic for greater center stability. Again, monophonic summing (listening to all the mics in mono) will reveal problems in phase coherence and may cause you to increase or decrease the relative level between the mics. Orchestral recordings for use in film soundtracks often employ the Decca Tree because it can produce a stable stereo image that holds up well when processed for surround-sound applications.

Mid/Side (M/S)

The mid/side technique uses two mics with two different microphone patterns, one cardioid and one figure-8 (sometimes called bipolar or bi-directional). The cardioid mic is for center (or mono) information and is generally aimed at the sound source. The figure-8 mic is placed in close proximity (usually above or below) the cardioid mic and aimed at a 90 degree angle to the cardioid so that the two areas that it picks up are each offset 90 degrees from the center mic. The figure-8 microphone encodes stereo information by picking up from the two opposing sides of the microphone's capsule. The single channel that is recorded by the figure-8 mic (side channel) is decoded by duplicating that channel and reversing the polarity (also called "inverting the phase") on the duplicated channel and then panning the original and polarity-reversed channel hard left and hard right, respectively. Some DAWs, such as Nuendo, have a Stereo Tools VST plug-in that will automatically configure the side channel (figure-8 recording) as described here. If you group the left and right (side) channels together, you can raise or lower their volume relative to the mid channel (panned center), and in doing so you will increase or decrease the sense of stereo spread.

The biggest advantages to the M/S technique are in mono compatibility and in the way you can control the stereo versus mono relationship. Because all of the stereo information is provided by two identical but reversed-polarity tracks, they completely cancel each other out when played back in mono (such as playback on old mono AM radio receivers or television sets). This leaves only the original mid or mono channel, without any of the phase anomalies of other two-channel stereo miking techniques. It also eliminates any room ambience that has been added by the side channels, which may or may not be desirable in the mono playback setting. Because all of the stereo information comes from one microphone, and all of the mono information comes from another, you can balance the two, keeping a clear differentiation between stable mono and highly phased stereo.

Mics and DAWs

Mic selection and positioning are critical elements that affect the quality of your recording. Quality, in this case, means both the fidelity and the aesthetics, or "sound," of what has been captured by each microphone. In many instances, the signal path from the mic into the computer is the only time your audio will be processed in the analog domain. You may wish to access analog gear

WHAT NOT TO DO

Do not get hung up on having to use your stereo recording in maximum stereo configuration—with the two channels panned hard left and hard right. "Collapsing" the stereo image by bringing the panning of either or both channels in from hard left or hard right is often desirable in mix situations.

such as compressors or EQs as part of this chain to avoid sending your signal back from digital to analog for this kind of processing. There are other, less frequently used kinds of mics (Soundfield mic, binaural mics, etc.) and miking configurations (Blumlein pair, baffled stereo configurations, etc.) to explore, but they fall beyond the scope of this book. In any event, you will want to pay close attention to the role that the microphones are playing in your overall recording strategy.

2.4 Mixing Boards and Control Surfaces

Traditional routing for analog recordings goes from the microphone to a mixing board (mixer) to a tape recorder. Microphones may be connected to a DAW in a wide variety of ways, and the mixer/recorder paradigm from the analog world has been expanded. DAWs include a mixer-style interface as part of the software; some DAW interfaces include hardware mixers and a whole new world of control surfaces that may replace a traditional mixer in a DAW setup.

Mixing boards and control surfaces: What are they?

To begin, it is necessary to define what is meant by mixing boards (usually referred to as mixers, but also called consoles, desks, etc.) and control surfaces. A traditional *mixer* includes all of the elements necessary for routing audio to and from the tape recorder and the speaker/amplification system, as well as the capability of controlling the audio for most other routing or processing that may be desired. This means that most mixers have microphone preamps, some amount of signal-processing capabilities (generally at least some EQ), and routing capabilities for incorporating all varieties of external gear, such as other signal processors, cue/headphone systems, and other recorder and/or playback devices. A *control surface* is a subset of a mixer that generally provides only for the control and routing of the audio, without the mic preamps or signal-processing capabilities. There are numerous hybrid products that incorporate some, but not all, of the capabilities of a traditional mixer. Software mixers (such as the "mixer" page in your DAW) are really just virtual control surfaces, although they become more mixerlike by using plug-ins to give the user signal-processing capabilities. Mic preamps are hardware by nature—the mic must be able to physically plug into them.

Here, I am concerned primarily with software mixers (the mixer in your DAW), which might be better described as a virtual control surface. However, your DAW's mixer is modeled after its hardware predecessors, so much of what I cover here translates to the hardware world as well, and I include a discussion of mic preamps also. I follow a typical order of controls from top to bottom on a typical channel strip, but this order will vary with different software. The general function of each of these controls is found in almost every mixer. At

PHOTO 2.7

A Solid State Logic (SSL) G+ series analog mixer

PHOTO 2.8

A Digidesign C24 digital control surface

the end of this chapter, I have a more thorough examination of software versus hardware mixers.

The mixer channel strip

Each channel strip duplicates a set of controls for the individual channels on a mixer. The number of channel strips defines the capacity of a hardware mixer (e.g., a 16-channel mixer or a 24-channel mixer), but the software world has pretty much ended that distinction. With most DAW programs, channels can be added as needed, often up to a very large capacity. Even some systems that restrict the number of audio channels still provide a large number of auxiliary channels, as well as virtual tracks (covered in section 4.2) that multiply the mixer's capacity enormously. By examining each of the principal functions of the channel strip, I survey all of the primary operations that a mixer is used for.

Shown on this page are a couple of screenshots of software channel strips from two different DAWs. Note the labels for the functions, including Inserts, Sends, I/O for inputs and outputs, Panning, Solo, and Mute, plus the main fader including volume readout, the scribble strip for labeling the channel, and other functions depending on the DAW. Note that many DAWs do not have labels for every function on the channel strip, requiring you to learn your way around the DAW, using the manual and/or trial and error.

Types of mixer channels

Because of the increasing number of capabilities within a DAW, there has been an increase in the number of channel types. It is not possible to thoroughly discuss them all in this context, but you should be aware that great flexibility is derived from using the proper channel for the proper function. Here, I cover audio channels in depth; and in the section on sends and returns (section 5.2) and building a mix (section 6.1), I look at uses for auxiliary input channels (aux channels). Master fader channels are also covered under the topic

SCREENSHOT 2.1

A channel strip: Pro Tools

SCREENSHOT 2.2

A channel strip: Digital Performer

of building a mix (section 6.1). Besides these channels, your DAW may include the ability to create channels specifically for MIDI use and for instrument use (usually "soft synths," or software-based synthesizer and sampler programs that operate within the DAW environment). See your DAW user guide for more specific information on these and other specialized channel strip capabilities.

I/O—input and output

In the previous section on signal path, I covered some of the general principles of input and output (I/O). Somewhere in your channel strip you must have the option for choosing the primary input and output for that channel (as seen on the previous screenshots, this may be located at different places in the channel strip—top or middle—on different DAWs). *The primary input sets the path that audio takes to get into each channel.* The signal is typically coming from a microphone, but it could be from a synthesizer, from another already recorded audio track, or from any other audio source. *The primary output sets the audio destination when it leaves the channel.* Usually this would be the stereo buss that feeds the playback (speakers), but it could be going to an outboard processing box, another track, or any other audio destination.

Interface or buss routing

In the digital world, there is an important distinction made with regard to inputs and outputs that did not exist in the world of hardware mixers. Within the software mixer, the choices for I/O routing may be either through interfaces or through busses. This distinguishes audio routing that takes the audio out of the computer (external) from routing that keeps the audio within the computer (internal). *External routing*—routing out the audio interface through which all audio must travel to get in or out of the computer—is used when the audio needs to access external gear, such as speakers, amplifiers for headphone mixers, or any analog processing. *Internal routing* uses busses to move audio around within the computer software—such as to other tracks or to computer-based processing tools (plug-ins).

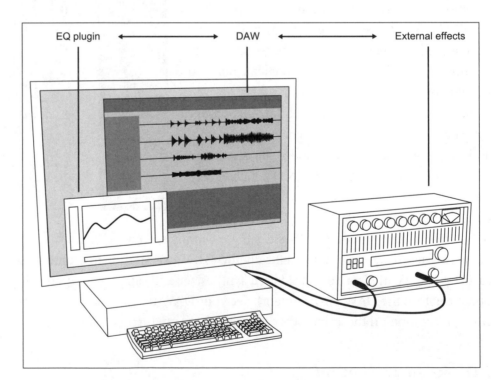

DIAGRAM 2.8

Internal and external routing

Mono or stereo

Audio channel strips may be configured as mono or stereo in both their input and their output status. Mono input and stereo output is the most common configuration, but stereo inputs are also common when stereo recordings are being made or when stereo samples are accessed. Mono outputs are available and are valuable if you are routing audio from the DAW to a mixer or control surface channel where they are then given stereo-output capabilities. Most hardware channel strips are configured mono in and stereo out, so the output of the DAW to the input of the hardware channel strip is a mono signal path. (See the section below on panning for more on mono and stereo outputs.) There is increasing need for and use of expanded I/O options to deal with surround sound (5.1, 7.1, etc.), but that is beyond the scope of this book.

Mic preamps

Microphone preamps are necessary to amplify the low-level output from a microphone. They provide a variable level to supply the proper output to be effectively recorded. Different microphones have very different levels of output—and, of course, sound sources differ enormously in volume as well—so the ability to control the output from a mic with a preamp is essential to the recording process. With the prevalence of DAW systems, where mic preamps are not necessarily a part of the hardware interface, more attention has been paid to outboard preamps (any mixer-related hardware, such as mic preamps or processing units, that is not built into a mixing board is referred to as *outboard equipment*). Mic preamps (whether onboard or outboard) are also able to supply the special phantom power needed for condenser microphones, and they often include a phase-reverse switch, as well.

Mic preamps, as with most electronic audio gear, come in two basic designs: vacuum tube and solid state. They also come in a staggering array of quality and price ranges. As with microphones, the selection of mic preamps should be based on a combination of access, intended use, and experience. In selecting all audio gear for purchase, it is a good idea to keep in mind that every link in the chain is critical. It probably does not make sense to buy a $1,000 mic pre to amplify a $100 mic (though it does no harm), and it certainly isn't advisable to buy a $25 mic pre for use with your $1,000 mic. Because of the proliferation of interfaces that provide only line-level input to the DAW, it has become more common for studios to accumulate a variety of external mic pre's in order to have a range of

PHOTO 2.9

A Solid State Logic (SSL) mic preamp

33

options for different mics and different situations. This proliferation of stand-alone mic preamps also eliminates the need for the typical mixer with built-in mic pre's, and this is part of the reason for the rise in hardware-control surfaces as alternatives to mixers.

In a typical hardware mixer each channel contains an onboard mic preamp. It is generally located at or near the top of the channel strip. The onboard mic pre ranges from a barebones model that has only a gain control to a more elaborate preamp with individual controls over phantom power, pad, and phase reversal and a separate level control for line-level signals, such as in the photo on the previous page.

Inserts

Inserts are such an important part of a software mixer's applications that I devote a separate section to their use (see section 5.1). Here, I simply note that the insert portion of the software mixer is the point at which all manner of processing functions, as well as software instruments, are integrated into the mixer environment. This is one of the areas in which software mixers differ considerably from hardware mixers. The use of inserts to dramatically increase the control over and creation of audio has far exceeded the comparably minimal use that inserts found in the hardware world. (There are more details on this at section 5.1.)

Auxiliary sends

Auxiliary sends (or "aux sends," or most commonly, just "sends") are another essential part of mixer functionality, and their various uses are outlined in two independent sections in this book (sections 3.2 and 5.2). Here, I cover only the basic controls found on a typical aux send.

An aux send functions similarly to the main fader on any mixer channel. The primary routing for audio on any given channel is through the primary channel output, and the main channel fader controls the level of that output. The channel aux sends provide further routing options for the same audio—the audio on that particular channel. This is why they are called aux sends—they are auxiliary (or "in addition") to the main send, which is output controlled by the channel fader (usually located at the bottom of the channel strip). When an aux send is created on a software mixer, typically a pop-up consisting of a new fader appears along with a variety of other controls. Additional aux send controls include the ability to select the output for the send, panning control, solo and mute capabilities, and the pre-fader or post-fader status for that send.

Pre-fader and post-fader aux sends
The terms *pre-fader* and *post-fader* describe a critical element in the routing status of an aux send (and the settings are often shortened to simply "pre" or "post" when describing the send's status in this regard). Because the aux send

is in addition to the primary channel output, you must set its routing status relative to the primary output. The channel's main fader controls the primary output. Any aux sends on that same channel access the audio on that channel, either before (pre-fader) or after (post-fader) the audio is routed through the main channel fader. If it is selected to be pre-fader, then its level control of the channel audio is unaffected by the position or movement of the main fader and the level is controlled only by movement of the sends fader. If it is selected to be post-fader, its send level is affected by both the position and the movement in the main fader, as well as by the sends fader.

In practice, the decision to set a send to pre or post depends on the intended use for the audio being sent. The two primary uses for aux sends are headphone mixes and access to effects via sends and returns; and these are prime examples of the need for the two different routing options (pre and post). Because headphone mixes need to be completely independent of the control-room mix, the sends used will typically be set in the pre-fader position. Because effects added in the sends and returns routing model need to maintain a consistent relationship to the level of the primary output, the sends used will typically be set to post-fader. (Details are covered in the sections on headphone mixes and sends & returns, sections 3.2 and 5.2, respectively.)

Aux send outputs

Sends have output routing that is separate from the channel's primary output routing. As with the primary outputs, however, these outputs may be either through the interface or via busses (explained in the section on I/Os, above). When sends are used for things such as headphone mixes, it is necessary to use the interface outputs in order to get to the headphone system. For

SCREENSHOT 2.3

Send control

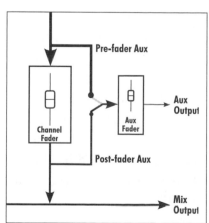

DIAGRAM 2.9

Pre-fader and post-fader auxiliary sends

internal processing, such as that done when using the send and return model, busses are used to route the signal. (Again, details are covered in the sections on headphone mixes and sends and returns.)

Panning

The channel pan function controls the placement of the audio in the stereo field. *Panning* requires a stereo output, allowing you to move the sound from the left speaker through the stereo field to the right speaker. If you create a channel with a mono output, you will notice that the panning function has been eliminated—there can be no panning with a single channel of output. This seemingly simple distinction between mono and stereo—and the ability to pan audio in stereo—is often misunderstood. A mono sound source (a single sound) can be panned (placed) anywhere in the stereo field as long it has access to a stereo output (typically, outputs 1 and 2—with output 1 feeding the left speaker and output 2 the right speaker). Both elements of a stereo sound source can be panned across the stereo field independently, though placing one hard left and the other hard right is commonplace for stereo audio. (More on this in building a mix, section 6.1.) When something is playing "in mono," this means that there is no difference between what is feeding each of the two speakers. A mono system has only one output to the speaker(s), whereas a stereo system must have two outputs and two speakers. Here are the input and output options for panning capabilities:

Input	Output	Panning
Mono	Mono	No panning possible
Stereo	Mono	No panning possible
Mono	Stereo	Sound can be panned anywhere in the stereo field
Stereo	Stereo	Sound from each output channel can be panned anywhere in the stereo field

What, then, is meant when the sound coming from a channel with stereo output is playing in mono? This means that the sound is center-panned (panned evenly to both the left and the right channel). This is sometimes where the confusion comes in. When a sound is center-panned, it is effectively "playing in mono"—it is not using the capabilities of panning because the same level of output is feeding each speaker equally. If all channels are center-panned, the entire piece is effectively "playing in mono" (even though channels with stereo outputs have stereo capabilities). As soon as the sound is moved by the use of panning, even slightly, to create an imbalance between the right and left speakers, then the sound is "playing in stereo."

Output fader

The main fader control (generally at or close to the bottom of the channel strip) controls the output level. It is important to remember that it is at the end of the channel's signal path, controlling only the level of the signal as it leaves the channel to its destination, as set by the main output. The destination is frequently the stereo buss, but it may be any interface or buss output. This means that the position of this fader has no effect on the input to the channel, and therefore, it has no effect on the level of the recording (a common novice mistake is to try to turn down the recording level by lowering the channel's main output fader). The fader sets the monitor (listening) level and the final output volume when mixing.

Groups

In every DAW, there is the capability for grouping channels together to facilitate a variety of functions. In the most basic group configuration, the output faders of each channel are grouped so that moving any one fader moves all fader levels in the group by the same amount. This allows you to easily raise or lower the level of many channels used for the same instrument (like multiple tracks often used to record a piano or a drum set) or many channels of related elements (such as backing vocal tracks). Other group controls include solo and mute functions, panning, input or output assignments, automation controls, or arming the channels for recording. Whether or not the groups share all of these functions is usually determined by the user and will depend on the nature of the elements in the group. Most of these controls provide added convenience with the exception of panning position, which will often be best left individually variable, as different panning positions are usually an important part of the group settings.

In many DAWs, the groups made by the user are given a particular designation (a number or a letter) that is indicated on the channel strip. Channels may be color-coded by groups as well. It is necessary to have the ability to temporarily suspend the group functions, so that you can adjust individual tracks independently and then return to group status (perhaps the hi-hat is too loud relative to the rest of the drums, or one background singer's voice is getting lost in the mix and needs to come up in volume).

Channels may be part of more than one group. Larger groups can be helpful in complex projects where groups involving whole sections (such as strings, or percussion) may be used at times, and then suspended while smaller groups (violins, or hand percussion, for example) are kept active for more fine-tuning. The ability to group all channels in a project allows for editing entire sections of the arrangement, such as when eliminating or rearranging whole sections of a piece (as described in section 4.4 under "Global

Edits"). In almost every recording project, there are instances when using groups makes the workflow simpler.

Track name/Track notes

At the bottom of the fader, there is typically a place that allows you to name the channel. This is roughly the equivalent of the track sheet used to keep track of what was recorded on individual tracks of analog tape, or the "scribble strip" at the bottom of a mixing console where tape is generally placed to write track names. The track name has the additional function of supplying something other than a default name for the audio files as they are recorded. This means that if you name your track *Gtr* (for guitar) or *Vox* (for voice), then each audio element recorded on that channel will be tagged with the label *Gtr* or *Vox*, adding a numbering scheme each time a new recording is made. For example, the first audio recording on the track might be labeled by the DAW as *Gtr.01*, the second as *Gtr.02*, and so on. This can be very useful in both finding audio files at a later time and being able to identify the order in which they were recorded. If the default track name is not changed when creating new tracks, the audio will be labeled with the default name (such as *Audio1.01*, *Audio1.02*, etc.). This leads to a huge number of audio elements with very similar names and no means of identifying them. Naming tracks before recording is a beneficial practice in the DAW recording process.

SCREENSHOT 2.4

Track naming and scribble strip

Kik	Snare	Hat	Rack Tom	Floor Tom	OH	Room	Drum Verb	Drum Rm	Bass	Rh Gtr	Lead Gtr	Gtr Verb
D112 Kevin	57	452	421	421	KM84's	U87's			DI Frank	57 Steve	121 Paul	

Below the track name there is often an area for making notes or comments about the track. Again, this is information that was generally kept on the track sheet for recordings made on analog tape recorders. The two most common bits of recordkeeping done here are the name of the musician who was recorded and the name of the microphone (if any) that was used. Other information, both technical and creative, can be entered here. You may want more complete input path information, such as the type of mic preamp or compressor that was used, or you may want to make mix notes such as "filter the low end rumble." You may also want to note particularly strong or weak elements ("great solo"). The ability to name tracks and make notes and comments becomes even more useful when using virtual tracks (described in section 4.2).

Other kinds of channel strips

Besides the typical audio channel, mixers (both hardware and software) have other kinds of input and output capabilities, such as auxiliary inputs (aux inputs) or master fader outputs. DAWs now come equipped with a large array of specialty channels. Besides aux inputs and a master fader, a DAW mixer may

WHAT NOT TO DO

Don't postpone keeping tracks labeled and organized as a session progresses. Even in the heat of a rushed session, it is worth the few seconds it takes to label a new track with the name of what is being recorded, making a quick but essential note in the scribble strip (e.g., "mute this track during the guitar solo"), and creating a group if you're recording multiple related elements (e.g., three backing vocalists on separate tracks). Labeling saves time in the long run and is always worth the little bit of time it takes.

include MIDI channels for handling MIDI data, as well as instrument channels for software instruments/synthesizers (soft synths).

Auxiliary input channels

Aux inputs provide additional routing capabilities that are used primarily for internal routing and processing duties. An aux input cannot record or playback audio. Instead, the aux track passes audio through a channel and this can be used for processing or monitoring. Whenever you wish to use signal processing (EQ, compression, etc.) as part of the recording or on groups of already recorded tracks, an aux channel can provide the appropriate signal path. An aux channel can also be used to monitor a talkback mic that isn't being recorded. Unlike audio tracks, aux tracks receive audio without having to be in record mode (or record ready), as long as audio is routed to their input path (either interface or buss).

Unlike a DAW mixer, every channel of a hardware mixer functions like an aux channel, as opposed to an audio channel. This is because the channels of a hardware mixer don't actually contain audio recordings (the audio is handled by the separate recorder)—they simply pass the audio signal through for processing and mixing. What are called "aux channels" in a hardware mixer (often included in the center section) are really just more input channels with limited routing and processing capabilities. The integration of the actual recording, as well as the added flexibility of software over hardware, gives the DAW channel paths much broader functions than found in any hardware mixing console. (For further information about aux track functions, see section 5.1 on insert/ plug-in uses and section 5.2 on send and return routing for signal processing.)

Master fader channel

Most hardware mixers incorporate a stereo master fader that gives you single-fader control over the sum of all the individual channels. DAW mixers do the same thing, though as with all channels in the DAW mixer, it is up to you to create a master fader or to work from a template that already has one created.

The master fader is used to control global level movements such as fade-outs at the end of the song. It can also be used to adjust the overall level of a mix before it is rendered or bounced to a file for use outside of the DAW (such as burned to a CD, podcast, or e-mailed as an mp3) The master fader also allows you to see what the overall (summed) level is so that individual tracks might be adjusted up or down to put level operations into a comfortable range. The master fader itself can also be used to adjust overall output if the sum of all the tracks is not at a comfortable operating level. It is a good idea to create a master fader in your DAW at the beginning of your project, to help monitor your overall gain structure.

MIDI channels

MIDI is an acronym that stands for Musical Instrument Digital Interface. MIDI channels allow for the recording and playback of MIDI data. MIDI is not audio; it is digital data that is used to control synthesizers and other computer-based music gear. MIDI information is stored and controlled differently from audio information, so MIDI channels are an essential part of every DAW (many DAWs began as MIDI recorders/sequencers). MIDI production techniques fall outside the scope of this book, which specifically addresses audio recording. There are plenty of books about MIDI and I encourage you to study and explore the MIDI capabilities of your particular DAW.

Instrument channels

One of the most explosive areas of development in the world of DAWs has been the integration of software synthesizers (soft-synths). These software instruments run the gamut from traditional synthesizer-type sound generation to elaborate sample-based instrument playback. The instrument programs are often capable of running either as stand-alone software or integrated into most DAWs. Many DAWs now include dedicated instrument channels that can be created within the mixer environment to best integrate the functions of the soft-synth program. Implementation will vary depending on the DAW and the particular soft-synth.

Hardware versus software mixers and control surfaces

The focus of this book is on the DAW, but every DAW software program requires some amount of hardware to get audio in and out of the computer. The differences between software and hardware control of audio has led to some confusion over the need for a hardware mixer. At the same time, the typical software version of a mixer that you find in a DAW has now been recreated in the hardware world, and to differentiate it from the traditional hardware mixer, it has been renamed a "control surface." So, software "mixers," or mix pages, or whatever they are labeled in your particular DAW, are really more akin to the new generation of hardware control surfaces than they are to the traditional hardware mixer. The main differences between a control surface and a mixer are in the ability of the mixer to process audio (primarily with EQ, but some mixers have other processing capabilities, as well) and the existence of mic preamps (which by their nature must be hardware).

The one item on a typical hardware mixer channel strip that cannot be reproduced through software in the DAW is the microphone preamp. Instead, many DAW manufacturers integrate mic preamps into their interface units, and there is a proliferation of stand-alone mic preamps available in all price ranges. Whether through the use of integrated mic preamps or stand-alone units, if you are going to record using a microphone, you will need a hardware mic preamp to amplify the signal before it goes to the DAW. Audio processing (signal processing such as EQ or compression) can be handled with hardware or through the use of software plug-ins. Hardware processors can be either digital or analog, but are built into the mixer rather than accessed as plug-ins. Plug-ins can be part of a software mixer (the one built into the DAW) or accessed from a digital mixer or control surface. If this all seems confusing, it's because it is—there is a lot of crossover in functions between the hardware and the software world. Here's a breakdown of the main features for the basic types of mixers and control surfaces:

- *Analog Mixer.* This is the traditional-style mixing console. Analog mixers generally include mic preamps and some signal processing, though most often just EQ.
- *Digital Mixer.* The digital mixing console includes analog mic preamps so that it can function as a true mixer. Digital mixers sometimes include built-in hardware signal processing, as well as the ability to access and control your DAW's software processors via plug-ins (some even include plug-in software).
- *Analog Control Surface.* There is no such thing. If it is a control surface, it is the digital control of a DAW, though it may have some analog elements. See Digital Control Surface, below..
- *Digital Control Surface.* The hardware-based digital control surface offers physical control over a DAW (fader controls, panning knobs, etc.), but typically does not include mic preamps or any processing capabilities—outside of the ability to use and control plug-ins.
- *Software Mixer or Control Surface.* The built-in mixer in a DAW is really a control surface (though it is often labeled as the mixer or mix page). The DAW software cannot include mic preamps and it handles all signal processing via plug-ins. By their nature, software elements are completely digital.

Deciding between using a hardware mixer or control surface (digital or analog) and relying solely on the DAW's built-in software control surface (the virtual mixing board) has become a major dilemma for many recordists. Below,

I examine the pros and cons of each and I offer the rationale for my own working methodology. Having a hardware mixer or a control surface does not restrict you from using the DAW's control surface, but it does add expense.

Using analog mixers

Analog mixers offer the most elements not found in a DAW. Besides the essential mic preamps, these mixers may provide analog EQ, as well as other processing gear, such as the compressors and noise gates found in some high-end analog consoles. They also offer the advantage of physical faders that give tactile control and are much easier to operate than trying to move software faders with a mouse. Analog mixers also provide analog summing, which is to say that they combine all the individual track outputs into the stereo buss in the analog realm. Some argue that digital summing is one of the weak points in software mixers.

The downside of analog consoles are that they require conversion from digital to analog and back again in order to be used (assuming the source is a DAW and not an analog tape recorder), and there is some loss of detail in any conversion process—the extent being determined by the quality of the conversion. The mic pre's on the console might not be of the same high quality available in stand-alone units because of the demands of providing mic preamps (and EQ and routing, etc.) on each channel, which is expensive in the analog world. Top-end consoles provide excellent mic pre's and processing, but they also command relatively high prices. Although there is physical fader control, these faders don't provide access to the highly flexible and reliable automation of the DAW. Of course, they don't prevent you from using the DAW automation, but then the advantage of the physical fader is minimized. Finally, there is disagreement about the summing issue. DAW manufacturers have sponsored shoot-outs that would indicate that digital summing in the DAW is not audibly different from analog summing (and comes without the added layer of conversion), but others claim a dramatic difference between digital and analog summing.

So, is a hardware mixer an advantage? Personally, I believe it is an advantage on large recording sessions if a high-end console is available. This gives you access to a lot of good mic preamps and EQ. Stand-alone mic pre's are fine—maybe even preferable, depending on make and model—but having enough for a large session is expensive and complicates routing and operation. Analog EQ on the best mixers sounds great and has a quality that is not exactly reproducible in the digital world. In smaller sessions, stand-alone mic preamps are often the best choice. Not all elements want or need EQ when recording (or mixing, for that matter), and there are a variety of hardware "channel strip" options that combine a mic pre with EQ and compression, so only in large sessions with many elements that might benefit from EQ does the analog mixing console provide a substantial advantage. Personally, I love having an SSL or a Neve for a large tracking (full band or large ensemble) recording date, but outside of that,

I find that the overlay of duplicated functions—not to mention the expense—outweighs the advantages of a hardware mixer in most instances.

Using digital hardware mixers and control surfaces

Digital mixers (as opposed to digital control surfaces, covered below) imply the presence of analog elements, most especially mic preamps. They may also have hardware or software processing built in (EQ, compression, reverb, etc.). Otherwise, hardware digital mixers and control surfaces do the same thing: they provide physical, tactile control over the digital mixing functions found in the DAW. The advantage is in the tactile control over faders and other mixer functions, such as panning or plug-in parameter control. This is generally easier than mouse control over the same functions. The mixer or control surface interface also offers quick access to several elements at once because of the physical faders and knobs (including two-handed operation).

The disadvantages to these kinds of digital hardware (besides expense) is that they do not provide the graphic-based automation found in the DAW, and for many of us, this is preferable to physical control over faders. Also, most hardware mixers and control surfaces of this type offer a limited number of channel controls and require paging through different screens in order to access all the channels from a larger DAW session. Personally, I find a few elements in hardware mixers and control surfaces convenient for some operations, but because I prefer graphic automation, it is difficult to justify the expense. For many, the physical requirement of having a large console in your workspace is also problematic.

Using only the DAW control surface

Using what is often labeled as the DAW's mixer is essentially using a control surface. You can control all routing and automation functions, but signal processing comes in the form of plug-ins and mic pre's must be accessed from the hardware world. The DAW provides excellent automation (especially in graphic mode) and controls all mixer functions. Certainly in terms of cost, the DAW is the most efficient mixer, as it requires no additional mixer or control surface hardware. (For more on maximizing your use of the DAW's mixing capabilities, see chapter 6.)

Many home and project studios have no hardware mixers or control surfaces, using only the DAW for all mixer-type functions and using either the mic pre's built into the DAW interface, external stand-alone mic pre's, or some combination of the two. Manufacturers have responded to this situation with a variety of mic preamp options at a wide range of price points. Units with two, four, or eight mic preamps in a single rack space are common, and some of them have built-in digital conversion to access the DAWs digital inputs. Channel strips—typically one or two channel units that often incorporate mic pre's, EQ, dynamics processing, direct box functionality, and even analog to digital conversion—have also proliferated to meet the needs of smaller facilities or to add variety in signal-path options at larger studios.

2.5 EQ: General Information

EQ stands for "equalization" and it has become the default name for what was traditionally termed "tone controls" in consumer audio hardware. The term *equalization* comes from the original intent to "flatten" or equalize frequency responses. Now, EQ is used to alter and reshape (and, it is hoped, to enhance) sounds, with many different goals in mind. EQ is capable of altering frequency characteristics from low to high. Frequencies are expressed in Hertz (symbol Hz, named after the German physicist Heinrich Hertz), which is the scale used to pinpoint any particular place on the frequency continuum. EQ allows the user to shape the tonality of the sound by either boosting or dipping various frequencies. EQ is the most powerful, and most frequently used, of all the signal processors. Most hardware and software mixers include the capability of applying EQ in one form or another.

EQ parameters

There are three primary parameters in most EQ operations, although there are a multitude of specialty EQ functions that provide somewhat different tone-shaping capabilities. The human ear, operating at maximum capacity, can typically hear sounds from about 20 Hertz (or 20 Hz on the low end) to 20,000 Hertz (expressed as 20 kilohertz or 20 kHz on the high end). In typical EQ operation, you can either boost (add) or dip (reduce) the level of certain frequencies in the sound to change its sonic characteristics or frequency shape. The degree of boost and dip is expressed in decibels (dB), which provide a volume scale ranging anywhere from .1 to 15 dB in standard operation.

Two of the three primary EQ parameters are pretty obvious: (1) boosting or dipping by a variable degree (more or less boost or dip); and (2) the frequency (from low to high) that you are boosting or dipping at. The number of "bands" available refers to the number of different frequencies an EQ can operate on at the same time. The typical "tone controls" in consumer electronics provide two-band EQ, meaning you can boost or dip frequencies in two different ranges, and those are typically labeled treble (highs) and bass (lows).

If you can find the specifications on a typical piece of consumer electronics, you will find the specs for the tone controls. They read something like, "Treble control: ± 12 dB @ 8 kHz, Bass control: ± 12 dB @ 80 Hz." This means that the knob marked "treble" will allow for up to 12 dB of boost or dip at the preset frequency of 8,000 Hz (8 kHz), and the knob marked "bass" will allow for up to 12 dB of boost or dip at the preset frequency of 80 Hz.

The third parameter of EQ manipulation involves bandwidth, which refers to the breadth of the EQ activity over the frequency range. You might ask,

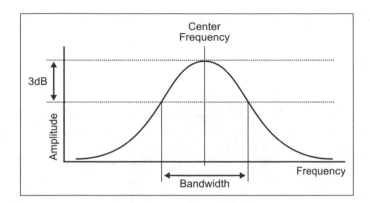

DIAGRAM 2.10

Bandwidth filter parameters

"When the specs say that the treble control operates at 8 kHz, does that mean that it boosts or dips only at exactly 8 kHz?" The answer is—of course, not! Not only would it be very difficult to limit the EQ's activity to one exceeding narrow frequency, but it wouldn't be very helpful in shaping the sound. The designation of a frequency (such as 8 kHz) for a particular EQ function indicates the center frequency. In typical EQ operation, there is a bell curve spreading equally above and below the center frequency. The breadth of the bandwidth is expressed in a range of Hertz or in portions of musical octaves (reflecting the musical scale's relationship to the frequency scale). The bandwidth setting is also referred to as the "Q," which is short for the "quality factor" of the signal process because changes in bandwidth affect the quality, meaning the characteristics, of the sound. The bandwidth is defined by the breadth of the equalizing effect when it falls 3 dB down from its maximum boost or dip at the center frequency.

The current generation of software EQ plug-ins is especially user friendly because they provide a graphic representation of the EQ curve along with the standard knob controls with numerical readouts. Here is a screenshot of an EQ set to boost 3 dB at 3 kHz using a two-octave bandwidth:

Here is a screenshot of a four-band EQ with three of the bands in use. The first band is set to boost 3 dB at 80 Hz, the second to dip 1 dB at 250 Hz, and the third to boost 5 dB at 2.5 kHz using this EQ's preset bandwidth (Q) setting.

SCREENSHOT 2.6

Four-band EQ with three active bands

The type of EQ shown here—one that has control over all three primary EQ parameters—is called *parametric EQ*. Fully parametric EQ has control over boost and dip, frequency, and bandwidth. The consumer audio paradigm usually provides two-band EQ with user control limited to boost and dip—both frequency selection and Q (or bandwidth) are preset. Because of the flexibility of software EQ (there is no more expense in providing full-range controls once the code has been written), most plug-in EQs offer full parametric control along with other EQ functions. Some of the common variations on the three standard EQ parameters described above are:

Shelving EQ
This refers to a different approach to setting the Q. Instead of the bandwidth's being a bell curve as shown above, the Q setting refers to the starting frequency and (when set to shelving) the boost or dip will affect all frequencies above (high shelving) or below (low shelving) the frequency selected.

Here is an EQ setup using +5 dB of high-frequency shelving at 8 kHz:

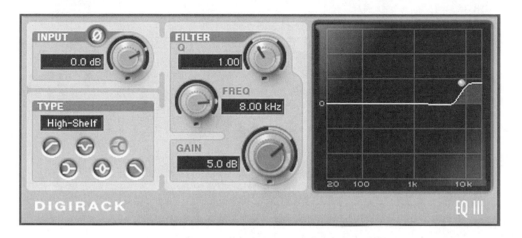

47

SCREENSHOT 2.7

High-frequency shelving

Here's another set of parameters using -5 dB of low-frequency shelving at 120 Hz:

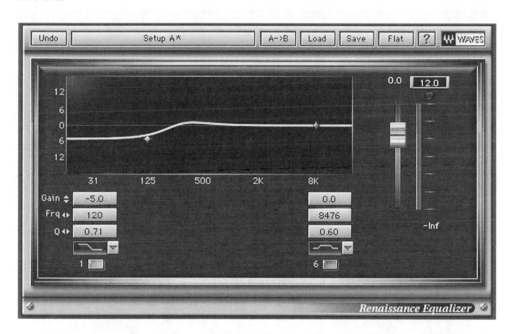

SCREENSHOT 2.8

Low-frequency shelving

Shelving provides particularly smooth-sounding alterations in frequency and is commonly used when a broad increase or decrease in either high or low frequencies is desired.

High- and Low-Pass Filters

This refers to EQ that sharply limits either high- or low-frequency sounds while allowing all other sounds to "pass" through the filter unaffected. The terminology can be a little confusing: high-pass filters reduce (filter) the low frequencies and allow the high frequencies to pass through, while low-pass filters reduce the high frequencies and allow the the lower frequencies to pass through. You may be able to adjust both the frequency for the passing filter and how steep the drop-off is on the filtering.

Here's a high-pass filter set to 50 Hz with a steep drop-off curve of 12 dB/octave:

SCREENSHOT 2.9

High-pass filter

Here's a low-pass filter set to 5 kHz with a gentle drop-off curve of 6 dB/octave:

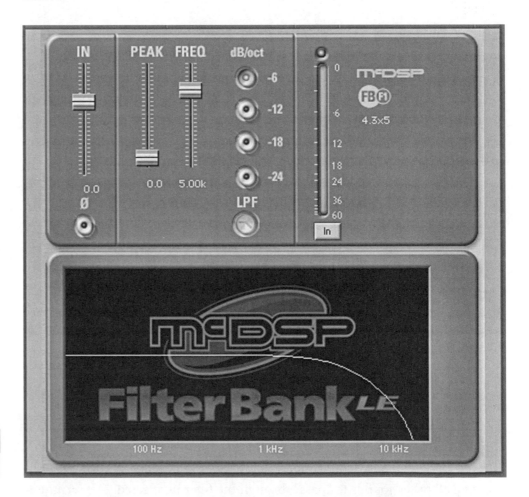

SCREENSHOT 2.10

Low-pass filter

High-pass and low-pass filters are particularly useful in clearing up problems such as low-frequency rumble or high-frequency buzzes. Of course, if some of the desirable sound occupies the same frequencies as the problem sounds, the filters will be removing both, causing unwanted effects along with desirable ones. These filters can be especially effective when used to clear subtle resonant

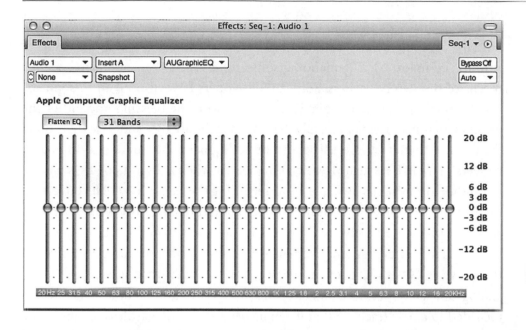

SCREENSHOT 2.11

31-band graphic EQ

and/or leakage when the problems are in frequency ranges that have no significance to the element being retained. A high-pass filter on a hi-hat track can help filter out low-frequency bass-drum leakage without affecting the sound of the hi-hat at all, and a low-pass filter on the kick drum can do the reverse, filtering highs that are not a significant part of the kick-drum sound. Band-pass filters combine high-pass and low-pass filters to limit the frequencies on both sides of the spectrum.

Graphic EQs

Graphic EQs were used extensively before the more flexible parametric EQs became common. They are not frequently seen in either software or hardware processors anymore. The "graphic" in the name refers to the fact that the layout of a graphic EQ allows you to see the EQ curve as a graphic representation. To create this graphic effect, a graphic EQ uses fader controls rather than rotary knobs for boosting and dipping frequencies. The frequencies are typically evenly spaced (based on their relationship to the musical octave), and the Q setting is predetermined (not user-controllable). The most flexible (and sometimes employed in professional settings to "tune" large monitor speakers to the acoustic anomalies of the room) are the 1/3 octave EQs that cover the range of frequencies at 1/3-octave intervals (requiring 31 bands to cover the entire audible frequency range).

Analog and digital EQs

The debate over whether digital EQs are as good-sounding as their analog predecessors continues, or perhaps I should say that it actually exists now, because up until fairly recently most professionals agreed that the high-end analog EQ sounded considerably better than any of the software alternatives. As software developers have become more and more sophisticated in their programming (and the computers have become more and more powerful, and thus capable of running complex, CPU-demanding software), a true debate about the relative merits of the two has arisen. Software developers have also taken to sophisticated modeling of analog units (often either with the blessing and aid of the original manufacturers or actually developed in-house by a software division of the original manufacturers). There is the additional matter of digital-to-analog conversion (and back again), which is necessary when using analog EQs on digital audio; this raises its own questions regarding the extent to which conversion might negatively affect the sound. And, of course, relative cost is often a factor as well, with the best software EQs costing much less than the high-end analog units. There is the additional benefit with software that separate instances of the software EQ can be used on many channels in the same session, while the analog unit is limited to a single use in any given session (unless its effect is recorded to a new track, so that it can be used again). Regardless of where one stands on the digital versus analog EQ debate, most agree that the newest digital EQs continue to sound better and better.

EQ and phase

It is inherent in the nature of normal operation that applying EQ will alter the phase relationship of the sound that is being processed. This is because there is a certain amount of time required for the EQ to process the frequencies that it is acting on, and so those frequencies get shifted in their time relationships to other frequencies that make up the sound. This time shift creates changes in the phase relationship. Developers have found ways to minimize the negative effects that such phase shifting might cause, but it is not possible to eliminate the effect completely. As with virtually every kind of processing, there is a something sacrificed in exchange for what is gained. Using EQ will compromise the sound in certain ways, but it may enhance the sound in others. You need to balance the trade-offs.

Recordists may speak about EQ in terms of decibels of boost and dip, and refer to certain frequencies with various Q settings or shelving characteristics, but to many musicians this will be meaningless. Finding the right nontechnical words to communicate about EQ and other recording qualities can be a valuable skill in managing the creative give-and-take of making recordings. (This is explored further in section 6.4).

Human hearing and the use of EQ

When it comes to understanding EQ, it is valuable to consider the characteristics of human as controlled by the capabilities of the human ear. Two researchers defined these characteristics in 1933, and their description, known as the Fletcher-Munson curve, became the standard for understanding the biases of human hearing. Since then, the curve has been further analyzed and refined, but for our purposes it isn't necessary to go into the details of this analysis (it is available in many other sources). The critical information supplied by the Fletcher-Munson curve and its successors is the nature and extent of the loss in sensitivity of human hearing to certain frequencies. That is, sounds become more and more difficult for us to hear as they get higher and higher, or lower and lower, until they pass into frequency ranges beyond our capacity to hear at all. What's more, this effect is compounded when sounds are played more quietly. The quieter the sound, the less capable the ear is of hearing its higher and lower frequencies, instead focusing its abilities on the upper midrange (where the primary harmonics of singing and talking reside; these are the frequencies that help us differentiate vowel sounds). This is sometimes explained as natural selection for our ability to understand the human voice without distraction—especially important when external forces threaten lives and the focus is necessarily on communication.

At the same time, musical sounds are, to a large extent, defined by their *timbre* (the quality of the sound), and the timbre is primarily determined by the nature of what is called the *overtone series*. This is what explains the difference in sound between a piano that plays the note middle C and a guitar that plays the same note. The note is defined by its fundamental pitch (or frequency), and the fundamental frequency of these two notes is the same (middle C). Why, then, does the guitar's note sound so different from that of the piano? The difference is in the timbre, or quality of the sound, that is a result of the particular process used to create the sound, interacting with the physical qualities of the instrument being played. Thus, the overtones of a middle C created by a piano string struck by a piano hammer and resonating within the chamber of a piano are much different from those created by a guitar string struck with a plastic pick (or finger) and resonating inside the body of the guitar (or in the speaker of a guitar amplifier). The differences create the timbres that make it easy for us to distinguish between a piano and guitar, even when they play the same note, such as middle C.

The overtones series is made up of a series of higher tones than the fundamental or root tone that gives the note its name (and its primary pitch). If we combine these two facts—(1) the human ear loses sensitivity in the higher and lower frequencies; and (2) the musical quality or timbre of a sound is largely the result of the higher frequencies created by overtones—we start to see some of the reasons for a particularly common approach to EQ-ing, which is the basis for an EQ approach sometimes referred to as the *loudness curve,* or the smile curve. On some consumer-electronic units, there is a button marked "loudness," and this button introduces EQ that is a response to the factors listed above. The loudness curve boosts high and low frequencies, leaving midrange frequencies unaltered. In doing so, it seeks to make up for the loss of our ability to hear these frequencies when music (or anything else) is played more softly (that's why it is called the "loudness" function—it is intended to increase the "loudness" during soft playback). By enhancing the lows and the highs, the loudness button is emphasizing the tonalities that our ear starts to lose at lower volumes, and it is emphasizing the overtones in order to maintain the musical timbres of the sound.

The loudness curve is intended to enhance the tonalities that are lost during low-level listening, but the same approach might be applied to louder sounds. That is to say, even at louder volumes, the qualities that are a crucial part of musical timbre—the overtone series—may be enhanced with the use of high-frequency boosting. This application of the loudness curve is also referred to as the *smile curve* because of the shape it creates on a graphic EQ. The following is a typical smile curve on a graphic EQ.

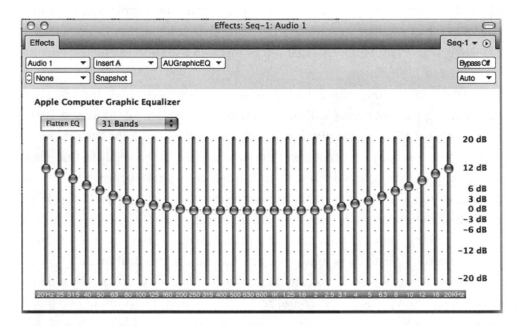

SCREENSHOT 2.12

Graphic EQ set to a smile curve

While EQ remains the most powerful and frequently used tool for signal processing, it can certainly create unintended effects. For example, EQ can enhance the natural resonances of musical sounds, it can shape the timbre of sounds to help them fit well with other sounds (covered in section 6.2), and it can fix problems that have specific frequency characteristics (covered in "Filtering and Fixing Problems," below). As already noted, EQ always alters the phase relationships, and this in itself reflects a certain compromise with every application of EQ. EQ can also diminish the quality of recorded sounds in ways not understood or necessarily noticed by the recordist.

One of the biggest pitfalls in using EQ is that when it is used to boost selected frequencies, EQ also boosts the overall volume (gain) of a sound. Our ear tends to respond favorably to louder sounds (up to a point, of course), so when you boost the high frequencies of a sound, this can be irresistible; as you turn the boost knob up, your ear is causing you to think "That sounds better!" until the boost becomes obviously overdone. Unfortunately, what a recordist

might perceive as "better" is too often simply "louder," and in the process the recordist has created excessively thin and harsh sounds or excessively boomy and indistinct sounds. We are lulled into thinking positively about a sound because it is louder, even though a true comparison between the EQ'd and un-EQ'd sound (played at relatively the same volume) might make us chose the un-EQ'd version.

Learning to EQ is a process that involves a lot of back and forth—trying more and less boost and/or dip and then listening both to the isolated sound (in solo mode) and the sound within the ensemble. A/B-ing between the EQ'd sound and the flat sound (no EQ), trying to adjust your decision-making process to the understanding that the EQ'd sound has changed in volume as well as tonality, is an essential part of using EQ. Most books on recording encourage you to take a minimalist attitude toward EQ-ing, and some promote the "all cut" approach, which makes the gain issue work in reverse (the un-EQ'd sound is louder and therefore perhaps more appealing because all the EQ-ing is cutting frequencies). Minimalist approaches are often the right way to go, and even the "all cut" approach is sometimes best, but there are times when extensive EQ-ing is called for. My own experience indicates that most recordists do quite a bit of boost EQ-ing in mixing, and that even as much as a 10 dB or more boost on certain elements may be right for the mix when and if the situation calls for it. Of course, there is really no right or wrong when it comes to EQ-ing (or any other recording practice), but there is a difference between making decisions based on understanding and mistakenly identifying changes in volume as improvements in sound.

Using EQ on input and/or output

When to EQ is sometimes just as important as how to EQ. The question arises especially in regard to whether EQ should be applied during the recording process (on the way in to the DAW) or during mixing (on the way out of the DAW). Logic argues for delaying the application of EQ until the mixing process. That is, signals that are EQ'd during input are permanently altered by the EQ, whereas EQ applied during mixing can be repeatedly revised without affecting the original recording. For the most part, this logic represents wise operating procedure and personally I apply very little EQ during recording. However, there are exceptions to this rule—no blanket operating procedure will be right for every situation.

Several different circumstances might warrant the application of EQ during the recording practice. The most common is when recording sounds that typically end up being processed with a considerable amount of EQ. This is dictated by the sound itself and the musical and technical circumstances of the recording. An example is recording a drum set for most popular music genres. On

the technical side, drum sets consist of so many different-sounding instruments (from kick drums to cymbals) that it is often desirable to EQ out frequencies that don't relate to the specific drum-set element being recorded (e.g., removing low frequencies from the mic that is recording the hi-hat). On the creative side, contemporary drum sounds often involve highly processed sounds (very bright snare drums and/or booming kick drums). When a lot of EQ is going to be used to achieve the final sound, it is usually desirable to use moderate amounts when recording and moderate amounts again when mixing. This doesn't overly tax the capabilities of the individual EQ, and it can help minimize phase problems by boosting at different frequencies between input and output.

The availability of hardware EQ may also dictate some EQ usage when recording. If you are working in a DAW and want to remain in the digital domain throughout the project, then input is the one chance to use analog EQ without going through an extra stage of conversion out to analog and back to digital. If you have access to a particularly desirable-sounding analog EQ when recording, and if you're pretty sure about some degree of EQ-ing that you're going want on a particular element of the recording, you might take advantage of the situation and apply some of the analog EQ during input. Creative use of EQ means responding to your circumstances and planning for the likely use of each element that you are recording, while at the same time recognizing the advantages of postponing EQ-ing decisions where possible.

Filtering and fixing problems

EQ is primarily a creative tool, but it also can be a problem solver. Buzzes, hums, fan noise, machine noise, and the like are best eliminated prior to making the recording, but this is not always possible. EQ can be used to minimize the effects of unwanted sounds, though there is usually some compromise in doing so. *Filtering* refers to the dipping of chosen frequencies—they are being filtered out. You can filter out buzzes and hums, but that often requires pretty broadband action (dipping across a fairly wide spectrum of the frequency range). Doing this often impacts the sound that you are trying to preserve. For this reason, it is usually impossible to completely filter out unwanted elements, and you have to make a creative decision about what point is the optimal compromise between diminishing the unwanted sound and negatively affecting the parts of the sound that you want. There's no right way to make such a decision—though, again, listening to a variety of options both in isolation (solo) and integrated with the rest of recording is a good way to go about coming to that decision.

Occasionally, problems are completely resolved using filtering, such as the need to get rid of a 60-cycle hum (a hum at 60 Hz sometimes created by bad AC grounding) for a recording of the triangle. There is no discernable part of the triangle sound at 60 Hz, and this particular grounding hum is restricted to a

very narrow band of sound. A good filter can make the hum inaudible without affecting the sound of the triangle.

There are other EQ-type tools that can be valuable for fixing problems, such as de-essers and multiband compressor (sometimes called dynamic EQs). Although these tools really function primarily as EQs, I discuss them in the following section on dynamics because you must understand the basics of compressors to understand how they function.

2.6 Dynamics (Compressors and Noise Gates)

The most mysterious and misunderstood tool in signal processing is the compressor; however, it is also one of the most valuable and widely used. What does a compressor do? Why do you use compressors and limiters (and what is the difference between the two)? What about expanders and noise gates? What is a brickwall limiter? The answers to these questions, along with details of the use and operation of dynamics processors, are covered in this section.

What compressors/limiters do

Dynamics refers to the changes in volume found in almost any audio program material. Certain elements (words, notes, beats, etc.) are louder or quieter than others, and the combined effect of these variations in volume create audio dynamics. Compressors and limiters are dynamics processors, which means they operate to control these changes in volume (dynamics). Compressors and limiters function very similarly; the fundamental difference is in the strength of the processing. Limiters are strong compressors. I clarify this point below, in describing the specifics of compressor/limiter operation.

Dynamic range is described as the range between the quietest sound and the loudest sound in any particular piece of audio. The basic action of compression is to limit the audio's dynamic range. That means that a compressor reduces the range (or distance) between the quietest sound and the loudest sound. It does this by reducing the volume of the loudest sound without affecting the volume of the quietest sound. Below is a screenshot of a single vocal line before and after compression. The height of the waveform indicates the volume, and you can see that the louder sounds have been reduced while the quieter sounds remain at the same height (or volume).

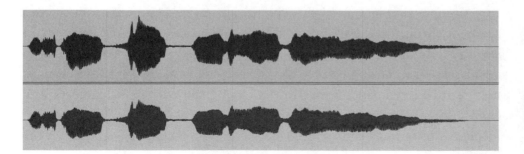

SCREENSHOT 2.13

Vocal recording before and after compression

Why use compressors/limiters?

Controlling the dynamics is an important part of contemporary audio production, but compressors and limiters have a more technical function in regard to making recordings, as well. As a technical aid, compressors and limiters help prevent overload—distortion caused by audio levels above the recorder's or DAW's capability. Because a compressor/limiter reduces the volume of the loudest sounds, it can prevent an unexpectedly loud sound from exceeding the recorder's capacity and becoming distorted. In the studio environment, it is usually possible to do enough level checking to set recording levels within a safe range, though not always (the unexpected can still happen). In live recording situations, with more unknowns, compressor/limiters are especially useful in protecting against audio overload.

In terms of production uses—as enhancements for audio—compressors/limiters are used in both subtle and obvious ways. The most typical use of compression is quite subtle—unlike EQ, where effects are often obvious even when used in moderation. Compression is also somewhat counterintuitive: why reduce the dynamic range of a musical performance? Isn't it dynamics that provides some of the most expressive and creative aspects of a performance? Yes, but reducing the dynamic range can enhance recordings, and so compression is widely used in popular music production. Consider a vocal performance on a recording with many other instruments. In the final mix, many elements might be competing with the vocal for space (bandwidth) in the musical spectrum. Because we often wish for the vocal to be very present—for the listener to be able to hear all (or at least most) of the words and even to understand all (or at least most of the) of the lyrics—a wide dynamic range in the vocal performance can frustrate the attempts to create a satisfying blend of elements. If you make the vocal loud enough to hear the quiet words, the loud words may be too loud and seem out of balance with the band. If you balance the loud words with the band, the quiet words may be lost. Compression evens out the dynamics and allows you to consistently hear the vocals without passages that are either annoyingly loud or so quiet as to get lost among the instruments. When used in this way, recordists usually want the compressor to be as transparent as possible. That is to say, you don't want to hear any audible change in the vocal sound, only a reduction in the dynamic range. This effect is often quite subtle, though its overall effect on the balance of instruments would be obvious to a trained ear.

Compression may also be used more aggressively to produce much more apparent changes in the sound of certain instruments. The most obvious case is with the compression effects used on many popular music recordings of the drum set. When strong compression effects are used on percussive sounds, there can be a dramatic change in the tonal quality of the instruments. Percussive sounds have a lot of energy—complex waveforms in brief sounds that include a lot of transients (short bursts of high frequencies)—and when this

energy is compressed it can produced explosive-sounding effects. Highly compressed drums have become a hallmark of certain genres of music, including a great deal of rock.

How to record with compression in a DAW

As a practical matter, using a compressor when recording into a DAW requires either a hardware compressor before the signal enters the DAW or proper routing within a DAW. Just putting a compressor plug-in on the track that you're recording does not allow you to record with compression. That's because plug-ins are inserted in the record channel after the audio has been recorded. A compressor on your recording track will apply compression to what you are hearing, but it will do so after the signal has been recorded, so even though you're hearing the compressor working, its operation will not have been recorded along with the signal. To record with compression in a DAW, you must route your signal through the compressor before it arrives at your record track. To do this, you need to create an aux track, place a compressor plug-in on that track, and then route the signal from the aux track to the track you are recording on. This means that the input of the aux track will be the microphone input, and then the signal will be output from the aux track via a buss to the recording track.

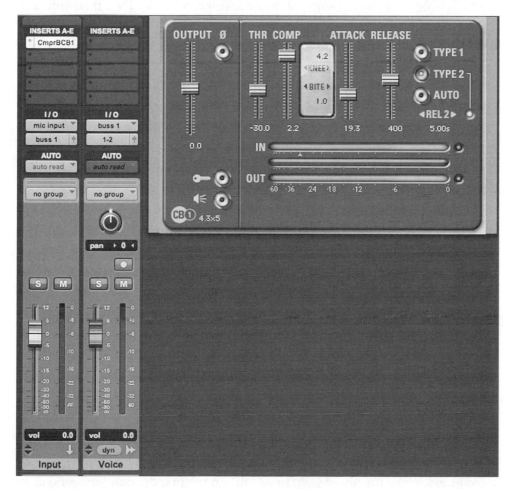

SCREENSHOT 2.14

Recording with compression in a DAW

The recording track's input will match the output of the aux track (let's say they are both set to buss 1), and then the output of the recording track will go to the stereo buss as usual. You set the compressor controls as desired by monitoring the input (see compressor operations, below). In this way, the compressor is processing the signal being recorded.

How to use compressors/limiters—basic controls

Compressors and limiters operate by detecting dynamics (volume) and then reducing the volume of louder sounds and allowing the quieter sounds to pass through unaffected. The detection devices vary and will be covered in a later section that discusses types of compressors and limiters.

Every compressor has two primary parameters: *threshold* and *ratio*. You always control the threshold, whereas the ratio may either be preset or user controllable. The threshold controls the compressor's actions; it controls what elements are compressed (reduced in volume) and what elements are unaffected. The ratio reflects the extent to which the elements that are compressed have their volume reduced.

The threshold is expressed in decibels because it sets a decibel level (volume) at which the compressor is activated. You can think of the threshold as a doorway to level reduction. If the audio does not achieve enough volume to get up to the door (the threshold), the audio is unaffected. If the volume gets past the doorway—is loud enough to go over the threshold—the compressor reduces the volume of the sound. Any portion of the sound that is louder than the threshold will have its level reduced. Once the volume drops below the threshold, the sound is no longer affected. The lower the threshold, the greater the amount of original audio will exceed the threshold and the more compression will take place. With a higher threshold, fewer elements of the original audio will be affected.

The ratio setting on a compressor defines the extent to which the volume that exceeds the threshold is reduced. Two numbers describe ratios: the first indicates the amount in relation to the second number, which is always 1. Thus, a ratio of 2:1 describes compressor action that will reduce the volume of any sound over the threshold by a factor of 2 to 1, meaning that for each 2 decibels that the sound exceeds the threshold, the compressor will reduce that volume to only 1 decibel. A ratio of 4:1 means that the compressor reduces each 4 decibels of volume over the threshold down to 1 decibel. In this latter case, the portion of the sound that originally exceeded the threshold by 8 dB would exceed the threshold by 2 dB when exiting the compressor. Compressor ratios can also be variable; see the following section on advanced controls and the discussion of compression knee variables.

The following diagram shows a graphic of a waveform being processed by a compressor. The threshold is set to –24 dB. In the first diagram, the ratio is set to 2:1. The left side shows that for each 2 dB above the threshold, the audio has been reduced to 1 dB above the threshold (and fractions thereof: 5 dB above the threshold will be reduced to 2.5 dB above the threshold, etc., maintaining the 2:1 ratio). The right side of the diagram shows the same audio with the same compressor threshold, but with a 4:1 compression ratio.

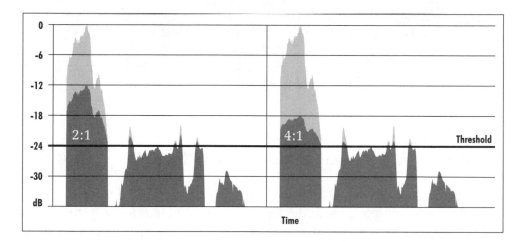

DIAGRAM 2.11

Compression ratios

Compressors have a third primary control function, after threshold and ratio, and this is *gain control*. This control is sometimes labeled as "make-up gain" and that describes the reason for its existence. Because a compressor reduces the dynamic range of audio by reducing the volume of the loudest sounds, the overall effect is that compressed audio is quieter. It is apparent from the diagram above that the compressed sound has been reduced in volume because the waveforms are smaller. This can make the audio difficult to use because the volume may no longer balance with other elements, especially if aggressive compression (a high ratio and/or a low threshold) is used. For this reason, compressors have an output gain control, allowing you to turn up the overall gain of the signal exiting the compressor, allowing you to "make up" for the lost gain caused by the action of the compressor.

Compressor and limiter metering

The meter on a compressor shows the degree to which it is reducing the audio signal level and may also show both input and/or output levels. Some compressors show all three at once, and some have the ability to switch the meter function to allow you to view any of these three levels on a single meter. The metering function that indicates the amount of compression is displayed in the reverse direction of a normal meter, because it is indicating a loss of gain. This means that a typical VU-type meter will begin at the 0 dB designation, and as the compressor acts on the audio, the meter will show deflection moving to the left, indicating the amount that the signal is being reduced. The screenshot on the following page shows a compressor meter prior to any compression activity and then with 3 dB of compression (a reduction in level of 3 dB).

60

SCREENSHOT 2.15
Compressor metering

The difference between compressors and limiters

Up until this point, I have either used the compressor/limiter designation or just referred to compressors in the discussion. As I noted in the introduction to this section, compressors and limiters function similarly, the fundamental difference being in the strength of the processing. Limiters are strong compressors. Limiters are made into strong compressors by their use of high ratios. There is no exact definition of what ratio turns a compressor into a limiter, but it is generally understood that ratios of 20:1 or higher may separate limiters from compressors. Brickwall limiters are a different kind of processor (though they share the basic idea of a limiter) and are covered in a later section of this chapter.

How to use compressors/limiters—advanced controls

Some compressors provide more extensive control over the compressor and limiter functions. The most common kinds of more advanced controls regulate the attack and release characteristics of the compressor, and what is called the "knee" function, or variable ratio control. When these functions are not controlled by the recordist, they are either preset in the processing unit or (more frequently now in plug-in processors) are program dependent, which is to say they vary depending on the program material (sound) that is detected by the unit, automatically adapting settings to fit the nature of the sound.

On the one hand, the detection circuitry in compressors is remarkable in its ability to detect sound levels as they approach and pass the threshold level so as to begin acting on the sound very quickly. Software compressors can detect signal levels in as little as .01 milliseconds (one ten-thousandth of a second!). This allows the compressors to control levels without any audible delay. However, it is not always desirable to "attack" a sound with compression very quickly. Many sounds contain a lot of leading-edge high-frequency components (transients) that are an essential part of the vitality of the sound. Sometimes these transients are problematic and can be tamed with a compressor set to a fast attack, but more frequently compressing these parts of the sound creates dull-sounding audio and robs the sound of its most distinctive characteristic. For this reason, using a relatively slow attack often produces a desirable compression on certain types of program material, such as most percussive sounds (drums, etc.) and any sound made by striking an instrument (such as piano and guitar).

Release times on compressors may also be set by the recordist, preset by the unit, program dependent, or some combination of the above. The manner that a compressor "releases" the effects of compression needs to correspond to the dynamic slope of the audio in order to prevent obvious compression arti- facts (such as an audible "pumping"). If the audio decays slowly and the com- pressor releases quickly, there will be an unnatural rise in volume. If the audio decays quickly and the compressor releases slowly, the following audio may be compressed even if it is not loud enough to cross the compressor's threshold. Because audio release characteristics often vary within a single musical per- formance, it is frequently desirable to use some form of program-dependent release setting, if available.

Variable knee characteristics describe the ways that compressors might adjust ratio settings depending on the extent that the audio exceeds the thresh- old. *Hard-knee* settings maintain a constant ratio regardless of how far over the threshold a sound might be. *Soft-knee* settings vary the ratio so that the further the audio travels beyond the threshold, the higher the ratio and thus the stron- ger the compression. Generally speaking, soft-knee operation provides com- pression that is more consistent with musical dynamics as it scales the degree of compression to the level of dynamics. User-set ratio settings act as an overall scaling factor when in combination with soft-knee operation.

Types of compressor/limiters and their effects

There are endless variations on compressor technology, especially now that they are created using computer code instead being of restricted by hardware ca- pabilities. Nonetheless, there are two basic kinds of compressor and limiters that reflect the two most common hardware designs. The first type is compres- sors that operate using tube technology or that simulate tube-based compres- sors. These earlier compressors used optical sensors to react to dynamics and thereby apply gain control. The optical-type compressor has a natural variation in release times that is slower when sounds do not exceed the threshold too far (typically about 3 dB of gain reduction or less) and faster for greater levels of reduction. The second type is the more recent compressors that use electronic sensors (VCAs, or voltage control amplifiers). These have the reverse release characteristics—faster on smaller levels of reduction and slower on greater lev- els. There are other technologies (tubes themselves; FETs, or field effect transis- tors; and now proprietary digital processors) that may be used for "riding gain" (compressing). In each case (and within each technology as well, depending on how it is implemented), there are variations in attack, release, and ratio characteristics that affect the sound.

As a rule of thumb, it is the more contemporary-style compressors using VCA detection circuitry that will be the most transparent. That is to say, they will change the characteristics of the sound the least. Optical compressors tend to have more "personality," which means they change the sound more audibly. This may or may not be desirable, but it continues to find widespread application and is often considered to enhance certain elements, especially vocals, bass, and drums in popular music production.

Compressors can also vary in how they read audio level. The RMS-level detection—root of the mean (value) squared—looks at average level over time, whereas peak-level detection reacts to the momentary audio peaks in level. Some compressors offer a choice between the two, and some offer control over the "window" size of the RMS readings; that is, as the RMS detection looks at a smaller and smaller window of sound for its average, it becomes more and more like a peak-detecting compressor. In general, RMS detection is better at general "leveling" compressor function, and peak compressors do better at taming sounds with a lot of quick dynamic changes (like snare-drum tracks). Some recordists like to use the two in tandem, compressing peaks first and then leveling the output using a compressor that is reading the average level (RMS), or sometimes the opposite, if more dramatic leveling is desired. In general, the RMS-level detection functioning is going to producer gentler results. Variations in attack time also function similarly to peak versus RMS detection, with slower attack times producing more gentle leveling-type results and fast attack times better at taming sharp dynamic transitions.

With the advent of software compressors came the capability of *look-ahead operation*. This means that the compressor processes the sound with compression and delay the output of the audio while it performed complex frequency and waveform analysis to provide the most transparent and musical kind of compression algorithms. This enables complex operations and some unique kinds of compression (see the following section on brick-wall limiters), but it may introduce significant delay times that need to be accounted for, either through delay compensation or used in circumstances (such as mastering applications) where delay is not a significant factor.

Frequency-conscious compression: de-essers and multiband compressors

Another whole school of compressors falls into this category of *frequency-conscious compression* because the compressor's actions are also affected by variations in frequency—the compressor is "aware," or conscious, of changes in level within certain frequencies, as opposed to only responding to overall changes in level. These compressors bear a relationship to EQ that also works on specific frequency ranges, and sometimes it is not clear whether it would be more accurate to call these processors EQs or compressors. In reality, these processors are both EQs *and* compressors, working in combination.

The most common kind of frequency-conscious compressor is the de-esser. A *de-esser* reduces sibilant elements in vocal performances (or in other sounds that have sibilant-like qualities). Because the *s* consonant is the most frequent cause of sibilance, the processors are called de-essers, but they also operate on other parts of vocal performances—anything with a lot of very high-frequency information. De-essers work by using EQ'd versions of the original vocal signal to trigger a compressor. The technique for doing this uses a side-chain capability within the processor. *Side-chain routing* allows the user to send a second signal into the process and use that signal to trigger the processor's action.

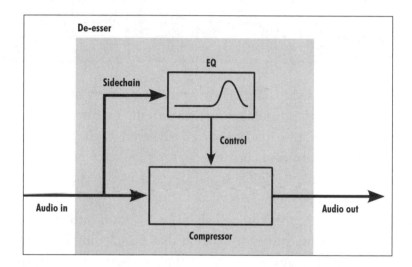

DIAGRAM 2.12

De-esser plug-in routing

The signal path used to de-ess a vocal track is as follows: the original vocal is routed to the de-esser, which is typically a plug-in that has been inserted on the vocal channel. The de-esser provides an EQ function that allows the processor to EQ the vocal in a way that greatly emphasizes the most prominent frequencies in *s* sounds and other similar sounds (very high frequencies). You don't hear the EQ'd sound, but it is sent to the compressor within the de-esser. Because the *s* sounds have been so emphasized with EQ, they are the only (or at least the primary) sounds that will trigger the compression. The gain reduction that has been triggered by the exaggerated *s* sounds effectively turns down the original (un-EQ'd) sound. Only the elements triggered by the side-chain (the EQ'd signal) get compressed. The effect can be quite dramatic, turning down sibilant sounds considerably (depending on the threshold) and leaving every other part of the sound unaffected.

Multiband compressors work on a similar principle, but they offer side-chaining at a variety of frequencies so that frequency-dependent compression can occur at several frequencies at once. This is similar to a multiband EQ and,

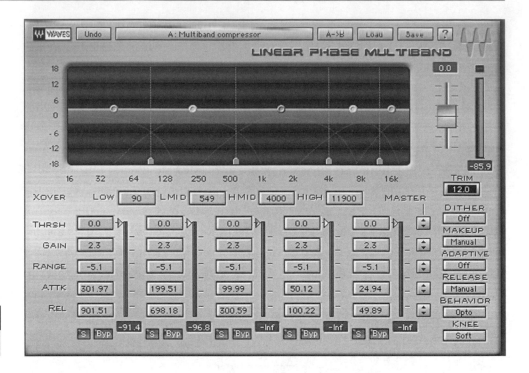

SCREENSHOT 2.16

Multiband compressor

like an EQ, it can be used to either boost or dip at a variety of points along the frequency spectrum. These multiband processors dip by compressing, but they can also be set to boost by expanding when triggered. Rather than side-chaining an EQ'd signal, multiband compressors use frequency analysis to identify frequency ranges from the original signal and use these to compress or expand at the frequencies set by the recordist.

Multiband compressors can be helpful with certain problems, especially when you are mastering program material that has already been mixed. For example, with a track that has a harsh-sounding vocal, you could use EQ to roll off some of the high mids to reduce the harshness, but that would tend to make the track sound dull all of the time. With the multiband compressor set to compress the high mids, you could probably set the threshold for the high midrange compression to trigger off the lead vocal. In this way, the high mids would be reduced only when there was vocal, leaving the track unchanged during passages with no vocal.

In general, program material that has unwanted buildup in certain frequency ranges at certain times might best be handled with a multiband compressor. This means that mastering is the most likely place for multiband compressor processing, and fixing problems is the time it is most appropriate to be put it into action. Beware of using multiband compressors too frequently—EQ and standard compression produce more consistent and predictable results.

Brickwall limiters and maximum level

Digital audio has changed the meaning of "maximum volume." With analog, the final maximum gain of any particular audio element was limited by a variety of factors, including the ability for a needle to track high gain on a vinyl record. In an absolute sense, there is a limit to the volume in any analog system or storage medium if the goal is to prevent distortion and other compromised audio artifacts, but it is confused by the perception that certain kinds of analog overload distortion, on certain instruments and in certain circumstances, may be considered desirable. There is no such confusion in regard to maximum level in digital audio.

Digital audio converts gain from analog sources using a scale that culminates at digital zero. Digital zero represents a "brick wall," in the sense that digital audio is unable to effectively process any incoming sound that exceeds digital zero. Any such sound will turn into distortion (digital noise). Unlike analog distortion, where the sound may break down gradually as distortion increases, all digital distortion is characterized by the same basic qualities (which are exceedingly unpleasant by any typical musical standard).

In order to prevent digital overload, and to maximize gain potential, a variety of software processors known as brickwall limiters has been developed. While these are a part of the larger compressor/limiter family—they reduce the level of loud sounds based on a user-definable threshold—they function quite differently and are used for different purposes than the typical compressor or limiter. A typical brickwall limiter has two basic controls: the threshold and the output ceiling. The *output ceiling* represents the loudest level that the processor will allow the audio to achieve. This functions as a brick wall, or infinity to 1 (∞:1) limiting ratio, which means that it allows no overshoot beyond the ceiling that is set. While this ceiling might be set to digital zero to attain maximum level, it is typically set just shy of digital zero—often to -0.2 dB—to avoid problems that processors may have trying to reproduce a lot of audio at digital zero. In order to create an absolute brick wall—no overshoot—these processors use look-ahead technology that utilizes complex algorithms to analyze and process audio prior to its output.

Unlike a typical compressor, the *threshold* control on a brickwall limiter increases the overall volume of the incoming audio. The threshold increases

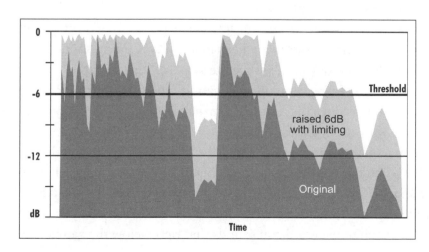

DIAGRAM 2.13

Brickwall limiting

the gain linearly—for each 1 dB in lowered threshold, there is a 1 dB gain in overall level. As a result of the increase in gain, any elements of the incoming audio that exceed the output ceiling are limited to the absolute maximum set by that ceiling. For example, if the threshold is set to -6 dB and the output ceiling is set to -0.2 dB, the incoming audio will be boosted by 5.8 dB (the difference between the 6 dB threshold and the -0.2 dB ceiling), and any of that audio that would exceed -0.2 dB of gain on the digital scale will be completed limited, to stay within a maximum output of -0.2 dB. The effect of this action is to make the overall level of any audio that has not reached the output ceiling louder by up to 6 dB, while any audio that would have exceeded that limit is set to -0.2 dB. The primary use of brickwall limiters is for mastering and their use is discussed more thoroughly in chapter 7.

Expanders/noise gates

Expanders and noise gates are the opposite of compressors and limiters. Rather than decreasing the dynamic range of audio, they increase it. *Expanders* operate using the same basic control parameters as compressors/limiters. *Noise gates* are simply more powerful expanders (they utilize a higher ratio), following the same model as limiters, which are more powerful compressors (utilizing a higher ratio). Although expanders and noise gates find a variety of applications in audio, they are much less frequently used than compressors and limiters.

Expanders allow the audio that exceeds the amplitude threshold to pass through unprocessed while it processes (reduces the gain) of the audio that does not exceed the threshold (again, the exact opposite of compressor action). The level of the quieter sounds is reduced based on the ratio (with high ratio settings yielding greater gain reduction). Expanders do not need to have gain make-up controls because the louder sounds have been unaffected.

Expanders and gates are useful in certain circumstances when you wish to reduce background noise or leakage from adjacent sounds. This is particular true in live recording situations. There has been progressively less use of expanders in studio applications because of the capabilities of digital audio, which allow relatively easy elimination of unwanted parts of recordings. Functions such as "strip silence" work like an expander in separating sounds based on a user-definable threshold, but they operate as an editing tool rather than as a real-time operation, offering more flexible gating-type functions. The editing process allows you to adjust the results of expansion in many more ways than would be possible with an expander operating in real time. A typical example is a noise gate set on a snare-drum track to reduce the level of leakage from other drum-set elements when the snare drum isn't playing. If a dynamic drum roll were played on the snare (from soft to loud), the soft hits would likely be gated by a typical real-time expander. By using "strip silence" to edit the track, you can go back and retrieve the soft snare-drum sounds that were below the gating threshold.

2.7 FX: Delay

The most common effects are all delay-based, generally emulating what happens to sound in different environments. This means that these effects add delayed versions of the original sound, just as acoustical environments add delays caused by the sound's bouncing off of surfaces and returning to the listener slightly later than the direct sound that comes from the sound source (as shown in Diagram 2.1 at the beginning of this chapter). Delay-based effects include reverb—the most complex and natural simulation of acoustic environments—and echo effects (delays) that provide simpler, more stylized simulations.

Long and medium delays

Although single, discrete repeat delays (sometimes called "echoes") that are nearly identical to the sound source do not actually exist in nature—any natural delay is somewhat compromised (less discrete than the original)—they are used frequently in recording to simulate the effect of acoustical environments. Long delays simulate larger environments where the sound travels to a distant wall or surface and the time it takes for the sound to return to the listener makes it discernable to the ear as a delayed signal. The most obvious example of this effect is in a very large concert hall or church (or something like a rock quarry), where the listener can hear a very distinct echo of a word after the entire word has been spoken. In a very "live" environment (one with highly reflective surfaces), the delay or "echo" will repeat many times as it bounces back and forth between walls, diminishing in volume each time as the sound waves lose energy with each trip through the air. When we simulate this effect using a delay processor, the ear perceives the sound as having been made in a large acoustical environment.

A typical delay unit has a control for the length of the delay and for feedback. The length of delay is usually set in milliseconds, though there may also be settings based on musical time (e.g., one quarter note, one half note, etc.). The feedback controls the number of repeats, with each repeat diminishing in volume to simulate the occurrence in nature. A setting of 0 feedback yields one discrete delay.

Long delays are usually about 250 ms (1/4 of a second) or longer. Long delays are usually used with some feedback to simulate the repeating echo of large spaces. Delay times between 100 and 175 ms are medium delays

SCREENSHOT 2.17

Single delay plug-in

and are sometimes referred to as *slapback delays*, as they provide a short but audible delay that suggests a medium to large acoustical environment. Slapback delays are typically just one discrete delay, no feedback. (In section 6.2, I explore more specific uses of long and medium delays when mixing.)

Short delays—chorusing, doubling, phasing, and flanging

Short delays, typically between 1 and 50 ms, provide a very different kind of effect than the medium and long delays described above. Short delays are not primarily used to simulate room environments; rather, they are used to provide doubling or thickening effects. The primary model for short-delay use is chorusing. *Chorusing* refers to the typical effect of choral singing when no two singers are perfectly aligned with each other. Neither are any two singers perfectly in tune with each other. The combination of slightly time-shifted and slightly pitch-shifted performances creates the thick and pleasing sound of a vocal chorus. This effect is simulated with digital signal processors by the use of a modulated short delay. Chorusing effects typically use delay times between 20 and 40 ms. There may be only one discrete delay or multiple discrete delays with slightly different delay times.

Modulation is the technique used to create small changes in pitch. Typically, a low-frequency oscillator (LFO) is used to oscillate (shift) the pitch of the incoming audio. The waveform of the LFO nudges the pitch in a regular pattern back and forth from sharp to flat. The depth setting controls the extent to which the pitch is shifted and the rate controls the speed that the pitch is shifted.

Doubling uses one or more short delays without any modulation. This can thicken a sound (though it may make it more artificial sounding) without the regular cycling that is created by modulation. *Phasing* and *flanging* are similar to chorusing but typically use shorter delay times. Definitions vary (there is no "standard") but phasing is usually considered to use delay times in the 3 to 6 ms range and flanging in the 1 to 3 ms range. Both use modulation, often deeper and faster than with a typical chorusing effect, and sometimes with feedback to produce even less naturalistic sounds.

Many unusual sounds can be created using these kinds of delay-plus-modulation effects. Settings can vary widely in regard to delay times, modulation depth and speed, type of waveform used for the LFO, and feedback—producing a wide variety of effects. Other controls such as phase reversal, EQ, filters, and

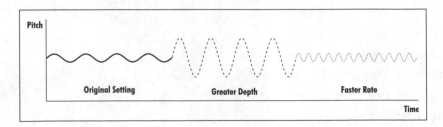

DIAGRAM 2.14

Sine wave LFO

multiple delay lines can increase the variety of these modulating effects. (In chapter 6, I explore more specific uses of short delays when mixing.)

2.8 FX: Reverb

Reverb is short for *reverberation* and is the most realistic of the delay-based effects. Generally, reverbs simulate or reproduce the kinds of complex delays found in an acoustic environment. Reverb consists of early reflections, which are the quickest and most direct reflection of sounds; and reverb tails (or late reflections), which are the multiple reflections that continue from the early reflections. The large number of delays that make up the reverb tail are heard as a "cloud" of sound rather than as discrete delays. The early reflections cue our ears in regard to the size and shape of the space, whereas the reverb tail cues our ears to the general "spaciousness" of the environment.

The reverberation time, or length of the reverb, is generally defined by the time it takes for the delays to decay 60 dB from their original value. The reverb time is controlled by a combination of the size and surfaces of the room. The larger the room, the longer it takes for the sound to travel to the various walls and ceiling and return to the listener. The more reflective (rigid) the surfaces in the room, the longer the sound will continue to bounce back to the listener. Concrete, brick, tiles, glass, and so on will provide longer reverb times, whereas carpets, drapes, and people (audiences, for example) will reduce the reflections and the length of the reverb.

Reverb devices

Over the history of recording, many different devices have been used to create the reverb effect. The most basic approach is to use a microphone to capture some of the natural reverb of the space as a part of the recording. It's almost impossible to avoid doing this completely, but contemporary close-mic recording techniques do eliminate most of the natural reverberation of the recording space. Sometimes mics are moved some distance from the sound source to capture reverb along with the direct sound, and sometimes additional mics are used primarily to record the room ambience (reverb). Close miking became increasingly popular as techniques for adding reverb after the initial recording were developed. This gave the recordist more control over the size, quality, and amount of reverb.

In the 1950s, the *echo chamber* became a popular technique for adding reverb. The echo chamber is a relatively small room (from the size of a closet to the size of small bedroom) that is generally all concrete and therefore very reverberant for its size. A speaker is put in the chamber along with two microphones. The original signal is broadcast through the speaker and the microphones pick up the reverberated sound, which is then mixed in with the original recording.

69

The size and reflective characteristics of the room, along with the position of the microphones, will affect the length and quality of the reverb.

Other hardware reverb units are variations on the echo chamber—they feed the sound into a unit that creates reverberant delays that can then be added back in with the original sound. *Spring reverbs* (often found built into guitar amplifiers) do this by using springs in a small metal box. They tend to have a somewhat crude (boingy) but distinctive sound. *Plate reverbs* do the same thing with large metal boxes and have a much smoother sound quality, but they are large and expensive.

Reverb lends itself very well to digital signal processing, and digital reverbs have pretty much replaced most of the other, more cumbersome techniques. Hardware versions of digital reverbs thrived for many years, but they have been mostly replaced by the software equivalent in the form of plug-ins. Digital reverb plug-ins operate using two distinct technologies. The older format simulates reverb characteristics using complex algorithms to approximate acoustical spaces. Many of these simulations are very realistic and natural sounding, but this also provides the capabilities for creating reverberation-type effects that don't occur in nature.

More recent developments have allowed for the recording of acoustical spaces and the transformation of these recordings into impulse-response samples that can be used in the same manner as any reverb device. The impulse-response reverbs require libraries of samples made from a variety of recordings. These reverb plug-ins are exceedingly natural sounding and some feature samples from famous acoustical spaces, including concert halls, auditoriums, churches, nightclubs, echo chambers, and recording studios. Digital reverbs can also either simulate or sample hardware versions of spring and plate reverbs.

Reverb control parameters

The most basic control for a reverb processor is the type of reverb, which is usually defined by the type of space being either simulated or sampled. Thus, reverbs typically have settings for concert halls, churches, rooms, plate reverbs, chamber reverbs, and so on. Because any environment can be simulated or sampled, sometimes this list is extensive and might include things like parking garages, stadiums, nightclubs, and bathrooms. The newer sampling reverbs often identify specific spaces (the Sydney Opera House, for example) that provided the source samples for the reverb.

The next basic parameter is reverb time or length. The reverb time is based on a combination of size and degree of reflectivity of the surfaces. The configuration of

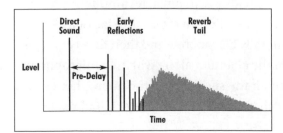

DIAGRAM 2.15

Reverberation impulse response

early reflections and reverb tail, as well as the spacing of delays in the reverb tail (density), might be affected by the size parameter. Some reverbs allow you to balance early reflections and reverb tail separately from the time parameter. Some split size and density into separate parameters.

The predelay sets the amount of time before the reverb tail is heard. This affects the perception of room size. Large rooms will naturally have longer predelay times because of the time it takes for the sound to get to the far walls and return to the listener. Predelay may also affect early reflections.

In addition, reverbs may offer diffusion, decay, damping, envelope, and EQ parameters. Because of the complexities of reverbs, there are an enormous number of subtle qualities that may be user controllable. In practice, most recordists pick reverbs based on the space or quality of the sound that is desired. From the preset it may be desirable to adjust the time or size parameter and perhaps the predelay. It can be interesting to hear the very subtle differences in small parameter changes, but it can also consume a lot of time and may have negligible results. If you have to make large parameter changes to get closer to a desired sound, it is likely that you started with the wrong preset. It is generally better to find a preset that is close to the desired effect and make only small changes (unless very unusual sounds are desired). (In section 6.2, I explore more specific uses of reverbs when mixing.)

2.9 Beyond Traditional DSP

There is a whole new world of digital signal-processing effects available since the advent of the DAW. Some, such as pitch correction, time compression and expansion without pitch shifting, and sophisticated noise reduction, provide capabilities never before available, and they have had a profound effect on music production. Others, such as guitar amplifier simulation and analog circuitry simulation, seek to reproduce some of the capabilities from the analog world that were previously lost in the digital domain. The following is not meant to be exhaustive, and there are frequently all manner of new products.

Manipulating rhythm and pitch

Some of the unique new capabilities that have emerged in the era of the DAW have to do with manipulating rhythm and pitch (the fundamentals of music) in new ways. Besides the tremendous new capabilities in editing music, and thus altering rhythmic placement and even creating new rhythmic content, the DAW has brought the easy time compression and expansion (shrinking and stretching) of audio. Of course, a variety of analog techniques were used for speeding and slowing audio, but these inevitably brought a corresponding change in pitch. The DAW can change tempos (speeds) without changing pitch. It does this by using algorithms to determine what to remove or add that conforms to the surround samples in a way to produce the most transparent results. Some-

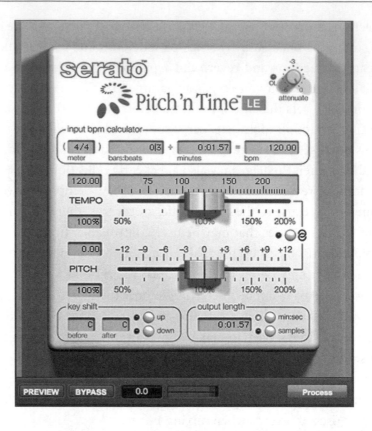

SCREENSHOT 2.18

Time compression or expansion

times changes in speed result in audible artifacts that render the result unusable in a typical musical setting (especially with large changes in the time base), but often the result is not apparent. There are more and less capable plug-ins that accomplish this, and it is an evolving technology. I've used some programs that have allowed me to speed up or slow down entire mixes by several BPMs without a change in pitch and without noticeable artifacts. Rhythm-altering software has also been used to match samples of performances with differing tempos so as to combine elements that would not have conformed to the same musical fundamentals. In practice, this allows for the combining of beats from samples of differing tempos and for more complex combinations of elements as found in mashups.

DAW software has also been developed that allows for alterations in pitch. There are relatively simple pitch-shifting devices that can alter pitch without altering the time of the audio. These plug-ins may be used to shift pitch in small ways that can be used, along with short delays, to create chorusing-type effects. The pitch shift doesn't modulate at regular intervals as it does with a traditional chorus, but instead remains constant (perhaps between 5 and 9 cents sharp and/ or flat). This technique can also be used for much larger pitch shifting that can create standard harmonies, typically from thirds or fifths, or you may choose more unusual harmony notes. Many of these plug-ins are "intelligent," in that they will make appropriate choices for harmonies if supplied with the music's key signature.

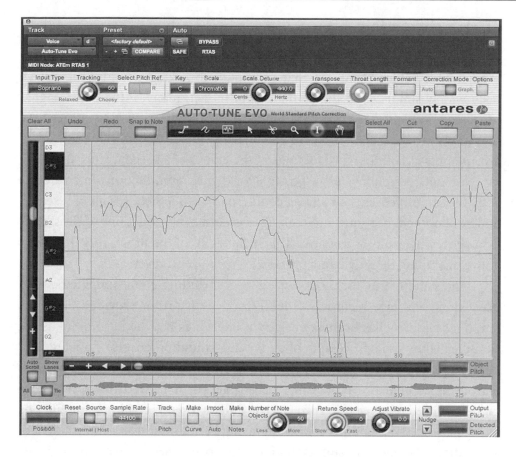

SCREENSHOT 2.19

Auto-Tune

Advances in pitch-shifting devices have incorporated pitch-detection capabilities, which then allow for the retuning of performances. Often referred to as *auto-tuning*, these plug-ins (Auto-Tune and its competitors) allow pitch fixing of vocal and instrumental performances either by automatically moving the pitch to the closest note in the scale selected or by allowing you to redraw the pitch graphically as desired. Besides being a tool for the correction of performances, Auto-Tune–type programs are being used to create new and unusual vocal effects that would not be possible for a singer to perform naturally.

Noise reduction

Tools for noise reduction originated with Dolby and dbx systems that were designed to reduce the tape hiss associated with analog tape playback. In the digital world, noise reduction has taken on much broader applications. Digital noise-reduction processors can reduce or eliminate broadband noise (including tape hiss and surface noise from transferred analog recordings), buzzes, clicks and pops, crackling, and so on. These processors have been used extensively to "clean up" old recordings for reissue on CD. Noise reduction is accomplished through sophisticated detection algorithms and then combinations of filtering and compression/expansion routines that isolate and reduce the noise while having a minimal effect on the remaining audio.

Analog simulation

For all the problems with noise created by analog audio, there have also been many highly valued properties that are unique to analog systems. These have been widely simulated in the digital realm. In fact, many of the digital signal processors available for DAWs are simulations of analog gear. Sometimes they are simply modeled on a variety of analog hardware units, and sometimes they are attempts at faithful reproductions of the effects of a specific piece of gear. I say "attempts" because it is not possible for digital reproductions to create exactly the same effect as their analog counterparts. Nonetheless, a lot of research and development has gone into making as accurate reproductions of classic analog processing units as possible. This includes all of the processors discussed above, including EQs, dynamic processors, delays, and reverbs.

The same is true for other analog gear, including guitar amplifiers, tube processors, and tape recorders. The distinctive distortion provided by guitar amplifier circuitry has been extensively modeled, as has the harmonic distortion created by tube processing of audio and saturation effects of analog tape compression. Elaborate software that models the many possible effects of these various kinds of analog processing is available. For many recordists, it has become standard practice to record electric guitars directly (with no amplifier or external processing) and to create the final guitar sound using these software simulations. Guitar amp simulators have also been used extensively on other instruments, and even vocals, to create distinctive effects. Other analog simulations of tube or tape recorder effects are routinely used on instruments and over entire mixes to subtly enhance the sonic character of recordings. There is endless debate in pro audio forums about the accuracy of these reproductions, but for most users the point is not whether the software is an accurate reproduction of the original but simply whether the software is producing a desirable effect. As always, it comes down to "What does it sound like?"

Vibrato and tremolo

A couple of standard effects that have been around for a long time, but they don't fit neatly into any of the above categories. *Vibrato* is a periodic shifting of pitch (frequency) and *tremolo* is a periodic shifting of volume (amplitude). Although these are the proper definitions, the two terms sometimes get confused, such as the tremolo bar on an electric guitar, which actually produces a vibrato effect, and the vibrato settings on some guitar amps, which actually produce tremolo. In practice, when produced by singers or on stringed instruments using finger and/or bowing techniques, there is often a certain amount of both effects being created at the same time.

Vibrato is related to the modulating effect of chorusing, but it tends to be more pronounced. It is generally produced by the musician, as opposed to being controlled electronically. The periodic pitch shifting adds interest to sustained notes, provides a thickening effect, and allows for a more forgiving relationship to the center pitch of the note. A deep and wide vibrato is associated with certain musical styles and with various historical periods (older operatic singing, for example). The use of finger vibrato on the guitar is associated with certain seminal electric guitar players, including BB King and Eric Clapton.

Tremolo is most frequently heard on electric guitar and as part of certain keyboard effects. Guitar tremolo is associated with certain styles of country and American roots music, and the spinning action of a Leslie speaker gives the traditional Hammond B3 organ sound a kind of tremolo effect.

Chapter 3

Recording Sessions
A Practical Guide

3.1 Setup

Setting up for a recording sets the tone for the entire session. Careful and complete setup makes for smooth running sessions. If you are at a commercial studio you may have help with your setup, but you will need to direct the assistants. Setups may range from the very simple to the very complex, but in any event it is best to do as much of the setting up before the session, and before the musicians arrive, if possible. This means having a good session plan. It's best if you've been able to consult with those involved beforehand so you know what they are planning and expecting. If the plan calls for a variety of recordings that require separate setups, you should consider what you think is a realistic goal for the time allotted. You don't want to set up for a bunch of things that you may well not get to, but you do want to do as much of the setup as you can in advance. This section divides setup into microphones, headphones, consoles, patching, DAWs, and then testing and troubleshooting. Careful and complete setup procedures will save time and foster a creative working environment.

Microphone setup

Setting up the mics also means choosing the mics and having a plan for the number and positions of mics for the elements being recorded. For complex setups, a written *mic plot* (or *input list*) is essential. Many studios have preprinted forms for mic plots that allow you to list the mics and the associated inputs. Except for simple setups involving three or fewer inputs, it is a good idea to write down the mic, the instrument, and the input points to avoid confusion in setup and patch-

Big Nut Studio

Artist Barry and the Examples

Engineer: Sam Jones

Date: 4/2/09

Input	Instrument	Mic	Comments
1	Kick	D112	
2	Snare top	SM57	
3	Snare bottom	KM184	
4	Hi-Hat	AKG 460	
5	Tom 1	421	
6	Tom 2	421	
7	Tom 3	421	
8	Ride Cymbal	AKG 460	
9	OH L	KM84	Spaced
10	OH R	KM84	Pair
11	Room L	U87	Spaced
12	Room R	U87	Pair
13	Bass DI	Countryman	
14	Scratch Guitar	SM57	Isolation room
15	Reference Vocal	U47	Isolation room

Big Nut Studio - 123 Abbey Rd, Townsville - Ph: 555-1234

DIAGRAM 3.1

Mic plot

ing. For very complex setups, you may also want to make a diagram showing where all the musicians and instruments will go (a *stage plot*).

Once the mic plot is established, the best mic stand and mic cable available for the job need to be selected. The cable should be attached to both the mic and its point of input as dictated by the mic plot so that it's ready to be tested. It should be properly positioned for recording, but if the musician hasn't arrived or gotten his or her instrument set up yet, the mic should be place close to where it will be used. For instruments held by the musicians (horns, strings, acoustic guitar, etc.) the final mic setup needs to be done in conjunction with the musician so the individual can show you exactly how he or she holds the instrument when playing. *You will want to consult with all the musicians to make sure that the positions of the mics and the stands are not interfering with their playing in any way.* The survey of instrument recording techniques later in this chapter has recommendations for specific mic and, in some cases, mic stand selection.

Headphone setup

Along with the mic setup, the headphones for each musician need to be set up and positioned. I devote the following section of this chapter to headphone (also called cue or monitor) mixes, so as far as the basics of setup go, you just need to make sure that each musician has a properly working set of headphones located for easy access. Closed headphone designs that are made to limit leakage from around the ear are necessary for studio work near an open microphone.

Headphones vary widely in terms of power requirements to achieve equivalent volume levels. This is why it is essential that either all of the headphones are of the same make and model or each musician has individual volume control for his or her own headphone. The overall headphone amplification system is also important; you need to ensure that there is adequate power for every musician. Each set of headphones that is added to a system increases the load on the amplification, so more power is required to drive more headphones. Headphones with higher ohm ratings require less power (and some models of headphones are available in different ohm ratings), so this should be considered when purchasing headphones.

Console setup

By console setup I am referring to a hardware console or mixer; setup for the internal or virtual mixer within the DAW is covered in a later section. There may not be any console setup for your session if you are simply plugging mics or line inputs (synths, etc.) directly into an interface and all processing and routing is done within the computer. Of course, all microphones require preamplification before going into a DAW, so this must be supplied by the interface, a stand-alone mic preamp, or a console with mic preamps. For this reason, many studios with larger session requirements have hardware consoles with mic preamps and routing capabilities to send audio to the DAW. Sometimes the console is used for headphone routing as well.

Input setup on a console

A hardware console is usually essential for large sessions, though this has been replaced in some studios with numerous stand-alone mic preamps and a patch bay. The advantage of a console is the ease of centralized operation, along with headphone mix and output monitoring capabilities. In a typical studio environment, the console is interfaced with the wall panels from the studio for input and the DAW for output. This means that if you plug a mic into input number 1 on the wall panel in the studio, it is hardwired to input number 1 on the console. The output of buss 1 on the console is hardwired to input number 1 on the DAW interface. More complex studio setups require that a patch be made in order to route the signal from the wall panel in the studio to the console and/or from the console to an input on the DAW interface.

If the console is acting as a series of mic preamps, then each channel strip will provide preamplification and phantom power, if needed. The preamp con-

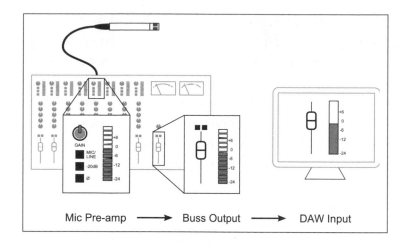

Mic Pre-amp $\longrightarrow$ Buss Output $\longrightarrow$ DAW Input

DIAGRAM 3.2

Mic preamp to buss output to DAW

79

trols the input level into the channel strip and the output fader controls the level from the console into the DAW via a buss. Setting the appropriate record level requires balancing the mic preamp input with the buss output, and reading the final record level as shown on the channel meter in the DAW. For initial setup, you simply want to verify that all the connections have been made and that you are getting signal from the mic into the DAW. Levels should be kept low until the musician is available and final record levels can be set.

Monitor mix and Headphone mix setup: Console or DAW?

The proper setup for control-room monitoring and headphone mixes depends on many factors, but the first question that needs to be answered is whether the mixes should be created at the console or within the DAW. There are advantages and disadvantages to each method.

Setting up all of your monitoring functions in the DAW means that all of your setup will be retained from one session to the next—simply recalled as part of your file. It also makes creating rough mixes in the computer (for burning to CDs or sending as mp3s) much quicker because what you are hearing is ready to be bounced down, all within the digital realm.

If you take all your DAW outputs and return them to separate channels on your mixer, and run your headphone mixes from the cue sends on each channel, you have the ease of using hardware controls rather than struggling with the mouse and the virtual mixer controls in the DAW. However, your setup will not be saved from one session to the next, and taking rough mixes to put on a CD requires some extras steps. You will need to either record from the console's stereo output back into the computer and then make the appropriate files or record into some other system such as a stand-alone CD recorder. However, if you are using a digital control surface you get the advantages of both systems: the DAW controls are mirrored in the control surface hardware, giving you the ease of using hardware controls, while all your level and processing functions are still retained within the DAW.

Overdub situations usually involve considerably fewer inputs than initial tracking sessions and they often require editing as a part of the process. Levels generally stay fairly constant for large periods of time as well, so it is easiest to control everything from a control surface or within the DAW when doing overdubs. If the DAW is interfaced to a console, this means simply monitoring the stereo buss from the DAW through two channels (or some other stereo return) on the console. Headphone mixes can also be routed to two channels of the console and those can be sent to the headphone mix as a stereo pair.

Patching setup

Patching, or interconnecting, all of the elements for a session can range from the very simple to the extremely complex, depending on the number of elements involved and the studios patching system. Studios have a variety of patching strategies and patch bays can vary widely in how they are wired. Problems with patching—whether incorrect patches, bad cables, or bad patch points—are some of the most common problems that slow down sessions, so an understanding of patching and attention to patching detail is critical.

Patching strategy

There is one simple rule for the best patching strategy: always patch from the source to the destination, following the signal path. In a typical patching situation, this means starting by plugging the cable into the microphone and finishing by patching into the DAW or other recorder. Sometimes some of this patching is already done with dedicated patches, such as console outputs that that are wired to feed DAW inputs. Each patch follows the intended signal path from the source through whatever series of outputs and inputs needed to record the signal.

Simple patching

A simple patch might be plugging a mic cable into a microphone and then plugging that cable into a DAW interface that includes a mic preamp. This completes the chain from source to destination. A slightly more complex patch might start with the mic cable into a microphone, from there into a stand-alone mic pre or channel strip, and then the output of the mic pre would be patched into the line input of a DAW interface or a console that is already interfaced with the DAW and requires no further patching. Even with simple patches like this, it is always best to patch from source to destination—from output to input, following the signal path.

Patch bay use

As patching gets more complex and studios wish to streamline the process of interconnecting a variety of elements from a variety of sources, patch bays be-

PHOTO 3.1

A console scribble strip indicating the stereo buss and two stereo cue mix returns

come an essential part of the studio. Many consoles have built-in patch bays to simplify access to all the patch points needed to get in and out of the various console functions. Patch bays can take on many different shapes and sizes and use a variety of types of connectors. Single-point patch bays may use 1/4-inch, RCA, or TT (tiny telephone) connectors and multiple-point patch bays may use a wide variety of D-subconnectors that have anywhere from 9 to 50 patch points at each connection point (though not all patch points may be wired for use).

Patch bays are centralized patching stations that facilitate the patching process. If a studio has a variety of recorders (DAW and/or tape based), outboard processors, mic preamps, and recording spaces, then patch bays become an essential element in functionality. Besides the fundamental in-and-out component of a patch bay, the use of normaled (and half-normaled) pairs of patch points allow patch bays to pass signal when connections are in their "normal" use but still allow the user to "break" the normal in order to create patches for alternative uses. The "logic" of normaled and half-normaled patch points is as follows:

Normaled

Two patch points are considered *normaled* when nothing is plugged into either jack and the signal is wired to pass from the top jack to the bottom (typically configured as one patch point above the other in the patch bay). For example, an external mic pre is wired to one jack and below that is a jack that is wired to line input number 1 on your console. With no plug in either jack, the mic pre goes right to input number 1 of the console. But plug a patch cord into either jack and the connection to the console is broken. When a patch cord is plugged into either jack, it separates the "v" part, breaking the connection between the two patch points. If, for instance, you want to send the mic pre to a compressor before it comes into the console, you would break the normal by plugging a patch cord into the mic preamp jack and routing it to the compressor. In a schematic normaled patch points look like this:

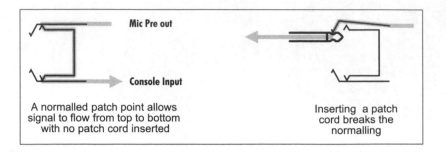

DIAGRAM 3.3

Normaled patching

Mic Pre out

Console Input

A normalled patch point allows signal to flow from top to bottom with no patch cord inserted

Inserting a patch cord breaks the normalling

Half-normaled

When two jacks are wired to be *half-normaled,* the connection is not broken unless there is a cable into both connections. The mic pre's input could be tapped at the top jack, but it would still go to the console. Plugging something else into the console's output, however, breaks the connection from the mic pre. This kind of patch is useful if you want to send the signal from the mic pre to two different recorders (that weren't both accessible from the console).

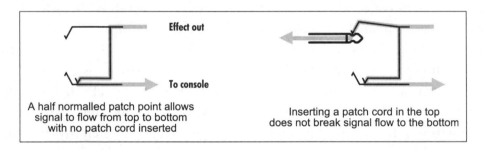

DIAGRAM 3.4

Half-normaled patching

Effect out

To console

A half normalled patch point allows signal to flow from top to bottom with no patch cord inserted

Inserting a patch cord in the top does not break signal flow to the bottom

While patch points that are half-normaled can be used to effectively split a signal, sending it to two places at once, many patch bays also have *mults,* which are used to split signals. Wired in parallel, mults provide multiple patch points that offer as many outputs as there are patch points in the mult—excluding one of the mult patch points, which serves as the input. Because mults are wired horizontally, any patch point in a mult can be used for the input. Mults are commonly used to send signals to auxiliary recorders (in which case, for stereo you will need two mults—one each for the left and right feed).

Complex patching

A complex patching situation might go as follows: a cable is plugged into a mic and from there connected to a wall panel in the recording room, the wall panel output has been wired to a patch point on a D-subconnector (D-sub) in the machine room, from there it is patched to another D-sub in the machine room

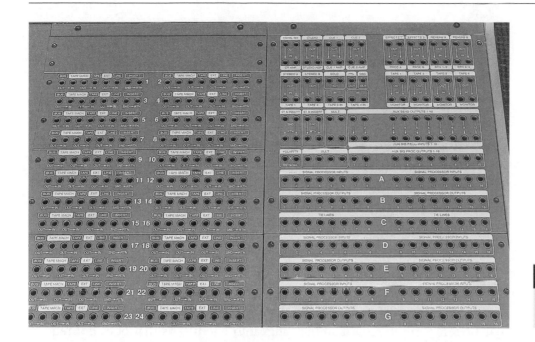

PHOTO 3.2

A TT (tiny telephone) console patch bay

that feeds the console inputs in the control room, the buss output of the console feeds a D-sub in the machine room, and from there it is patched into another D-sub in the machine room that feeds a wall panel D-sub in the control room, the D-sub in the control room is patched into a D-sub that feeds the inputs into the DAW. This signal path would be described by a series of outputs and inputs:

- Mic out to wall panel in
- Wall panel out to machine room D-sub in
- Machine room D-sub out to machine room D-sub console in
- Console buss out to machine room D-sub in
- Machine room D-sub out to machine room D-sub DAW in
- Machine room D-sub DAW out to control room wall panel D-sub in
- Control room wall panel D-sub out to DAW in

While patching can become very complex, as in the above example, if you adhere to the rule of patching by following the signal flow from beginning to end, it can be straightforward and you can have consistently good results.

PHOTO 3.3

A machine-room patch bay with Elco and other connections

84

DAW setup

Unlike a hardware mixer whose capacity is fixed, a DAW's mixer configuration can be set up for individual projects as needed. You can build your mixer as you work and you can also create templates that make complex setups much faster and easier. Although the specifics of each DAW will vary, the basics of DAW setup include creating the number of tracks needed for a recording session, naming the tracks, and assigning the appropriate inputs and outputs for each track. Some basic level and panning settings, creating sends for headphone feeds, and some effects such as a reverb that might be used for monitoring can also be set in advance.

Many files or one big file?

When starting a project that involves many songs (a typical CD project, for example) you will need to decide how you are going to manage the song files. It may be tempting to record all the songs into one file, as that does not require using a template and setting up a new file each time a new song is going to be started. It makes things easier at the basic session to have all the songs in one file and it can make mixing easier as well, but it is generally only a good idea for projects that are going to be very limited in the amount and variety of recording to be done.

If the project is solo piano, or acoustic guitar and voice, then one big file will be easier to manage and will save time. The same is true for live recordings, even if there are many tracks involved, because there are usually no overdubs (or very few), and a very consistent sounding mix for all songs is often appropriate. Of course, there isn't time to switch files during most live recordings, anyway.

For projects where there are going to be a lot of overdubs and a fair variety of instruments and/or arrangement elements (background singers on some,

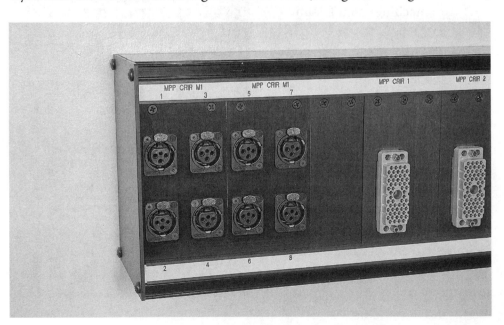

PHOTO 3.4

A studio-room wall-mounted patch panel

horns on others, etc.), then it is best to create a new file for each song. Ultimately, this makes the recording and mixing process simpler and more focused because there are not a lot of extraneous elements that don't relate to the song you are working on at any given moment. By using a template at the basic session, it doesn't take much more time to set up a new file for each song;, and in the long run this makes for more efficient work and better file management.

Regardless of how you organize your files, it is a good idea to periodically remove recorded and edited elements that you are not using. This includes multiple regions that may have been created in the editing process. Because each DAW file needs to keep track of all the elements recorded into that file, too many recorded elements can slow or even stop the operation of a file. DAWs have different ways of naming and identifying unused bits of recordings or edited pieces, so you will have to explore your own DAW to find the way to eliminate these elements; but it is important to do so, especially in large and complex projects. Simply remove these elements from the current file; don't erase them from your hard drive (two different choices in the "file management" function). Remember, if you maintain multiple files for each song or project, you can always return to an earlier file to retrieve elements that you may have removed in a later file. I name my files using ascending numbers, creating a new file at least once each day that I work on a song. For example, a song titled "Swing the Hammer" will be saved as *Swing the Hammer 2* the second day it's worked on and saved as *Swing the Hammer 3* the third day, and so on.

WHAT NOT TO DO

Don't record more than one song into an individual DAW file if you expect there to be a lot of recording (multiple takes and/or multiple elements) for that song. Too many recorded elements in one file will slow down the DAW's ability to function, and can even prevent it from functioning at all if the file gets too large. This is one of the most frequent causes of poor file performance and can often be fixed by removing unused audio files and regions from your session. You don't have to eliminate the audio from your hard drive to do this. Remember that keeping a separate session file for each day of work (or even more frequently, if a lot is done in a day) will allow you to recover previous material easily if needed.

Managing multiple takes

There are two basic options for managing multiple takes of the same piece of music (e.g., different takes of the same song). You can (1) place each take one after the other on the DAW's timeline as you would on a tape recorder, or you can (2) use virtual tracks and place each take "on top" of the other so that only one take at a time is visible in the DAW. The advantages to technique 1 are that you can see all of the takes at once and create markers for each individually. The advantage to take 2 is that your timeline is less cluttered and if you are working to a fixed tempo or click track, you can line all your takes up and more easily edit between various takes.

Many DAWs are developing new working protocols for handling multiple takes. Some are providing ways to manage virtual tracks so that they can all be seen at the same time and you can establish a hierarchy to automatically take care of muting when moving from one to the other. I have seen the various techniques debated in user groups, and it's clear that no one approach is best—use whatever approach seems most comfortable to you.

Line testing, setting levels, and troubleshooting

Once the setup for a session is complete, it is important to test your signal path, set rough levels, and, if necessary, troubleshoot before the recording begins. You can do most of this yourself, but if you have an assistant, it makes the process easier. It is always important to work as efficiently as possible, but if you have to involve the musician in the testing process it is doubly important.

Line testing

The first test is a line test, in which you verify that signal is passing as expected from the source to the recorder and then out to the monitoring system. This is easiest to do with an assistant lightly tapping each mic. If the mics are close enough, you can clap to see if they are active. You can also turn up the gain on the mic pre and see if you detect signal, but be careful as this can easily cause feedback.

As a part of the line-testing process, you also want to check to see if the headphones are working properly, both for talkback and playback. You might be able to hook headphones up to the cue system in the control room and check that way. If you already have something recorded, you can play that back and go out to the studio to see that the headphone playback is working and to check for

WHAT NOT TO DO

Do not ask a musician to put on headphones and proceed to playback audio for the individual without knowing that the level of that audio is not too loud. There are few things worse that blasting audio into a musician's ears at a recording session. Not only is it unpleasant and unnerving, it can actually affect the person's hearing for a period of time and make it more difficult for the musician to perform. Always check the headphone level before the initial playback for musicians.

level. You will want to check your talkback level, as well. You can do this if you have headphones in the control room or use an assistant or one of the musicians to check. It is always a good idea to start with the headphone level at a relatively low volume and to turn it up slowly to meet the musician's requirements. Many studios now have headphone boxes with volume control so each musician can control his or her own volume. Small units are available for home and project studios, and this feature is highly recommended.

Setting levels

Setting input levels for each instrument requires the participation of the musician being recorded. Once you have confirmed the signal path and the headphone operation (ideally before the musician arrives), you can ask the musician to play for you. Besides determining the quality of the sound, dependant on mic selection and mic placement (as explored in section 3.3 on recording various instruments), you will need to set the input level. Proper level setting requires discovering something close to the loudest volume the musician will be playing so that you can get a good amount of signal for your recording without overload and distortion. This can be a challenging process, but here are some rules of thumb.

Begin by explaining to the musician that you need to hear the person's loudest playing level in order to set a recording level. Ask the musician to play the loudest part from the piece that you're going to be recording, as different pieces will have different dynamic ranges. It's quite common for musicians to play their part louder when the recording actually begins, so always leave some headroom when initially setting levels. Some times musicians end up playing somewhat softer than they did when they were testing, so level adjustments may be necessary in either direction.

Nonetheless, it is most desirable to not change levels once recording has begun—especially not during an actual recording pass. With the heavy reliance on editing in many contemporary recordings, a consistent level makes it much easier to piece together performances from many different takes. Nonetheless, level does matter. There is the obvious problem of distorted audio if the level is too loud. If the level is too low, there is some sacrificing of resolution, as fewer bits are available to describe the audio's timbre.

There may well be a conflict between the desire to record at the maximum level without overload and the advantages of not changing level once recording has begun. Keep in mind that even the first run-through—sometimes the musicians aren't even aware that you're recording (you should *always* be recording)—may produce the best music of the day. Levels can be adjusted to compensate for level changes made during recording passes, but it can be difficult and time-consuming. Knowing when it is necessary to change your input level and when it's best to leave it alone, even if it's a little louder or quieter than optimal (without distortion of course), is part of the recordist's skill set.

Troubleshooting

Of course, you hope that there won't be any troubleshooting required at any session, but the reality is that with so many cables and knobs, and so many computer and software issues, there are likely to be some problems at many recording sessions. Fast, efficient troubleshooting is one of the primary ways topnotch recordists distinguish themselves from those with less experience.

The key to efficient troubleshooting is the ability to think logically through the signal flow to determine the most likely cause of the problem. The most common problem is no signal and the cause can be anywhere in the signal chain. Some consoles show input level, and that means you can determine if signal is getting from the mic to the console. If there is input level, then the problem is somewhere between the console and the DAW; if there is no input level at the console, then the problem is before the console. Problems can be anywhere in the signal path—bad mics; bad cables; bad connection points in the wall panel, patch bay, or DAW interface; or they can be computer related, such as software glitches that require program or computer restarts (or worse).

There are other typical problems, such as buzzes or hums. These can have multiple possible causes, from electrical to electronic to cell phone interference. There can be intermittent problems that can be almost impossible to track down until you can find the cause and reproduce the problem without having to wait for it to occur on its own. There can be dropouts. There can be computer freezes. There can be polarity problems from inconsistent wiring. The list is almost endless. Some problems can be easily solved, and some cannot be solved without sending gear out for repair, requiring sessions to be canceled in the meantime (the most dreadful outcome, of course). Following the signal path and using logical procedures to determine the most likely reason for the problem are the best companions to experience in troubleshooting.

One of the most valuable ways of correcting problems is the *workaround*. That means finding a way to eliminate the problem without necessarily identifying what is causing the problem. If there is a complex patching situation like the one described in the previous section, and you find that audio is not passing through to the DAW, you might start by plugging into a different patch point at the wall panel, which is going to bring the audio in to a different channel on the console. If that solves the problem, you don't necessarily know if it was a problem with the wall patch point, the patch point into the console, the channel or buss in the console, or the patch point at the computer interface. You make a note to track down the problem later (there is a trouble report form at most commercial studios) and simply move on. Workarounds are often quicker than identifying the specific thing that is causing the problem, and speed is the number one priority when it comes to troubleshooting—especially when people are waiting to start or continue recording.

3.2 Headphone Mixes

I have allocated a whole section of this chapter to headphone mixes (sometimes called cue or monitor mixes) because of how important they are to making successful recordings. However, before examining the process of making traditional headphone mixes, I explore some important alternatives.

WHAT NOT TO DO

Do not use headphones if the situation doesn't demand them. Following are some circumstances where headphones are not needed.

For most musicians, playing while monitoring through headphones is not as comfortable or familiar as playing without them. If you are recording a solo musician or an ensemble that plays together and balances their sound without the use of amplification (a string quartet or an acoustic duo, for example), then do not use headphones. Or, if you are able to bring the musician into the control room and work with the monitor speakers, this is almost always preferable to using headphones.

Working with the monitor speakers rather than headphones is easy to do with synthesizers and other instruments that do not require microphones (such as a bass guitar recorded direct), but it is also usually pretty easy to do with amplified instruments such as electric guitars. Place the guitar amp or speakers in a separate room, run a guitar cable to the amp, and then mic the speaker. If the amp head is separate from the speakers, the head can be in the control room and then run a cable from the amp to the speakers in a separate room. The guitarist can monitor his or her sound along with the rest of the recording in the control room with you.

If you are "sharing" the monitoring (through the speakers in the control room) with a performing musician, the performer should dictate the mix. Be sure to keep checking with the musician to see if the individual is hearing as desired, in terms of both his or her own volume relative to any other instruments and the overall volume of playback.

Some people even like to do vocals—and other recording that requires a microphone—in the control room. Of course, feedback and leakage can create problems if you're using speakers rather than headphones for monitoring, but there have been many great "live" recordings done with speaker monitors, so it certainly can be done. You can set up floor monitors in the recording room, as you would at a live gig, or you can use the control-room monitors. If you are monitoring in the control room, one trick is to put the control-room monitors out of phase so that there is some phase cancellation when the sound reaches the microphone. This can help reduce leakage.

Using your control-room mix for the headphones

An alternative to the traditional, independent headphone mix is using the same mix as you have for control-room monitoring for the headphones. The advantages of doing this are the ease of setup and the easy control of all the elements. Just as you are often making small adjustments in the control-room monitoring as performance dynamics change and the focus shifts to different elements, so might headphone mixes benefit from continuous monitoring and subtle shifts in balance. Sharing mixes with the performer also means that you are continuously monitoring the headphone mix so you will be much quicker to correct imbalances, such as often happens when a new instrument enters (a solo, for example) that hadn't necessarily been balanced in the initial headphone mix. I almost always use my control-room mix for the headphones when recording a single musician doing overdubs—especially vocalists.

A variety of circumstances will prevent your using the control-room mix for the headphone mix. When the musicians need to hear something that you don't want to hear (such as a click track), or when there is significant leakage in the studio but not in the control room (such as live drums), you need to adjust the headphone mix to account for the room sound. Often, when musicians are in the studio with live drums, they will need almost no drums in their headphones, as they get enough just from the sound in the rooms. Of course, you still need to hear the drums well in your monitor mix, as you aren't hearing the live drums in the room. The other disadvantage to sharing mixes is that you can't change your mix to hear something differently while the musician is recording. For example, if you decided you wanted to hear the background vocals as loud as the lead vocalist you are recording, to see how in tune they are, you wouldn't be able to do that because it would disrupt the headphone mix for the performing vocalist. Nonetheless, in many instances, the advantage of sharing mixes outweighs the disadvantages.

Creating separate headphone mixes

The typical situation, especially in larger sessions, requires a separate headphone mix for the musicians. Often two or more mixes are needed, especially if musicians are in different rooms. A classic example is a band recording in the main room and a vocalist in an isolation booth. The band needs a separate mix to account for the live drums in their room, whereas the vocalist needs sufficient drums and usually a lot more vocal level in order to sing. You might also be using a click track that needs to go to the drummer, but not to the other musicians. In that situation, three separate headphone mixes would be best: one for the drummer that includes the click; one for the other musicians in the main studio room that does not include the click or much drums, because they would be getting most of their drums from leakage; and one for the vocalist with a normal amount of drums and enough vocal to allow the vocalist to sing comfortably.

Once you have decided whether to use a DAW or your console for your separate headphone mixes (discussed above, under "Setup"), there are certain technical details that are essential to all headphone mixes. First is that aux sends will be used to control the levels for the separate headphone mix, and second is that all the aux sends must be set to pre-fader. *Pre-fader* means that the auxiliary send is tapping the signal before it gets to the main output fader (what you use for your control-room monitor mix) and is therefore independent of that fader. With pre-fader aux sends, you can create an independent headphone mix that doesn't change when you change levels on the channel's main output (post-fader sends follow the main channel output and are used primarily as effects sends in the send and return model, covered in section 5.2).

Besides separate pre-fader sends for each of your headphone mixes, you need separate amplification for each cue mix. There are a variety of small headphone amplifier and mixer options that provide from one to six separate headphone amps, and there are modular systems that allow you to add as many as you need (with some limits, of course). Some things to keep in mind are that different kinds of headphones have different power requirements and the number of headphones in use will also affect the ability of any given amplifier to supply sufficient level to all of the headphones. Some of the professional headphones come in different ohm ratings, meaning they have different power requirements. If you know that you'll be driving a lot of headphones at the same time, you can chose the model with a higher ohm rating that requires less power to drive each pair of headphones. Consider the needs of your studio situation and research the amplifier and headphone options that fit your needs and your budget.

Musicians make their own headphone mixes

It has become increasingly common for studios to have systems that allow each musician to make his or her own headphone mix. These systems consist of small mixers with headphone amplifiers that can easily be stationed near the musician. By feeding separate elements to the mixer (pre-fader, of course), the musician can then adjust the level and panning of each element to meet his or her own needs. There are several commercial systems available that provide varying features, including 4-, 8-, or 16-channel mixers. Some have built-in limiters to help guard against accidental overload.

Depending on the number of channels, it is likely that you will need to make some submixes for the headphone mixer boxes. With an eight-channel system, for example, you might make a stereo submix of the drums and then have individual channels for the bass, the guitar, the keyboard, the vocalist, and the click track. That would be a total of seven channels. As a result, you would still need to make adjustments depending on musicians' needs (more kick drum, less hi-hat, for example), but the bulk of the headphone mixing can be done by each musician.

The value of these personal monitoring systems is that they allow individual musicians to craft their own headphone mixes in the way that suits them best, and it allows them to adjust overall volume, as well as individual elements, instantly as needed. The disadvantage is that they do not allow the recordist to hear what the musicians are hearing, and as a result, they don't necessarily get the benefit from your experience. In the following section on the creative side of headphone mixes, I explore ways that headphone mixes might affect performances; what I have learned is that when the situation is appropriate for sharing mixes (control-room monitor mix and headphone mix), I do that, even at studios where there is the option for the musicians to control their own mixes.

The creative side of headphone mixes

Headphone mixes affect performance, and with experience you can help musicians create and alter their headphone mixes during the course of a recording in order to improve their performance. One example is working with a drummer who is playing to a click track. If the drummer is having difficulty staying with the click, it may be that the click isn't loud enough. Drummers without much experience playing to a click often don't realize how loud it needs to be in order to maintain the groove to the click. On the other hand, if the drummer is staying with the click but having trouble making appropriate transitions—as in changing his or her part for the chorus—then the drummer probably doesn't have enough guide vocal in his or her headphones so the musician is losing track of where he or she is in the song.

With singers, getting the headphone mix right is an essential part in helping them sing in tune. If their own vocal level is too loud in the phones, they will not have enough pitch reference from other instruments; and if the voice is too quiet, they won't be getting enough pitch reference back from their own voice. If extraneous elements are too loud (percussion or horn section, perhaps) and fundamental instruments are too low (bass and rhythm guitar or keyboard), then the singer will have trouble finding the pitch. It is often valuable to keep working with vocalists on their headphone mix over the course of a session.

An appropriate balance of elements in the headphones will affect the details of a musician's performance. A subtle shift in headphone balance can inspire a musician who has been overplaying to lay back more, and it can encourage a musician who has been struggling to find a part to come up with just the right thing. It isn't always possible to know what is going to work, which is why communication is such an important part of headphone mixes.

Talking about headphone mixes

At every session that involves multiple musicians, and each time I work with someone I haven't worked with before, I have a discussion about headphone mixes before we start working. What I say is essentially this: "It's hard enough to play music; it's much too hard to do so when you're not hearing well. So, *please*, let me know if you're not happy with your headphone mix. I don't care if you've already complained ten times and you're feeling like you're bringing everybody down; you must have a good headphone mix and I want to work with you until you do. The worst thing for me at the end of a session is to have someone say, 'I could have played better if I were hearing better.' *Please*, keep complaining about the headphone mix until it's right!" Even after offering this advice, it is still important to continue to ask the musicians if they are hearing okay. Over the course the session you want to ask "Are you hearing okay" every so often, just to remind the musicians to speak up about anything that might make them more comfortable with their headphone mix.

WHAT NOT TO DO

If you are using a click track or a loop for tempo control in a band recording, only allow the drummer to hear the click or loop. You want all the musicians to play to each other, especially to the drums—and not to the click. After all, the click will not appear on the final recording, so the groove that matters is the drummer's groove, even if it is being guided by a click track. Sometimes musicians need the click for a break when the drums don't play. In that case, print a track that has the clicks in the break and feed that to everyone in their headphones. Musicians will often ask for the click if the drummer is getting one, thinking that it will help them with the groove. Try to talk them out of it, if you can.

3.3 Survey of Recording Techniques for Instruments and Voice

Probably the most important elements in the final sound of any instrumental recording are (1) the way the musician plays the instrument; and (2) the sound of the instrument itself, including how it's set up and tuned. That said, the recordist's job is to capture the sound in the best way possible for the intended purpose. This survey is not intended to be exhaustive—that would be impossible—but the following represents many years of personal experience and research.

Using EQ, compression, and limiting when recording

Rather than addressing the use of EQ and/or compression for each instrumental recording technique, I am going to discuss this topic in more general terms. The problem with advising on EQ and compression usage is that it varies in every situation, depending on the sound of the instrument, the room, the musical genre, and the ultimate instrument configuration (e.g., solo instrument, small band, large band, etc.). Nonetheless, there are some general things I advise in regard to using EQ and compression when recording.

As a general rule, elements that will ultimately need a considerable amount of EQ and compression in the final mix should have some applied when recording; and elements that will need a small amount of EQ and compression, or none at all, should have none when recorded. For me, this translates roughly as follows: drums get EQ but no compression; bass, vocals, horns, electronic keyboards, and most acoustic instruments get compression but no EQ; electric guitars get no EQ or compression. These rules of thumb can easily be overturned by circumstances, but what really varies greatly is the amount of EQ or compression that might be applied. There is no substitute for experience in this regard, but again, as little as seems obviously beneficial is the best guideline.

Limiting can also be used as a guard against overload when recording, and this may be especially valuable in live recording situations. With studio recording, it is usually possible to do enough testing to be confident that overload is unlikely, but in situations where unexpected changes in level seem likely, a limiter in the recording chain that is set to limit near the top of the acceptable record level can be a worthwhile addition.

Direct boxes, reamp boxes, etc.

Direct boxes (or DIs, for "direct inputs") are an important part of many of the following descriptions of recording techniques. A direct box converts instrument level (and impedance) into microphone level (and impedance), and as a result provides a cleaner signal path that can be run for longer distances. Electric guitars and basses, synthesizers, samplers, drum machines, and so on put out various amplitudes of line-level signal that can benefit from a DI for recording. Most DIs provide two outputs so that the unprocessed signal can continue out of the DI to an amplifier while the converted signal goes to the mic preamp for recording. They also provide ground-lift capabilities that can help prevent hums and buzzes caused by improper AC grounding. Although direct boxes can be bypassed in many situations by plugging line-level sources directly into mixers or interfaces, DIs will generally provide better results.

Passive DIs require no external power whereas active DIs need to be powered, either by batteries or by phantom power from a console or mic preamp. Some active DIs require either batteries or phantom power and some are capable of using either. Passive DIs are less expensive, but they may introduce some high-frequency signal loss. Many contemporary mic preamps include a DI function so that instruments can be plugged directly into the preamp for conversion to mic level. Some direct boxes and mic preamps are tube based, and these provide a different tonality.

A reamp box is a relatively new device that converts the output signal from your DAW back to a typical output level from a guitar or bass. This allows for easy reamping, which means putting the recorded signal back through an amplifier, miking the amp's speaker, and rerecording the sound. This can be convenient for unsatisfactory guitar sounds or for situations where the desired guitar amp isn't available for the initial recording. Reamping works best when the initial recorded signal is the direct signal from the guitar, so some recordists record guitars both directly and through amps, just in case they decide they want to do some reamping later.

By the *etc.* in the title of this subsection I am referring to other boxes that can be valuable aids in recording, such as splitters and other level or impedance conversion boxes. Splitters that allow a guitar signal to be split out to two separate amplifiers without losing gain can be a useful tool, as can other conversion boxes, such as those that convert -10 dBV output level (consumer gear) to +4 dBu input (professional gear).

Drum set

Drum sets can vary enormously in their specifics. Here, I cover the basic types and principles for recording drums. The section in chapter 6 on mixing drums might provide some ideas about how these recording tactics play into various mixing strategies for a final drum sound.

Recording a drum set can be one of the most challenging jobs for a recordist. On the other hand, I read an interview with Mick Jagger in the 1980s in which he was asked what had changed most about making recordings between the '60s and the '80s. He answered that it was recording the drums. In the '60s, they used to spend an enormous number of hours—sometimes days—trying to get a decent drum sound, but by the '80s it would take less than an hour. Experimenting with drum-set recording techniques can be fun and can yield great results, but there is often a considerable limitation on time available, so the tried-and-true techniques that have been developed, and that prompted Jagger's response, are good starting points.

There are numerous potential strategies for recording drums, but there is a basic technique that has become pretty well standardized. This involves using separate microphones for almost every element in the drum set, and frequently two mics on the critical bass drum (more frequently called the kick drum) and the snare drum. Mics are also used on each individual tom-tom (usually referred to as either rack toms if mounted on the bass drum or floor toms). The hi-hat is miked and then a stereo pair of mics is used for "overheads" that cover all the cymbals and provide something of an overall drum sound. Frequently, a separate mic is used on the ride cymbal and, if the room the drums are in has an appealing sound, then a stereo pair of room mics is also used. On a typical drum set (configured with two rack and one floor toms), this could easily amount to 13 microphones as follows:

- (2) Kick drum: a mic inside the drum and one outside in front of the drum
- (2) Snare drum: a mic above and a mic below the drum
- (1) Hi-hat
- (3) Tom-toms: one for each tom, two rack toms and one floor tom
- (2) Overhead: a stereo pair
- (1) Ride cymbal
- (2) Room: a stereo pair

A more thorough explanation of the tactic for each drum follows:

Bass drum (also called kick drum)

Drums have two basic elements to their sound. The initial attack portion of the sound created when the stick (or bass drum beater, or hand, or whatever) strikes the drum and then the resonant vibrations of the drumhead and shell after the drum has been struck. While a mic can easily capture both of these elements, with an instrument as important to popular music as the kick drum, we often use two mics, each one optimized to capture the two different elements of the sound. On the bass drum, this means having either a hole in the front head of the drum, no front head at all, or an internal mounting that allows us to place a mic within a few inches of the front head (from behind the beater side, inside

PHOTO 3.5

An AKG D112 microphone positioned inside a kick drum

the drum) to best capture the sound of the attack when the drum is struck, and another mic—often a couple feet away from the front head—to capture the resonance of the drum.

The close mic can be either directly across from the beater or set off-center for a slightly softer attack sound. It can be anywhere from 2 to 10 inches inches away from the beater, the closer positioning providing a more pronounced attack. Experimenting with this mic position can be productive, though a simple standard (across from the beater and about 4 inches away—or some variation on this that you prefer) can provide excellent results very quickly. A dynamic mic is almost always the best choice, and certain mics have become industry standards (Electrovoice RE-20, Sennheiser 421, AKG D-112), but there are many new mics coming onto the market all the time that have been specifically created for recording kick drums and these can also do a great job.

The outside mic can be a large-diaphragm condenser mic as long as it isn't too sensitive to loud sounds (most contemporary non-tube mics will hold up fine). The classic mic to use is the Neumann U-47 FET, but it is expensive (though it can also be used for many other things, including vocals). Because the mic is outside the drum, in front of the drum set, it is subject to picking up a lot of leakage from the other drums and cymbals. It is a good idea to isolate this mic by creating a tunnel that effectively extends the shell of the kick drum. This is most commonly done with mic stands and a bunch of packing blankets, but it can also be done with a rolled-up carpet. I like to refer to this structure as the "tunnel of love" because the tunnel creates such a lovely kick-drum resonance.

As an alternative or in addition to the mic outside the drum, you can use the speaker "trick" for capturing the very low end of the kick drum. This involves placing a speaker very close to the bass drum so that the speaker cone is vibrated when the drum is struck and then wiring the speaker with an XLR connection and taking its output as though it were a microphone. Remember, a microphone and a speaker are at the two ends of the same process—one captur-

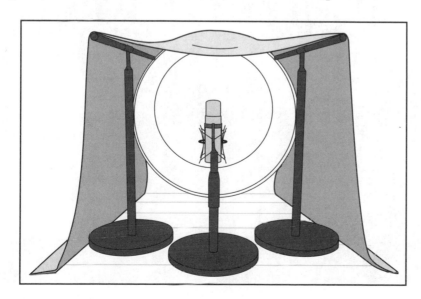

DIAGRAM 3.5

Kick-drum miking with a "tunnel of love"

ing and one reproducing sound—and as a result they use very similar technologies (a vibrating membrane). A Yamaha NS10 speaker, at one time the standard for small monitor speakers in studios, is often used as a "faux" microphone to capture the low end of the kick.

Snare drum

The snare drum is often the most prominent drum in a final mix, and it is frequently one of the loudest overall elements as well. Although many other mics and techniques have been tried and are used sometimes, the standard is a Shure SM57 placed a few inches in from the rim and a few inches above the drum. The mic can be placed at varying degrees off-axis, and this will affect the sound slightly. Many people also use a second mic underneath the snare drum, pointing up at the snares. A small-diaphragm condenser is a good choice for this mic, but many different mics, including a second SM 57, will work fine. This mic allows you to add more of the rattling "snare" sound if you want it. Because it is facing above the snare mic (180 degrees out of phase), it needs to have its polarity switched for the two mics to be in phase. Although I sometimes record a second mic under the snare, I find that I rarely end up using it in the mix.

If miking a snare is so easy, why is it so difficult to get a great snare sound? The key to the snare drum is in the way it is hit and the way it is tuned. These two elements can vary so greatly as to completely alter the sound of the drum, no matter how it is miked. The drum itself is important as well, but unless it's really poor quality or in really bad shape, almost any snare drum can sound great if it is struck and tuned well. How the drum is struck really changes the sound (normal hit, rim shots, hit in the center, etc.—consult a drummer!). Snare drums are also complicated to tune because of the interaction between the two heads and the snares. Damping is often used on the top head, and this can alter the sound dramatically.

PHOTO 3.6

Miking the top of a snare drum (Shure SM57)

Anything from small bits of duct or gaffer's tape, a small square of folded paper towel, a wallet, or some "moon gel" (a gel-like substance that sticks to the drum and is sold at music stores) can be used for dampening the snare drum. If you are not happy with the snare drum sound, there is a good chance that the mic or mic placement is not at fault; it's more likely to be a combination of how the drum is being hit, how the heads are tuned, and what, if any, dampening is used. Using EQ and compression on the snare drum in the final mix (as discussed in section 6.2) will also play a significant role in the final sound of the drum.

WHAT NOT TO DO

Don't assume anything about the sound of a snare drum.
Shallow snare drums don't necessarily sound higher in pitch and metal snare drums are not necessarily brighter than wooden ones. It's a good idea to have several snare drums available at a session and to audition each—but remember, tuning and dampening can really change the sound of the drum.

Hi-hat

Recording the hi-hat is generally accomplished best with a small-diaphragm condenser mic placed a few inches in from the outer edge and above the hi-hat cymbals. You will want to check how far up the top cymbal is when the hi-hat is open and how loose the two cymbals are to make sure that the mic has a few inches of clearance. You can aim the mic slightly away from the drum set to minimize leakage from the other drums.

PHOTO 3.7

Miking a hi-hat (AKG 452 EB)

Tom-toms

Tom-toms are recorded much like the snare drum, generally using dynamic mics with similar placement above and in a bit from the rim. The Sennheiser 421 has become the default microphone for the tom-toms and it does a great job, but there are many equally good alternatives on the market these days. Some people prefer condenser mics on the toms, and it is a different sound—more detail but less of the woody warmth. If you use a condenser, make sure it can withstand the level or be sure that the drummer isn't going to hit the toms very hard.

Positioning the tom mics can be a challenge, depending on where the drummer's cymbals are placed. It's important that you find a spot that doesn't interfere with the drummer's stick movement and won't get hit by a swinging cymbal. As discussed in section 8.1, do not ask the drummer to move any of his or her drums or cymbals to accommodate the mike positioning!

Although I list drums as one of the few elements that I tend to EQ while recording, the tom-toms are the one part of the drum set that I often do not EQ until the mix stage. I've found that when tuned and recorded properly, tom-toms require very little EQ, so it is best to reserve it for the mix stage.

PHOTO 3.8

Miking tom-toms
(Sennheiser 421s)

Overheads

There are many ways to approach overhead miking. The size of the drum set, the sound of the room, whether or not you are using room mics, and the kind of drum sound you prefer will all be factors in choosing a strategy for your overhead mics. In most cases, my preferred overhead setup is with small-diaphragm

PHOTO 3.9

Overhead drum miking using the ORTF stereo configuration—insert shows mics configuration in close-up (Neumann KM-84s)

condenser mics centered two to three feet over the drums in an ORTF stereo configuration. For larger drum sets you may want to use a spaced-pair configuration to capture all the elements of the set more evenly. This may produce slightly more phase problems, but it will give a good stereo spread. You can also use a classic X/Y stereo pair for a tighter, virtually phase-free sound but with a narrower stereo field.

If you have room mics, then the overhead mics may be closer to the drums, really focusing the attention on capturing the cymbals. If you don't have room mics and like the sound of your room, you may want to consider using large-diaphragm condenser mics for overheads and putting them another foot or so higher above the drums. In this way, you capture some of the room acoustics along with the overall drum sound. If the room sound is problematic, then you'll want to keep the overheads pretty close to the drums.

Ride cymbal

Even with overhead and room mics, it is a good idea to put a separate mic on the ride cymbal. Generally, a small-diaphragm condenser mic positioned a few inches above the ride cymbal is best. Although the overheads will pick up a lot of ride cymbal, there may be times in mixing that you want more ride cymbal relative to the crash cymbals, and a separate ride track allows you to balance the two. It used to be that the limited number of tracks made it hard to accommodate a separate track for the ride cymbal when it isn't always needed, but the expanded track count of most DAWs has eliminated that problem. The question may be whether you have enough mics and mic inputs, and if you do, I recommend a separate ride cymbal track.

PHOTO 3.10

Miking a ride cymbal
(AKG 452 EB)

Room mics

Room mics can be a wonderful addition to an overall drum sound if the drums
are in a nice-sounding room. Placement may vary depending on the room and
the amount of ambience desired. A pair of large-diaphragm condenser mics
works well, and typical placement is eight to ten feet from the drum set, pointing down from above. Some recordists swear by a mic placed a few feet above
the drummer's head pointing at the set.

PHOTO 3.11

Stereo room mics for
drum recording (Neumann
U-87s)

Percussion

There are literally thousands of percussion instruments (including the drum
set), so it is impossible to cover them all. Instead, I have divided percussion into
three basic "families" and will cover the general principles for each.

WHAT NOT TO DO

Don't skimp on drum mics.
There seem to be endless stories about how great drum sounds have been captured using minimal miking setups. The stories are no doubt true, and you may indeed want to use the three-mic drum sound (kick and two overheads) or the five-mic drum sound (kick, snare, two overheads, and room) or whatever. But none of these tactics precludes having many more mics to choose from. I recently made a record, and during the tracking the artist (who favored the sound of blues records from the '30s and '40s) said, "That's too many drum mics." I said, "We don't have to use them all." And indeed, in the final mix we often only used a few of the drum mics to get the best sound for the record. However, at one point during one mix, the artist said "Can I get more hi-hat?" and at that point we were both glad that I had used a mic on the hi-hat.

Drum percussion

Here, I include congas, bongos, timbales, djembe, taiko, and other drum-based percussion instruments. Also in this family are the drums in the drum set, and a similar strategy for recording may be employed for all of these instruments. This means that a dynamic mic, placed a few inches in from the rim and above the drum, is a good starting point. When placing mics, the recordist needs to be sensitive to how the drum is played so as to not interfere with the musician's technique.

PHOTO 3.12

Miking conga drums
(Sennheiser 421s)

High-pitched percussion

Here, I include cymbals, tambourine, chimes, triangle, bells, and other percussion that produces primarily high-frequency sounds. Because of the fast-moving transient frequencies of these instruments, their sound is very effectively captured by large-diaphragm condenser mics. The mic should be reasonably close to the instrument, but take care not to interfere with the playing.

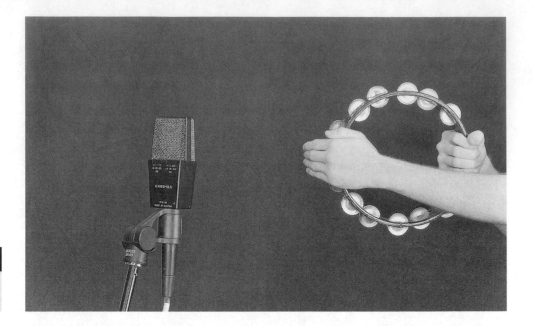

PHOTO 3.13

Miking a tambourine (AKG C-414 ULS)

Clacking-type percussion

Here, I include cowbell, woodblock, castanets, guiro, and other percussion that is struck and that produces sharp clacking or scraping sounds. These thick, strong sounds are generally best captured by a dynamic mic. You will notice slight variations in tonality depending on which part of the instrument the mic is facing.

PHOTO 3.14

Miking a cowbell (Sennheiser 421)

Bass

The low frequencies of bass instruments are easily compromised by amplifiers and room acoustics, so take care if you wish to capture the purest sound possible (certain genres may encourage all kinds of experimentation that does not value a "clean" bass sound). For obvious reasons, electric and acoustic basses require different recording tactics.

Electric bass

Electric bass is often recorded very simply, using a direct box (DI) to transform the output from the instrument into a mic level output that is fed into a mic preamp and then directly to the DAW (or through a mixer and then to the DAW). The advantage of direct recording of bass guitar is that it bypasses the various problems that amplifiers and speakers can cause (low-level distortion and unwanted effects caused by room acoustics). There are a variety of direct boxes available and they will affect the sound of the bass, as well. Some recordists swear by the sound of tube DIs for bass. I often include some compression in the input chain. The Empirical Labs Distressor and the Urei 1176 are frequent choices for bass compression, though many compressors—including plug-in versions—will compress the bass without noticeable artifacts.

Some bassists like to record the amplified sound along with the direct sound and combine the two when mixing. If doing so, I like to place the mic about 12 inches away from the bass speaker to allow for

PHOTO 3.15

Miking a bass guitar speaker (AKG D112)

some greater contrast to the direct sound. Sometimes it is best to just take the direct out from a bass amplifier without using the speaker. This allows you to record the effect of the amplifier's preamplification, as well as any onboard effects that you might want from the amplifier without the additional diffusion created by speaker reproduction. Although I usually simply take the bass DI, I am happy to record the preamp or mic the speaker as well if the bassist feels that it is an important part of his or her sound.

Acoustic bass

Acoustic bass can be a challenge to record effectively, especially if it isn't isolated from the drums or other sounds. A small-diaphragm condenser mic often works best for acoustic bass. It should be placed about 12 inches from the front of the instrument facing one of the f-holes—this usually allows the musician sufficient freedom of movement when playing. Most bassists have a pickup that they use to amplify the bass, and this can be ex-

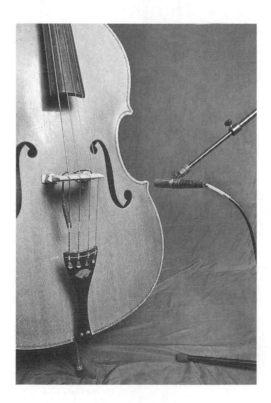

PHOTO 3.16

Miking an acoustic bass (Neumann KM-84)

ceedingly valuable when there are leakage issues, but it never has as good a sound as the instrument when properly miked. Unfortunately, where there is a lot of leakage, you sometimes have to use the pickup sound primarily.

I've found the acoustic bass pickups are sometimes wired in reverse from the typical mic cable, and so the pickup signal and the mic signal are 180 degrees out of phase. This is easily fixed by switching the polarity of either one of the signals. It's a good practice to check the phase and polarity any time you are getting two distinct signals from the same sound source.

Guitar

Recording guitar has become an elaborately studied art, as guitar has occupied such a central role in so much popular music. The most widely practiced basics are covered here.

Electric guitar

The sound of the electric guitar is intimately tied to the sound of the amplifier and speakers used to reproduce the sound before it is recorded. The elements in the chain, from the guitar itself to any stomp boxes in the chain, to every setting on the amp, to the type and size of the speaker used, to the mic, mic placement and mic preamp, all combine to create the final sound of the electric guitar when recorded. All kinds of mics, combinations of mics, and mic placement strategies have been used to record electric guitars. The classic approach—a Shure SM57 placed halfway between the center of the speaker and its edge, slightly off-axis (the plane of the mic's diaphragm at a slight angle to the plane of the speaker cone), and an inch or two from the speaker grill cloth—still produces excellent results and is sometimes the best approach to capture the desired sound.

Other frequently employed strategies include using a "far" mic (or a stereo pair of "far" mics) in conjunction with the close mic, placed anywhere from 2 to 20 feet away from the amplifier (even mics just 2 feet away from the amp will produce a much different sound than mics 2 inches away). Far mics are often either small- or large-diaphragm condensers. Other dynamic mic models are sometimes used, and ribbon mics

PHOTO 3.17

Miking an electric guitar speaker (Shure SM57)

have become very popular as close or far mics, either in combination with a close dynamic mic or as a replacement.

On-axis placement, varying degrees of off-axis placement, angling toward or away from the center of the speaker, up against the speaker grill cloth or anywhere between 1 and 3 inches away, closer to the center or closer to the edge of the speaker—all of these represent variations on close-mic strategies for capturing the sound from guitar amplifier speakers, and each will make a small but audible difference. When there is time, it can be valuable to explore any or all of these variations and/or additional miking options, but sometimes it is necessary to simply "throw a 57 up to the speaker and go!"

As mentioned above, recording the direct sound from the guitar has become more popular so as to allow for either reamping or using one of the many amp modeling plug-ins now available for DAWs.

Acoustic guitar

Recording acoustic guitar has also been explored extensively, and there are many possible tactics. However, the one that many of the most experienced recordists have settled on involves using two small-diaphragm condenser mics. The primary mic is placed across from the 12th fret (one octave) on the guitar and aimed toward the sound hole. This placement coincides with the most resonant spot on the neck. The second mic is aimed from the other side of the guitar and can be positioned the same distance as the first mic or a bit farther away if you want to capture more of the guitar's fullness.

Many alternative approaches may also produce great results with acoustic guitar, including using large-diaphragm condenser mics, ribbon mics, alternative mic placement, and so on. However, if you are using only one mic, I recommend the positioning across from the 12th fret as the starting point.

PHOTO 3.18

Two-mic technique for recording acoustic guitar (Neumann KM-84s)

Vocals

Recording vocals is one of the most complex of studio activities, and there is information at other points in this text regarding headphone mixes and talk-back techniques that are essential parts of the vocal recording process (sections 3.1 and 8.2). From the technical standpoint, it can be pretty straightforward: a large-diaphragm condenser mic set to the cardioid pattern, with a pop filter in front of it and the mic about 8 to 10 inches from the vocalist is the standard. However, within that context there are many subtle variations. The type of mic, the distance from the mic, and the exact placement relative to the singer's mouth are all elements that can be adjusted depending on the musical genre, the volume of the singer's voice, and the style of his or her delivery.

Although large-diaphragm condensers are generally the first choice, there are other mics, especially dynamics such as the classic Shure SM57 or the Shure SM7, that may be right for your particular singer. Within the ranks of large-diaphragm condenser mics, there is a broad choice, including tube-based mics. It is likely that a good-quality large-diaphragm condenser will sound good for pretty much every vocalist, but when you are getting down to the subtleties, certain mics will sound better for certain singers, and it can be difficult to predict. One can go with a warmer mic on a male vocal to capture the generally lower tonalities or a brighter mic to provide more clarity. You can choose a warmer mic to soften a female vocal or a brighter mic to accentuate the presence. If you have more than one mic for vocals, and if you have the time (both pretty big "ifs" in many cases), it can be valuable to test to see which one is most appealing. It has been very interesting for me to discover that, when there has been an opportunity to compare vocal mics, there has almost always been an immediate agreement among all involved as to which mic sounds best.

PHOTO 3.19

Miking a vocalist—
Michael Moorhead
(Neumann M49)

Large-diaphragm condensers are very sensitive and can be overloaded by a loud vocalist who is too close to the mic. However, a more intimate and detailed sound can be captured when the vocalist is very close to the mic (a couple of inches away) as long as the mic doesn't overload. All directional (cardioid) mics exhibit the *proximity effect* (a bass boost when a singer get very close to the mic), but the large-diaphragm condensers are smoother and richer in proximity so it can be desirable. Ideally, the vocalist works the mic—coming in for quiet passages and leaning back when belting—but even if the vocalist doesn't, you might play with his or her distance from the mic to get the most detail without overload or unwanted proximity effect.

Finally, I offer a note about the mic position relative to the mouth. I prefer to have the mic very slightly above the singer's lips, so as to encourage the vocalist to tilt the head just slightly up and thereby keep his or her throat open. Some singers are not comfortable with this and prefer the mic directly across from the mouth, and some singers prefer to tilt slightly downward. As in all things, the desire of the musician comes first unless you're convinced that it is truly detrimental to the performance and then you can discuss it. Some recordists like to place the mic well above the singer's head, angled down at the mouth. Again, experimentation is helpful in determining the best approach for any individual singer.

Piano and keyboard percussion

The piano is often considered a percussion instrument because of the hammer actions in striking the strings. Other keyboard-based instruments, such as the vibraphone and marimba, are also considered part of the percussion family. The key to recording these instruments is to achieve a good balance between the percussive attack and the resonant sustain. Because these instruments are rather large, and their sounds cover the entire frequency spectrum from low to high, they are usually recorded in stereo (at least two microphones).

Grand piano

The piano is a wonderfully complex instrument, with very rich sonorities covering a huge spectrum of fundamental frequencies and overtones. It is also used in a wide variety of setting so there are many strategies for recording the grand or baby grand piano. Although you can record the piano with one mic, it is typical to use at least two mics to capture a stereo image of the piano. A stereo pair of small-diaphragm condenser mics is most commonly set in one of the standard stereo configurations, such as ORTF or a coincident pair. The mics are usually placed 6 to 8 inches above the strings and can be put parallel to the hammers or the bridge. I prefer the ORTF configuration and an over-the-bridge placement. I also use a third "centering" mic to capture a little more ambience and to fill the "hole" that can be created with a stereo pair. I typically use a large-diaphragm condenser, placed above the lip of the piano casing and aimed to capture the

110

PHOTO 3.20

Three-mic technique for recording a grand piano (Schoeps CM-5s and Neumann U-87)

entire piano. The centering mic is used to stabilize the stereo image and to balance the percussive sound of the stereo pair with additional ambience.

Other strategies for recording piano vary from the best isolation techniques to the most elaborate miking plans. The best strategy for isolation—when the piano has to be recorded in the same room as the drums, for example—is to use a stereo pair up over the strings, with the piano lid in its lowest position (using the short stick to hold the lid up). This takes some careful placement in order to get the mics as far from the piano strings as possible while still being able to lower the lid (short pencil condensers such as Neumann's KM-184s are helpful for doing this). Once the mics are set and the lid lowered, you completely cover all of the openings around the lid, using as many as 20 packing blankets (or other blankets—though packing blankets are relatively cheap and a great asset in a variety of studio setup applications). This does deaden the sound of the piano a bit, but a remarkably good recording is still possible while achieving enough isolation to be able to adjust piano tone and level independently.

For solo or small ensemble recordings where the piano is central, and where there is isolation from other instruments, it is best to remove the piano lid altogether (the hinges have removable pins to make this a relatively simple task). You can start with the same three-mic setup described above and add mics as desired. I have used as many as nine mics on a grand piano by adding a stereo pair 3 feet above the piano and another stereo pair 3 feet or so above that—both in the coincident pair configuration to minimize phase issues. Additional mics can be place at the foot of the piano, facing the player, and above the player's head, facing the piano (because these two mics are facing each other, whichever is most out of phase with the other mics will need to have its polarity switched). You can use either large- or small-diaphragm condensers for these mics, though the stereo pairs should be matched models. When mixing, you may not use all of these mics, and some of them may be used in very small amounts, but tremendously rich recordings are possible by using multiple mic configurations such as this.

Upright piano

A similar three-microphone technique as described above for grand pianos can be used for upright pianos. It is necessary to remove the covers over the strings and sounding board, both above and below the piano keyboard, and to open the top of the upright. A stereo pair of small-diaphragm condenser mics is placed near the bottom of the keyboard box, facing the strings in an ORTF or coincident pair configuration. A third, centering mic, is place near the top of the piano facing down toward the strings and sounding board.

Many other strategies can be used for recording an upright piano, including miking from the back and miking only from the top or bottom. Problems with leakage and access will affect the technique used to make the best recording, under the circumstances.

PHOTO 3.21

Three-mic technique for recording an upright piano (Shure SM81s and Neumann U-87)

Other keyboard percussion

There are a multitude of instruments that are laid out like a keyboard and struck with mallets, but the two most common are vibraphone (vibes) and marimba. These larger instruments can be miked very similarly to a grand piano, using the three-mic technique. Placing the mics over the instrument and leaving enough room for the musician to play comfortably requires careful placement and consultation with the musician. Smaller instruments, such as glockenspiel

PHOTO 3.22

Three-mic technique for recording marimba—Beth Wiesendanger (Shure SM81s and Neumann U-87)

or orchestra bells, can be miked with a single mic effectively, or with a stereo pair, probably best in the coincident-pair configuration.

Brass, reeds, and horn sections

Horns of all types can be recorded using a variety of techniques and a wide variety of microphone types, depending on the desired sound. Of all the instrument groups, they probably receive the broadest treatment—dynamics, ribbons, small- and large-diaphragm condensers all have valuable roles in possible miking strategies for horns.

Brass

The brass instruments include trumpet, flugelhorn, trombone, and tuba, as well as many instruments that are less common in popular-music settings, such as the bugle, French horn, and sousaphone. Although these instruments cover a wide spectrum of frequencies, ranging from the trumpet to the tuba, a basic miking technique will serve well for all brass: the mic is placed opposite the bell (the large opening at the end of the instrument). The mic can be placed closer or farther from the horn, depending on its ability to withstand high SPLs (horns can be loud!) and the degree of detail you wish to capture. Keep in mind that some of the "detail" of horn playing includes the sound of saliva in the instrument, so too close a placement may capture more undesirable elements, but too much distance may lose too much detail. I find 10 to 14 inches a good rule for the higher pitched brass (trumpet and flugelhorn) and 18 to 24 inches good for lower pitched instruments (trombone and tuba). The mics can be placed on-axis (pointed straight at the bell) for a brighter, clearer sound or off-axis for a softer, more diffused sound.

Selecting the type of microphone provides a variety of sonic options. Condenser mics, both small and large diaphragm, capture the truest sound of the instrument (and are generally preferred by the player), but they can yield an overly bright sound in an ensemble. Dynamic mics offer a warmer, rounder sound that may blend better with other horns and instruments. Dynamics also have an easier time handling the high levels that brass can put out, though many condensers (especially if they have a pad) can withstand the levels as well. Ribbon mics have also become popular for recording brass, especially with many

PHOTO 3.23a and 3.23b.

Miking a trumpet on-axis and off-axis—Brandon Takahashi (Shure SM81)

of the newer models able to withstand much greater levels than earlier versions. Ribbons provide a clearer high end than do dynamics (closer, though not equal to a nice condenser) and still provide the warmth typical of dynamics. Make sure the ribbon mic you are using can withstand the SPLs.

My preference for brass is generally the ribbon mics, though I don't always have one available (or one that is capable of handling the level). I will generally go for a small-diaphragm condenser if there isn't a ribbon option, and place it just slightly off-axis on trumpet and on-axis for most any other brass. If the horn is being used as a solo instrument, I will usually go for the condenser. For horn sections I will sometimes use dynamics to get a better blend. Ultimately, the nature of the player, the instrument, and the way the horn is used in the ensemble will all play a role in determining the best choice.

Woodwinds

Horns classified as woodwinds include the saxophone family (baritone, tenor, alto, and soprano) and clarinet, as well as the flute and the double reeds, such as the oboe and bassoon. Although classified as woodwinds, many of these instruments (saxes and flutes, most notably) are made from metal. Recording strategies will vary from instrument to instrument. Woodwind recording is not as straightforward as brass because the sound isn't necessarily coming primarily from the bell of the instrument (the flute doesn't have a pronounced bell). As with brass, a wide variety of microphones may be appropriate, depending on the goal. The instruments also vary greatly in frequency range, from the lows of the baritone sax to the highs of the piccolo flute, and this will affect your recording strategy.

Saxes do have a bell, and a strategy similar to that described above for brass is often a good tactic. A mic 10 to 24 inches from the bell (on the closer side of things for the alto and farther away for the tenor and baritone) captures most of the sound. Dynamics, ribbons, and small- and large-diaphragm condensers can all produce excellent results, with the dynamics and ribbons being warmer (or duller, depending on your point of view) with less high-frequency detail and the condensers being clearer and brighter, but with the potential to reveal too much of the harshness of the instrument. Generally on-axis positioning (directly facing the bell) will be best, but an angled, off-axis approach can be tried if you feel the need to soften the sound a bit.

PHOTO 3.24a & 3.24b

Miking a saxophone, one- and two-mic techniques— Joe Del Chiaro (Neumann U-87s)

Soprano saxes usually benefit from a different approach. With all of the saxes, a good deal of the sound emanates from the sound holes, where the keys are used to change pitches by closing certain of the openings. Because soprano sax is so bright sounding and has a relatively small bell, the more appealing sound tends to come from the sound holes rather than out of the bell. For this reason, I often simply mic from the side of the instrument, primarily capturing the sound that comes out of the sound holes. You can also use this aspect of the sax in a two-mic technique, capturing both the sound out of the bell and the sound from the sound holes. A tenor sax that is used as a solo instrument, especially in a small ensemble, can benefit from this recording tactic.

Clarinet is similar to a soprano sax and is usually captured best with a mic at the side. The lower notes come primarily from the keys, but the higher notes and high overtones come increasingly out of the bell. Placing the mic to the side, but down closer to the bell, can allow for a good balance through the frequency range. Because the sound emanates from different places in different frequencies, it is best if you can get some distance on the mic—preferably at least a foot and up to 3 or even 4 feet might yield the best results, depending on the room and the desired effect. Again, dynamic, ribbon, and condenser mics can all yield excellent, though tonally pretty different results. Ensemble playing often benefits from the warmer mics and soloing will benefit from the greater detail provided by the condensers.

The flute is generally captured from the side of the instrument. Most of the sound of the flute comes from the mouthpiece, so if you are using one mic, it should be across from the mouthpiece. In order to capture the instrument more evenly, and because the flute is so bright and benefits from more interaction with room acoustics to soften the sound, it is usually recorded from a distance of at least a foot away and usually more successfully from a couple of feet away. Interaction with other instruments playing in the same room may dictate a closer mic positioning. The less common alto, bass, and baritone flutes can be captured in the same way.

Double reeds, such as oboe and bassoon, are fairly rare in popular music, but you still need to be prepared if one happens to show up at a session. These woodwinds are related to the flute and the clarinet, in that the sound comes from different places depending on the frequency, so getting some distance on the mic is definitely recommended. The double reeds also produce a lot of hi-mid transients, sometimes heard as a nasal quality, so room ambience helps to soften the sound in a pleasing way. Again, all mic types can produce excellent results.

Horn sections

From 2- to 20- piece horn sections can be recorded with individual mics on each horn player, with mics capturing the section together (stereo pair(s), Decca Trees, etc.), with mics covering each section (brass, reeds, etc.), or some combination of the above. The horn players in a small section (two to six players) are usually miked individually. Mic placement may be a bit closer than with individual horn recordings in order to prevent too much bleed from the adjacent horn players, and you will probably need mics that can withstand the level that horns can produce when played aggressively. I find that dynamic mics often work well for section recordings because they tend to help the horns blend and to occupy less frequency space when mixed with other instruments. Unfortunately, I have found that experienced horn players are sometimes unhappy when they see a mic they associate with live gigs being set up in a studio situation. They know that condensers record a more "true" and detailed sound, and they prefer them, even for section work. I might suggest to them the logic behind using dynamics, but I will always go along with the players' wishes if I can tell they are unhappy about using a dynamic mic. Happy musicians trump subtle recording preferences every time!

Strings and string sections

By string instruments here I am referring to those instruments that are primarily bowed, including double bass, cello, viola, and violin, as well as numerous less common stringed instruments from other cultures, such as the Chinese erhu. The double, or acoustic, bass has already been covered in the popular music context, where it is much more frequently plucked (pizzicato) than bowed (arco).

One important guideline for successful recording of bowed instruments is to make sure that the mic has sufficient distance from the sound source. A bow on strings produces strong transients that can be very harsh sounding if not allowed to soften. The mic should be at least 18 inches from the instrument, and usually a distance of 3 to 4 feet produces the best results. Small-diaphragm condensers are preferred in ensemble situations because of the excellent off-axis response, but large-diaphragm condensers will yield outstanding results in solo recording situations and some recordists prefer the warmer sound of the ribbon mics. The mic is usually placed in front of and above the instrument.

String quartets and other string ensembles are usually best captured with a stereo pair or some form of Decca Tree mic configuration (as described in section 2.3). Because the mics need to have some distance anyway, it usually doesn't make sense to try to mic each instrument separately. Exact placement in terms of distance from the ensemble and height off the floor will vary with the size of the ensemble and the room acoustics. The musicians will balance themselves, so the mics should be placed in such a way as to best capture a balanced version of the entire ensemble. However, you may consider using a spot mic on the cello (probably a small-diaphragm condenser or a ribbon)—18 to 24 inches away. If the room has decent acoustics, you may not need to use any of the extra

PHOTO 3.25

Miking a violin—Reiko
Kubota (Neumann KM-
184)

cello mic, but sometimes the room mics will be a little light in the low end. If
the room is of a decent size, then a Decca Tree with at least two stereo pairs will
allow you to adjust room ambience by balancing the closer and farther of the
stereo pairs.

WHAT NOT TO DO

Do not close-mic bowed string instruments.
*A colleague tells the story of recording a violin for the soundtrack to a
horror movie. He wanted a very harsh, frightening tone, so he put the mic
a few inches from the violinist's instrument. After the recording, he invited
the musician to hear the playback. When she heard the sound of her violin,
she cried! Unless you're after a very special (and particularly annoying)
effect, do not close-mic bowed string instruments.*

3.4 Beyond

Of course, there are many other instruments not mentioned, but the above
should provide enough guidelines to get you started with almost any recording.
Exotic instruments usually fall into one or another of the categories covered;

pay attention to how the sound is created (struck, picked, plucked, bowed, blown, etc.) and where the sound is coming from (it may be more than one spot), and then mic according to a similar and more familiar instrument. When it comes to electronic instruments—synthesizers, samplers, and so on—see the section on direct boxes and use those guidelines for direct-input recording.

Editing
The New Frontier

I am calling editing "the new frontier" because of the tremendously expanded editing capabilities in the DAW. Not only is editing a much more important part of almost all recording projects than it was in the past, a lot of today's music is primarily *created* through editing within the DAW. Although all the major DAWs contain similar editing capabilities—and I use screenshot examples from several of them—the terminology for some specific editing functions in some DAWs does vary. For the sake of simplicity, where there are differences in terminology, I use the Pro Tools terms for these functions. It should be reasonably simple to determine which tools provide the same function in other DAWs.

4.1 Editing Features

The operating tools of editing begin with basic functions—such as cut, copy, and paste—that are familiar to anyone who uses computer programs. Functions that are somewhat more specific to audio, but still easily understood, include duplicate, repeat, loop, clear, and mute. The expanded editing capabilities within a DAW really take advantage of the computer environment. Becoming a capable audio editor who can work quickly requires a lot of experience making all kinds of edits and a familiarity with the idiosyncrasies of your particular DAW.

Audio regions

The building blocks for all editing features are audio regions. *Regions* are either a complete piece of audio as it was recorded from start to stop or some smaller segment of that initial recording that you have subdivided into a *sub-region*. This screenshot shows a region of a complete recording (beginning to end) and then, duplicated on the channel below, that region divided into sub-regions).

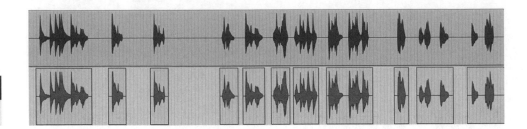

SCREENSHOT 4.1

Regions and sub-regions

120

Typically, all regions and sub-regions are simply referred to as regions, but the distinction may be important when editing. The region created by each full recording pass is a complete entity, whereas sub-regions created from smaller elements of these regions can be restored to include the entire region. The full region created from each complete recording pass is what is stored on the hard drive. The sub-regions are simply an instruction by the DAW program to play only a part of the original recording. In Pro Tools, the initial region is indicated in bold type in the regions list and the sub-regions are listed below it in regular type.

There may be several different ways to create sub-regions from the initial recording. These are basic editing operations that differ within different DAWs, but the principle—the ability to create very accurately timed sub-regions—is essential to much of the editing process. The segment later in this section on edit modes will define the ways that regions can be created and controlled before they are edited.

REGIONS
CAPO GTR
CAPO GTR-01
CAPO GTR-02
CAPO GTR-03
CAPO GTR-04
CAPO GTR-05
CAPO GTR-06
NYLON GTR
NYLON GTR-01
NYLON GTR-02
NYLON GTR-03
STEVE ELEC 2
STEVE ELEC 2-01
STEVE ELEC 2-02
STEVE ELEC 2-03
STEVE ELEC 2-05

SCREENSHOT 4.2

Region and sub-region list

Cut, copy, paste

The most basic kind of audio editing is just like editing with a word processor or just about any other computer program, and it begins with the ability to cut, copy, or paste audio regions. Cutting, copying, and pasting is made possible by the DAW's use of a clipboard, which is a temporary holding place for data. When any piece of data is either cut or copied, it is placed on the clipboard and available for pasting, but only one unit of data can be put on the clipboard at a time. It remains there until another bit of data has been either cut or copied. A whole universe of editing can be done with these most basic tools—cut, copy, and paste combined with the clipboard function that keeps data available to you as you work.

Duplicate, repeat, loop, mute, clear

The next set of edit functions expand on the basic cut, copy, and paste concept. As with many edit functions, these are often simpler and quicker ways of doing something that could be accomplished with more labor using the basic functions. The ability to work quickly and efficiently becomes very important when literally hundreds of edit functions need to be accomplished at a single session.

Duplicate allows you to duplicate an audio region with one step rather than copying and pasting (two steps). Once a region has been selected (usually by highlighting it), the duplicate function creates a duplicate region adjacent to the original region—that is, the beginning of the region is butted up against the end of the region being duplicated.

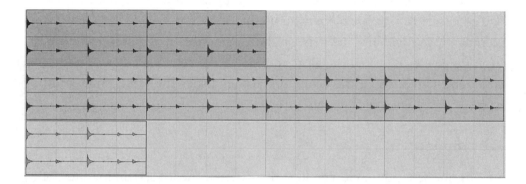

SCREENSHOT 4.3

Top track is a duplicated region; middle track is a repeated region; bottom track is a muted region

Repeat allows you to duplicate a selected region many times, one after the other. The repeat function requires that you enter a number of repeats into a dialog box. Repeat functions very much like a loop, continuously repeating an audio region, but it does so by actually creating new regions, stretched along the DAW's timeline (see screenshot 4.3).

Loop allows you to continuously repeat a section of the timeline. This can be valuable to check the ability of a region to loop seamlessly before creating multiple repeats of that region that stretches along the timeline. Some DAWs also have a loop record function that allows you record multiple takes while looping over one passage (e.g., you could take several guitar solos in a row while the audio looped over the solo passage and the DAW would keep each take as a separate virtual track).

Mute is a way of accomplishing the same thing as cut, but without completely eliminating the audio region from your timeline. When a region is muted, it no longer plays—just as though it had been cut—but a grayed-out image of the region remains on your editing timeline. This can be helpful when you're not sure what you want to do with a particular piece of audio. A classic example is editing guitar fills. You may be uncertain as to whether a particular fill should be included or not. If you mute the fill, you can audition the song without the fill, but it remains immediately available if you decide you want to use it after all. Sometimes there are many elements that you're not sure about, and by muting them they remain easily accessible and you are reminded of their presence by the grayed-out waveform. I've frequently had the experience of seeing a piece of audio that I had muted much earlier in the editing process and realized that it was now an element that would be a valuable addition to the music. Although too many muted regions can clutter the editing screen, a good philosophy is "When it doubt, *mute*, don't cut!" (see screenshot 4.3).

Clear is a form of cutting that can be useful in certain editing situations. It operates exactly the same as the cut command, except that it does not place whatever has been cut on the clipboard. Here's an example of how the clear command might be used: Let's say you've copied a piece of audio and are pasting it into many different places (a snare-drum hit or a sound effect, perhaps). As you navigate through the timeline and locate places to paste this sound, you run across a separate piece of audio that you want to cut. If you use the cut command, you will lose the item on the clipboard that you still need to paste in more places. By using the clear command you retain whatever was on the clipboard. Often, using the delete key accomplishes the same thing—cutting without placing on the clipboard.

Edit modes

An edit mode (with one exception) represents a way of restricting our ability to move and place audio regions. This may seem odd. Why would you want to restrict your ability to edit? It turns out that restricting the editing capabilities allows the recordist to perform some editing functions that would be very time-consuming and tedious without those limitations. Although I am using the terminology from the Pro Tools software, many of these same terms, and most all of these same functions, are applicable in every DAW.

First, the one exception: unrestricted editing mode. In the unrestricted mode (called *slip* mode in Pro Tools) you can place an audio region anywhere on the timeline, down to the smallest possible increment, which would be one sample. This will probably be the most frequently used mode, though it depends on what kinds of editing you are doing.

Grid mode is the restricted editing mode that is probably the most commonly used. In grid mode your ability to move or place audio is limited to a user-defined grid. This is frequently used when dealing with music that has been played or constructed to a regulated pulse by using either a click track to guide the musicians or loops set to a specific BPM (beats per minute), or both. The grid is then set up based on musical time, meaning a grid limited to quarter notes, eighth notes, or some other basic musical division of time. In grid mode you are limited to placing the beginning of an audio region at a grid point along whichever musical grid you have selected. The following screenshot shows a quarter-note grid with various regions, all starting at one of the quarter-note subdivisions.

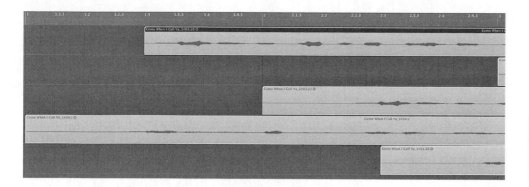

123

Grid mode is very useful in placing and moving musical events in a way that sets up or maintains an accurate relationship to musical time (beats and bars). Moving any part and maintaining its relationship to the beat, using loops, and repeating parts in various places (like copying and pasting a background vocal part into several different choruses) are all done much more quickly, accurately, and effectively in grid mode than with unrestricted editing.

Shuffle mode (as it is called in Pro Tools) restricts all editing movement to sliding (or "shuffling") an audio region from its current position to a position butting up against the end of any audio region that precedes it. This placing of audio from end to end can be very useful in doing things such as editing of narration, where you are often sliding cut up pieces of audio together and you want to be sure to have seamless transitions from one region to the next.

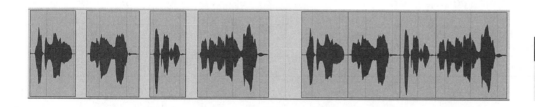

Spot mode represents the most restrictive of the edit modes and has very limited but very valuable functions. When you have selected a region of audio to edit in spot mode, you are presented with a dialog box asking where you wish to place (or "spot") the region. This comes from the film world, where audio frequently has to be placed at an exact location based on the corresponding frame of visuals. In this case, the film frame is identified by its SMPTE timecode—the timing code used to maintain and mark location along the film timeline—and the audio can be placed by inserting the SMPTE timecode location number in the spot mode dialog box start-time field. The beginning of the audio region selected is then placed at the timecode location indicated. Spot mode is essential for placing music, sound effects, and dialog in film and video work.

Spot mode can also be set to clock time or musical time (bars and beats), and audio can be placed anywhere on these grids in the same manner. This may be useful in placing audio events in certain circumstances, though outside of

SCREENSHOT 4.6

Spot mode dialog box

timing to visuals, there are usually simpler ways to place audio than using spot mode. Spot mode does have one other valuable function and that is returning audio to the place that it was originally recorded on the timeline (identified as its *time stamp*). Sometimes, audio gets moved accidentally and it can be difficult (or impossible!) to return it to its original location without help. When audio is recorded, it is time-stamped with its start time and when additional regions are created they are similarly time-stamped. If there is a discrepancy between the original time stamp (where the audio was recorded on the timeline) and the user time stamp (where the audio is currently sitting on the timeline), you can use the spot mode dialog box to reload the original time-stamp time into the start field, returning the region to its originally recorded position. (See the lower portion of Screenshot 4.6.)

One way to avoid the above problem is to *lock* audio in place. This is the ultimate editing restriction. When an audio region is locked, it cannot be moved or recorded over. This can be very useful, especially if more than one person is

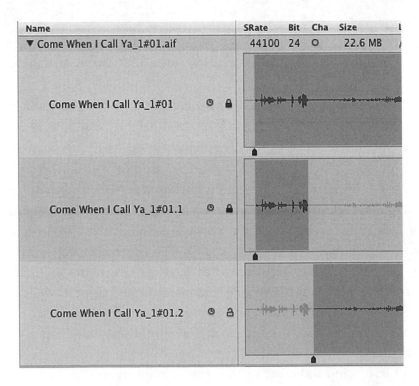

SCREENSHOT 4.7

Locked audio regions

working on a project. The user can always unlock the audio if needed, but the lock function prevents certain accidental or careless errors.

Edit tools

The edit tools represent the heart of an editing system. These tools are used to manipulate audio regions. As with edit functions, there are some edit tools that are familiar from almost any computer application. Again, although I am using the terminology from the Pro Tools software, many of these same terms, and most all of these same functions, are applicable in every DAW. Edit tools may also serve double duty and are revisited in section 6.3, where automation is covered.

The *selector* is the tool used to select portions along the timeline. Selected areas are highlighted. This tool is represented by a cursor like the one used in most word processors to select text. By positioning the cursor at any point along the timeline, engaging the primary mouse button, and sliding the mouse in either direction, the user can select any region along the timeline. This may encompass many audio regions, parts of one audio region, and/or areas of the timeline with no audio. If a portion of an audio region is selected, it may be made into a separate region and then cut, copied, pasted, moved, muted, and so on. A lot of editing begins by selecting an audio region.

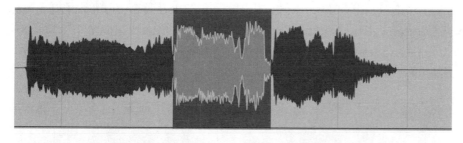

SCREENSHOT 4.8

A selected region

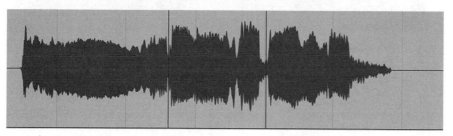

SCREENSHOT 4.9

A separated region

The *grabber* tool allows the user to "grab" an audio region and move it along the timeline. Using the grabber and engaging the primary mouse button allow the audio region to be slid in any direction by any amount in slip mode, or the movement may be restricted by the selected edit mode, as described above. Selecting, grabbing, and sliding an audio region to a new location is one of the most basic and common editing functions.

The *trimmer* tool enables the trimming of either the front or the back of any audio region. This is a convenient way of cutting unwanted material from

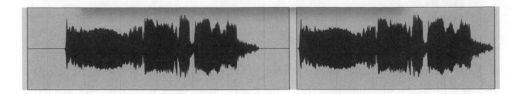

SCREENSHOT 4.10

A region before and after trimming

the beginning or end of any audio region. The trimmer tool also allows you to restore all or part of a sub-region that has been trimmed (or cut or deleted).

The *pencil* tool allows for a very specific (and generally fairly rare) editing function, but the tool becomes much more useful in its role in automation (covered in section 6.2). As an edit tool, its only function is to redraw waveforms. In order to use this function, the waveform has to be viewed in a small enough region to be represented by a line (rather than a filled-in waveform). You will need to magnify to smaller than 50 ms (milliseconds) on the timeline in order to use the pencil tool in this way. With the pencil tool selected, you can activate the primary mouse button and redraw small parts of a waveform by moving the mouse. This yields practical and desirable results in only a very few circumstances. Sometimes very short glitches in audio that are caused by timing errors or other kinds of interference can be corrected by redrawing the waveform. Attempts to redraw longer unwanted elements (such as an unwanted click, buzz, or other noise) will at best diminish the unwanted sound but not eliminate it and will often cause something worse than the original problem. It is best to duplicate your audio before attempting to use the pencil for redrawing waveforms to make fixes because you may be permanently altering the audio file.

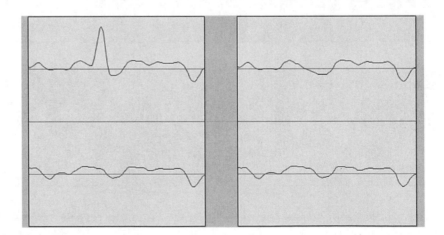

SCREENSHOT 4.11

A short glitch corrected by redrawing the waveform

The ability to *nudge* audio in user-defined increments is another very useful editing function. The nudge menu is identical to the grid menu, and it allows you to enter values in a variety of formats, including clock time, musical time (bars and beats), SMPTE timecode, or samples. Nudging can be very useful in fine-tuning the placement of audio events—for example, moving a guitar fill from one place in a song to another. If the recording was done to a click or loop, you can probably just use grid mode and move the fill by maintaining the relationship to the grid. However, if the recording was not done to a click, or even if the performance has wandered a bit from the grid, you may find that the fill does not feel like it's placed quite right against the existing rhythm. In this case, you might set your nudge value to 10 ms, highlight the audio region, and then nudge it earlier or later in increments of 10 ms until you find the place where it sounds like it is sitting right. You can do this by sliding the region with the mouse, but this is not as accurate and not repeatable. You can try several small differences in location using nudge, keeping track of the amount and direction nudged, and when you've settled on a location, you can go back to it easily and accurately.

Fades and cross-fades

Fades and cross-fades are essential editing tools. Fades and cross-fades can be accomplished by defining the desired fade graphically and then creating a new piece of audio that follows the fade instructions that you have defined (see screenshots 4.12, 4.13, and 4.14 for various examples of this). Fades can also be created by moving (or automating) the output channel fader. Small fades and cross-fades are almost always done using the first method, whereas longer fades, such as song fadeouts, are almost always done using the second method, which is explored in section 6.3, where automation is covered.

Short fades

Short fades can be very helpful in smoothing edits. One technique for creating seamless edits is through using zero crossing points. The *zero crossing point* represents the place in an audio waveform where the waveform crosses from positive to negative and the amplitude is zero. Whenever there is any audio right at the beginning or end of an audio region that isn't set right at the zero crossing point in the waveform, there may be a clicking or popping sound when playing through that region. You can locate a zero crossing point and trim to it, but it's usually faster and easier to avoid these clicks and pops by creating a very short fade-into or fade-out of the audio region. In most DAWs, there is a way to select many audio regions that you may have created in editing and apply a very short fade-in and fade-out of all of them. If short enough (5 ms is safe), this will be inaudible as a fade but will create a smooth transition in and out of all the regions.

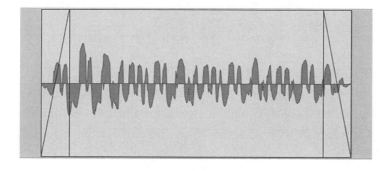

SCREENSHOT 4.12

A short fade-in and a short fade-out

Short fades are also useful when starting or stopping elements that are part of a continuous audio event. Ending a guitar lick early or starting a vocal line in the middle often means that you will need to create a short fade, not only to prevent a click or pop but also to make the new start or ending sound natural. The length of these fades will vary depending on the program material, and you will often have to experiment to find the most natural fade-in or fade-out of the edited audio event. The following screenshot shows a fade-out, a fade-in, and a region set to end at the zero crossing point.

Cross-fades

Cross-fades can be used on two adjacent audio regions. Cross-fades create fade-ins and fade-outs that intersect the two regions. Short cross-fades can be used to smooth the transition between regions and to avoid clicks and pops. Longer cross-fades can be used to make smooth transitions between sustained sounds—the crossfading action is like morphing—slowly transforming one sound into the other. This can be fun for special effects, but it also can be useful for certain, difficult edits. Editing in the middle of sustained vocal sounds where the idiosyncrasies in sound from one performance to another would make a normal edit obvious can sometimes sound very realistic by using long cross-fades.

Observing waveforms and editing with some visual aids can enhance the use of cross-fades. Using small cross-fades is the quick and easy way to make edits between audio elements that have only low-level sound or silence between them. Some more complicated edits, however, may require more than a simple cross-fade. Using the zero crossing for both sides of an edit will avoid many problems, and sometimes that is all that is required for a seamless edit. A zero crossing edit point plus a small cross-fade is even more likely to produce inaudible results.

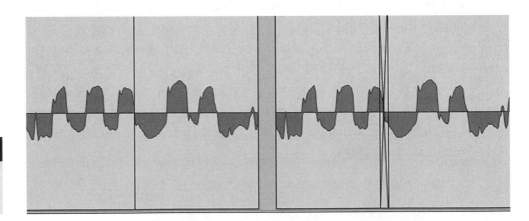

SCREENSHOT 4.13

A zero crossing edit, a zero crossing edit with a cross-fade

Choosing the edit point that is most likely to produce the best results can also be made easier using visual cues. Editing together sections that have equal gain at the point of the edit usually makes for smoother results. In most cases, you have some leeway as to exactly where the edit can be made, and you can search for matching adjacent regions with similar gain. In the following screen-shot, I show two audio regions with two possible edit points. The edit point where the gain (height of the waveform) is roughly equivalent is much more likely to produce the best results.

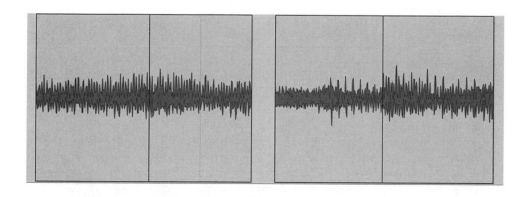

SCREENSHOT 4.14

Two possible edit points, the first being most likely to produce good results

Fade and cross-fade shapes and styles

The recordist can select from a variety of shapes for fades and cross-fades. Fades can be linear (straight line), have varying degrees of curvature, or even be "S" curves. A linear fade (a consistent change in volume characterized by

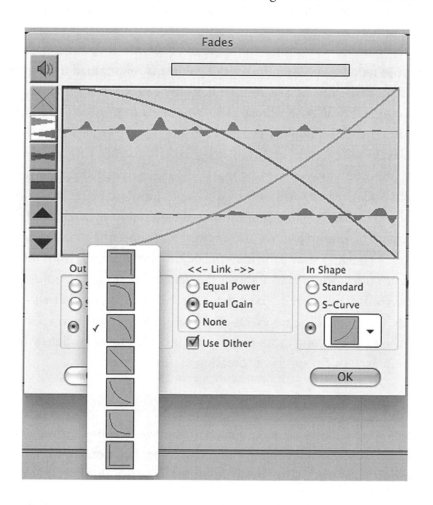

SCREENSHOT 4.15

A fades menu showing various options

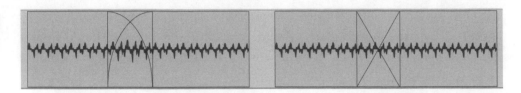

SCREENSHOT 4.16

An equal-power cross-fade and then the same cross-fade using equal gain

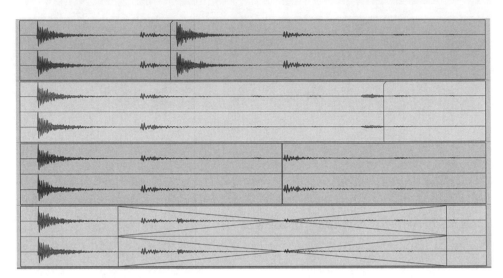

SCREENSHOT 4.17

Editing percussion recordings to avoid unwanted elements

a straight line) works for most situations. Cross-fades can also utilize various volume curves.

Cross-fades can be created to maintain equal power or equal gain. Equal-power cross-fades means that the overall volume is maintained throughout the cross-fade. Equal-gain cross-fades maintain the gain relationship regardless of overall volume. Equal-power cross-fades work best in most situations, though equal-gain cross-fades might work best for looping the same sound to avoid a spike in level.

It is important to keep in mind that with longer cross-fades, more elements from both audio regions will be heard. Cross-fades often need to be short in order for you to avoid remnants of unwanted material from one side of the fade or the other. The example above shows two recordings of percussive sounds—the top track (track 1) shows the material before the edit point from the second (right-hand) track, while track 2 shows the material past the edit point from the first (left-hand) track. Track 3 completes the edit and shows that with a short cross-fade there would be no extraneous material from either track included. Track 4 shows that a long cross-fade would include bits of earlier or later elements from each track—probably creating undesirable results.

4.2 Screen "Real Estate"

Effective editing requires careful management of what is showing on your computer screen at any given moment. Many editing functions are impossible if there is too much or too little showing on the screen. I think of the computer monitor as "real estate"—the territory that I have available to work on. Large screens are great for working with DAWs, but you can be effective on any size screen if you have good real-estate management techniques. Dual screens can be nice for spreading out, but I've done a fair amount of DAW work on my 12-inch laptop, and with good screen management it's not too bad.

Real-estate tools

Some of the edit tools are simply real-estate tools. They don't do any actual editing, but they help you manage what's on the screen and that allows you to edit properly. These tools, along with the strategies for using them to manage your workspace, are key elements in effective editing.

Managing the timeline

The fundamental real-estate issue for editing is how much of the timeline is showing. You need to see enough of the timeline for the editing function that you're doing, but you don't want to be seeing too much more than necessary, so that you can select and manipulate the relevant regions easily.

In most DAWS, there are many ways to manage the amount of timeline showing and being familiar with all or most of them will help speed the editing work. There is usually a magnifying glass tool that allows you to select part of the timeline by holding down the primary mouse button and sliding it across the region that you wish to occupy the screen. When you let go of the mouse button, the portion of the timeline you selected will occupy the entire screen. This is a great way to focus on the area you want to work on.

There are also usually some *quick key* (shortcut) methods for adjusting the amount of timeline that you are viewing. There may be a shortcut for expanding or contracting the timeline in increments, allowing you to zoom in or out without having to access the magnifying glass. There may also be presets that allow you to define distinct areas of the timeline with quick key commands. This is particularly useful, because you can create easily accessible view areas for each file. You might have one command to show the entire song on the timeline, one to show approximately one verse or chorus, one to show approximately one vocal line, and one to show approximately one word. On a different file with a much longer timeline—a suite of songs, mastering file, or audio book recording, for example—you can have different preset regions that are appropriate to that file's timeline.

Managing your overall workspace

There are many DAW features besides the timeline that require active screen management. You may be able to control the track height for editing; control the size of the waveform regardless of the level it was recorded at; pick which

SCREENSHOT 4.18

Recall options for screen setups

tracks are showing and which are still available but hidden; pick from a variety of timeline rulers to show or hide; decide if various submenus, such as a regions list, or secondary windows, such as a system usage window, are in view; configure some of the virtual mixing consoles features, such as number of sends to be visible or hidden; and so on. There are too many options to detail here and they vary among DAWs.

Some of viewing options, such as adjusting the height and size of the waveform, are key to the efficiency of your editing; and some of them, such as extraneous windows that are open, may be small annoyances. What is important is that you take an active roll in managing your real estate and trying to optimize your DAW working environment.

Most DAWs also have an elaborate recall system for storing and recalling a variety of real-estate setup features. You may be able to recall which windows are in view, which tracks are showing, track heights, timeline selections, and other features. This can be particularly useful for large-scale projects, such as movie or video soundtracks, where you may have multiple setups within one file, one dedicated to music, one to sound effects, and one to dialog. One day you may be editing music and the next day dialog, and the screen setups for the two jobs may be complex and very different. The ability to store and recall these screen setups can save you a tremendous amount of time.

4.3 Virtual Tracks (Playlists)

Virtual tracks are an essential part of the vastly expanded capabilities that computer recording provides over tape-based recording. Different DAWs use different names for virtual tracks, such as "playlists," "takes," or "comps." Beyond a basic understanding of virtual tracks, I cover the working models for using this capability in creating composite ("comp") performances.

In the analog world, each audio track was limited to one recording—in order to use a track for a new recording, whatever was already recorded had to be erased. But in the DAW, each track may contain many different recordings, each one represented by a virtual track. They are called virtual tracks because each track in the DAW is still limited to one track of playback at a time, though

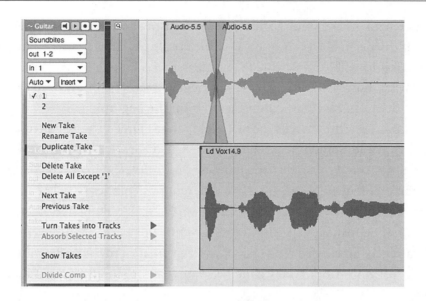

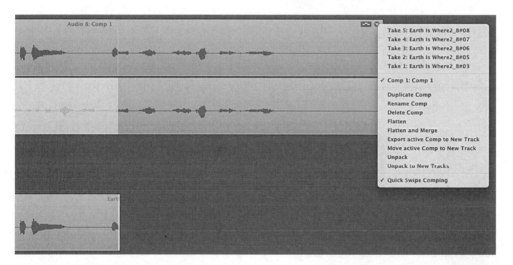

there may be many recordings to choose from on each track. The list of virtual tracks shows all the tracks that have been recorded separately using this one individual track. You can select any of the recordings from a virtual track for playback, or you can duplicate the current virtual track for editing or to rerecord a portion of the track, or you can create a new virtual track to record on.

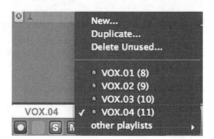

**SCREENSHOTS
4.19a, 4.19b, 4.19c.**

Virtual track pop-up menus

Duplicate virtual tracks

A duplicate virtual track can be made of a track that has already been recorded. These duplicates provide extra flexibility in the editing process. It is a good idea to make a duplicate virtual track before you begin any editing. This allows easy access to the original track at any point. Sometimes you can work yourself into a corner with editing and want to just return to the original track and start again. If the original track was created with multiple takes (punched in), it can be almost impossible to recreate the original after a lot of editing. With a duplicate playlist, however, the original is immediately accessible and you can make another duplicate and start editing again from the beginning

Duplicate virtual tracks for material that has already been edited can also be very valuable. Sometimes you may have edited a track or multiple takes onto a virtual track and think that the job may be complete. However, you want to try some different edits and see about different possibilities—perhaps you used a more conservative approach to picking performance elements and you want to see what happens if you select more adventurous performance elements. By duplicating an already edited version, you can create a revised edit without losing your previous work. Many edited versions can be stored on different virtual tracks.

New virtual tracks

A new virtual track is a completely blank track available to record on. Whatever has already been recorded on other virtual tracks is still available for playback if selected, but a new virtual track is an empty track. Although each virtual track acts as a new track, it doesn't make sense to treat it as a completely separate track. If you were to record a rhythm guitar on one virtual track and a lead guitar on another virtual track that is a part of the same original track, you would only be able to play either the rhythm or the lead guitar. Virtual tracks are typically used to record many versions of the same thing. It makes sense to record ten tracks of lead vocal on separate virtual tracks if you will only be using one lead vocal on the final recording.

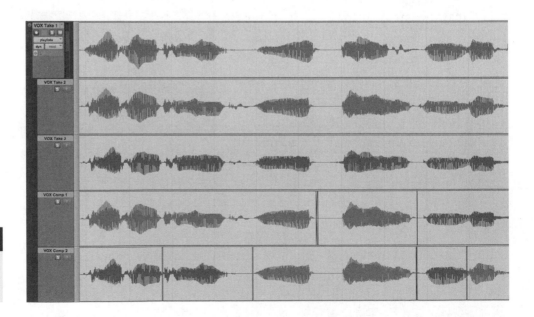

SCREENSHOT 4.20

Three tracks and two edited versions using virtual tracks

Virtual tracks versus many tracks

There are two ways to approach multiple recordings of the same part (such as a lead vocal) in a DAW: as virtual tracks or as many individual tracks. Virtual tracks offer some advantages over multiple individual tracks. It is simpler to select an individual track for playback using virtual tracks than it is to mute and unmute individual playback tracks. There's less screen clutter with virtual tracks playing back on a single track than there is with individual playback tracks. Virtual tracks provide a convenient way to store old takes and retain easy access to them— again, without cluttering up your screen. Virtual tracks may also reduce the load on your CPU (depending on your DAW) by demanding less in terms of track count and audio file accessibility. For these reasons, virtual tracks are a great resource when recording multiple takes of a single part. There is more on how to edit multiple takes on virtual tracks in the following section on composite editing.

Composite editing (comping) using virtual tracks

Making composite versions (comping) of multiple performances to create one complete performance has become standard practice. DAWs use different strategies for how to manage virtual tracks when comping, but the principle is the same. Elements from many recordings of the same part are pieced together onto a "master," or "comp," track of that part. Comp tracks may be made for just about any performance, from drums to solos to string sections, and in many cases, multiple tracks are grouped together and comped (such as with a typical drum-set recording). Probably the most frequently comped performance is the lead vocal, and I use that as the model for how comped tracks are made.

There are two common tactics for creating a final lead vocal. One is for the singer to sing the song through until the vocalist and/or the producer feels the performance is either complete or mostly complete. If complete, the task is done. If mostly complete, then punch-in replacement parts are sung for any line

135

SCREENSHOT 4.21

Three vocal takes as virtual tracks and three vocal takes on three separate tracks or section to be replaced until a satisfactory replacement is sung. In this case, either there is only one vocal performance or there may be earlier vocal takes as well, saved as virtual tracks, but they have not been used as part of the final vocal. A more common technique is for the singer to sing multiple takes and to then, often in collaboration with the recordist, make a composite performance by picking the best lines, or phrases, or words, or sometimes even syllables, from the available takes and editing them into the final vocal performance.

Comping tracks can be a relatively simple procedure, but it does require good management of virtual tracks and good editing practices to be done efficiently. Different DAWs manage virtual tracks differently, and this is also an area of further software development. Newer versions of DAWs have been integrating new ways to view and access multiple virtual tracks. Quick and easy access to many virtual tracks makes comping tracks faster and simpler. Nonetheless, it is a good idea to limit the number of takes you are managing when making a comp. I've found that between three and five takes is a reasonable number to work from. This may be the first three to five takes done, or you may find that you have recorded a few passes before the singing or playing really starts getting consistently good, and you end up comping by starting with Take 3 or Take 4 and including the following three or four takes. Some will want to use more takes when comping, but it becomes increasingly difficult to keep track of which parts you liked the best when listening to so many versions, and it can dramatically increase the overall time it takes to complete a comp.

The "It Could Have Happened" approach to making comps

Often, the primary objective in making comps is a final version that still sounds like "it could have happened." That is, it could actually have been played or sung in a single performance. Sometimes this is not important; sometimes we strive to create a performance that obviously could never have been sung or played as it is heard. But most recordings, even when put together from many different performances, still conform to the "it could have happened" ethic.

Adjusting pitch, timing, and gain while comping

Details about adjusting pitch and time are covered in the following section on advanced editing. This may or may not be part of the process of comping, though I recommend that you do integrate these adjustments as you work through a comp. Adjusting pitch is not always successful, so if you think you want to use a particular performance, but it has pitch issues that you want to correct, you had best try to do so while you're making the comp. If you comp together a performance and then go back and try to fix pitch concerns, you may find that some of the parts selected don't meet your particular standard of performance, even after being adjusted.

Where there are issues regarding the timing of a performance, these should also be addressed as a part of the comping process. Sometimes phrases or words are simply performed slightly earlier or later than desired, and a slight shift in timing makes this piece of the performance sound just right. Of course, pitch and timing are highly subjective. Even though there are theoretical standards for correct pitch, perfect pitch is neither possible nor desired for musical performances. "Fixing" pitch and time in performances should be something that is done within creative guidelines, and these vary greatly among artists and recordists.

Adjusting gain may also be a part of the comping process. Even though performances may have all been recorded using the same input level, sometimes when pieces of different performances are comped together, there are unnatural-sounding changes in volume from one element to the next. While these adjustments can be made with automation, you may want to avoid automation until the mixing stage. Once there is volume automation on a track, you cannot simply move the fader up or down for level changes without disabling the automation. For this reason, I often make gain (or level) changes by actually processing the piece of audio and "gaining" it up or down using an off-line plug-in. This gives me a new piece of audio with the gain more correctly balanced for the context and it allows me to avoid automation until I'm ready to start mixing.

Level of detail in comping

Comping can be done in large sections or down to the smallest level of detail. With vocal comping, I have made comps in a few minutes by taking whole verses or choruses from a couple of different takes and I've spend days comping a single vocal by taking lines, words, and even syllables from many different takes. Using the editing procedures described elsewhere in this chapter, you can edit very small elements—I have constructed three-syllable words using syllables from three different takes!—but this kind of work can be very tedious and time-consuming. Surprisingly, some of the most complicated edits end up sounding very natural—certainly like they "could have happened."

Besides the basic process of comping from different takes, and the additional possibility of adjusting pitch, timing, or gain, there are other comping procedures that can be used effectively. You can take bits of performances from different locations on the timeline and place them where they are needed. This is often done in the case of background vocal parts, which may be sung in one chorus and then copied and pasted into all the choruses. This works easily when the track was recorded to a click or a loop, but can be a challenge (or almost impossible) if the track is not referenced to a consistent tempo. Repositioning audio can be done with almost any part. Pieces of vocals can be taken from one spot and placed in another—either because it is a recurring part or, in the case of an ad lib, simply because you think it sounds better in a different location. Working with a grid when editing a recording that is referenced to a consistent tempo makes this kind of relocation work very easy.

137

Even more complex maneuvers are possible when comping. Elements can be recombined in ways that create completely new parts and pieces of music. I have taken bits from solos and rearranged them in ways such that new solos were created that were unlike anything that had been originally played. I have constructed "ad-libbed vocal vamps" from elements that had been sung at completely different locations, sometimes constructing lyric content by stringing words together from different contexts (you can make someone say almost anything this way!). Comping can be endlessly creative—and endlessly time-consuming, if you're not careful.

4.4 Advanced Editing

Our ability to manipulate sound through editing has expanded enormously in the age of the DAW. Although I list the following techniques as advanced editing, most of them really need to be part of every recordist's arsenal of capabilities. Implementation varies in different DAWs and new editing features are added on a regular basis. The following represent some of the most common and useful editing techniques beyond the basics already covered in this chapter.

Global edits

Global editing is used when you want to remove or add whole sections of a piece of music. Editing all the tracks in any file requires its own technique. One of the most remarkable capabilities of nondestructive editing is the ability to adjust the edit point of each track individually when making a global edit. This allows us to make edits that would have been impossible with analog tape, where all tracks were necessarily edited at the same point.

Global cuts

To discuss the process of making global cuts, I will consider one possible example. Perhaps you have decided that the song should go straight from the bridge to the outro without having a third verse in between, so you need to remove the third verse. The process for making such an edit is as follows:

1. Start by making a copy of all the tracks onto new virtual tracks so that you don't lose the song construction you had before making the edit. In most DAWs, this can be done with one keystroke by holding down one of the command, control, or option keys and selecting duplicate virtual tracks (or playlists or takes or whatever name your DAW uses to identify virtual tracks).
2. Group all of the tracks together so that you can cut, copy, and paste them all as a unit. Some DAWs have a default "all" grouping mode for all tracks.

3. Select the area that you wish to delete (in the example, this would be the third verse). If your music has been played to a click track or a loop, you can do this in grid mode, selecting the area from the downbeat of the verse to the downbeat of the outro—probably something like exactly 8 or 16 bars. If the music was not done to a grid, find some element that plays the downbeat of both sections (the kick drum often works well for this if drums are a part of your recording). Carefully select the entire verse from the beginning of the kick drum (or whatever sound) that starts the verse to the beginning of the kick drum that starts the outro. Separate all the tracks into regions that conform to this editing selection and then select them all—all the tracks for the part of the song that is to be cut should be highlighted.

4. Place the DAW editor into shuffle mode. This is the mode that automatically moves the material from later on the timeline and butts it up against the earlier material when audio is deleted (this mode may have a different name in your DAW). This edit mode can be seen at Screenshot 4.5 earlier in this chapter.

5. Hit the delete key. This will cause the selected verse to be deleted and the beginning of the outro to butt up against the end of the bridge.

6. Audition your edit. At this point, you should be able to tell if the timing sounds okay.

7. If you think the edit might work, you can then start going through each track in solo to "massage" each edit point individually.

8. Each track may require some trimming before or after your initial edit point to make a smooth transition. Each track will probably require a cross-fade, the length of which will depend on the nature of the material. Some edit points may need to be slid several beats. For example, the vocal at the end of the bridge may have hung over several beats into the following verse and now needs to be extended into the outro.

9. The screenshots on the following page show a global edit of this type both before and after the edit, with each track's edit point adjusted and cross-faded for a smooth transition.

Global additions

Adding material globally requires a similar approach as global cuts. To explore the process of making global additions, consider one possible example. Let's say you've decided that an already recorded song needs a verse added between the bridge and the outro. In order to do this you will need to copy an earlier verse

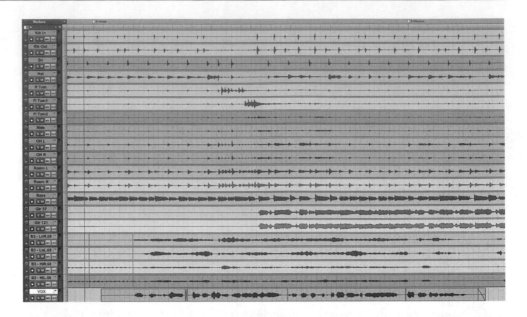

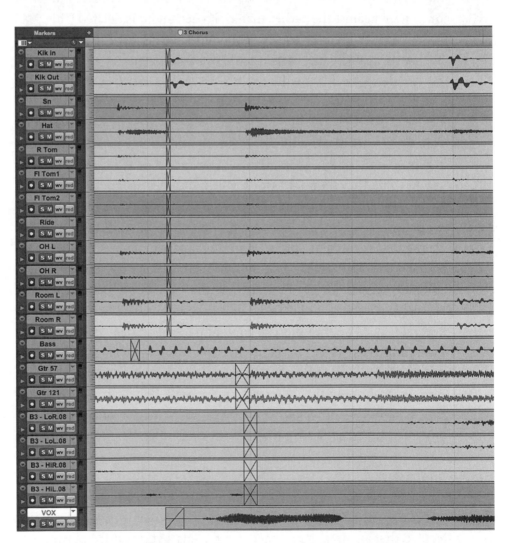

SCREENSHOT 4.22

(a) Global edit, before
the removal of a verse;
(b) Global edit, after the
removal of a verse

from the song and insert it in the spot where you want to add a verse. The process for making such an edit is as follows:

1. Start by making a copy of all the tracks onto new virtual tracks so that you don't lose the song construction you had before making the edit. In most DAWs, this can be done with one keystroke by holding down one of the command, control, or option keys and selecting duplicate virtual tracks (or playlists, or whatever name your DAW uses to identify virtual tracks).

2. Group all of the tracks together so that you can cut, copy, and paste them all as a unit. Some DAWs have a default grouping mode for all tracks.

3. Find the edit point for where you wish to place the new verse. In our example, this would be the downbeat of the outro. Separate all the audio regions at this point (this should require just one editing move, as all your tracks are grouped together). Grab all of the material after the edit point and move it farther along the timeline. You can either drag the material or cut and paste it. At this point, it doesn't matter exactly where the material is put; you just want to make sure that you leave a large enough gap between the end of the bridge and the beginning of the outro to insert the new verse.

4. Select the verse that you want to repeat for the new verse. This could be either the first or the second verse, and once the initial edit has been made, you may be able to use elements from either of the existing verses. If your music has been played to a click track or a loop, you can do this in grid mode, selecting the area from the downbeat of the verse to the downbeat of whatever section follows the verse, often exactly 8 or 16 bars. If the music was not done to a grid, find some element that plays the downbeat of both sections (the kick drum often works well for this if drums are a part of your recording). Carefully select the entire verse from the beginning of the kick drum (or whatever sound) that starts the verse to the beginning of the kick drum that starts whatever section follows the verse. Copy that verse.

5. Paste the verse into the area you created between the bridge and the outro (screenshot 4.32 on the following page).

6. Place the DAW editor into shuffle mode. This is the mode that automatically moves the material from later on the timeline and butts it up against the earlier material when audio is deleted (this mode may have a different name in your DAW). This edit mode can be seen at Screenshot 4.5 earlier in this chapter.

7. Grab the verse you pasted into the space and move it so the beginning of it butts up against the end of the bridge, then grab

141

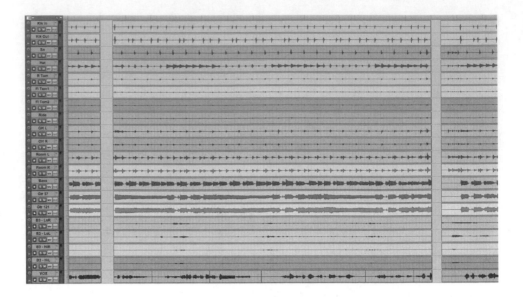

SCREENSHOT 4.23

Global edit, new verse inserted but transitions not yet made

the outro and butt it up against the end of the verse you have just pasted in.

8. Audition your edits. At this point, it may sound very rough, with a big pop at both edit points, but you should be able to tell if the timing sounds okay.

9. If you think the edit might work, you can then start going through each track in solo to "massage" the edit into shape. Each track may require some sliding before or after each of your initial edit point to make a smooth transition. Each track will probably require a cross-fade, the length of which will depend on the nature of the material.

10. The screenshot below shows a global edit of this type with each track's edit point adjusted and cross-faded for a smooth transition.

Adjusting timing and pitch

The capability to make adjustments in timing and pitch in a DAW has revolutionized the creation of music. We can quickly and easily make extensive changes in musical performances in regard to both rhythm and melody. For better or worse, we now often alter musical performances as a part of the editing process. I say "for better or worse" because there is considerable debate over the wisdom and value of altering timing and pitch. I believe that both sides have valid points. On the one hand, performances can be sapped of life when pitch and timing are flattened into very close adherence to absolute standards of intonation and rhythm. On the other hand, the ability to make adjustments that satisfy those responsible for the recording (artist and/or recordist) allows some great performances to be salvaged that would otherwise not be used. Before the DAW era I had to erase some spectacular musical moments because they

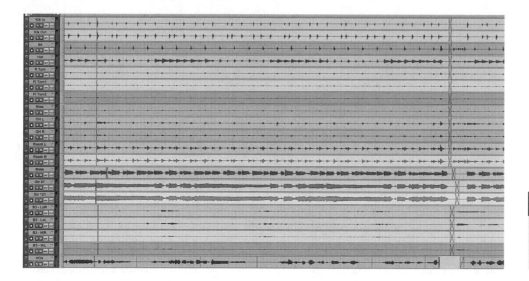

were slightly flawed in one way or another that was unacceptable to the artist. The ability to fix the timing or pitch of one note (or two, or whatever) within a performance has allowed me to save some wonderful bits of music.

The following discusses these capabilities without further comment on the advisability of their use. Suffice it to say that most people agree that musical performances are not meant to be as close to perfectly in time or perfectly in tune as possible. The extent to which they do conform to theoretical perfection varies widely, and all the more so now that we can make adjustments that can bring virtually any performance close to theoretical perfection. A lot of contemporary music employs constructed drum parts that play with metronomical accuracy, but many of the other instrumental and vocal performances may have a much more "humanly" typical kind of variation in beat accuracy. Many vocal performances are now more accurate in regard to pitch, but they aren't necessarily made "perfect" throughout. These tools are also used in obvious and creative ways, such as the machine perfection of the bass-drum hook in Christina Aguilera's breakout song "Genie in a Bottle," or the obvious pitch-adjusted vocals used for effect in Cher's song "Believe," and taken to new heights more recently by T-Pain and others.

Adjusting timing

There are many ways to adjust the timing of a performance within a DAW. The simplest is to move a portion of audio by selecting and then dragging it earlier or later along the timeline. Perhaps a guitar fill or a vocal line feels rhythmically a little early or late. You can select the piece of audio, slide it, and then audition the results. The screen view is important because the smaller the amount of overall time showing on the timeline, the smaller the increment you can comfortably slide the audio. While the sliding technique works fine in many instances, there are aids in making these kinds of adjustments. In some DAWs, you can "nudge" audio by a user-defined amount. The advantage to nudging over simply sliding is that you can repeat your actions exactly, trying a variety of positions for the audio and then returning to an exact placement when you've settled on a new location.

I have found that 10 ms represents a good nudge factor when trying to reposition audio that doesn't feel like it's sitting comfortably in the rhythm. This is a small enough increment to fine-tune location but large enough to hear the difference in one nudge (if you have an ear that is sensitive to rhythm). Sometimes the audio will feel out of place, but you can't be sure if it's early or late. You can select the audio and nudge it three or four times (30 or 40 ms.) in one direction and then three or four times in the other, audition the results each time, and by then it's usually clear which direction is solving the problem. You can place the audio back at its original location and nudge in 10 ms. increments, usually going beyond the proper point and then going back and forth among options until you settle on the one that sounds the best to you. With practice this can be a pretty quick process.

There are many variations on this basic nudging technique. Sometimes smaller or larger increments will work better. Sometimes you have to adjust different elements by different amounts. For example, you might find that an awkward-sounding vocal line seems to sit best when the first three words are nudged 30 ms later and the rest of the line only 10 ms later. Sometimes you nudge a piece of audio around for a while and decide that it sounds best where it was originally played!

Altering timing based on the relationship to a musical grid is another common way of adjusting performances. If the music was played to a click or a loop, then the DAW will provide a grid that shows the metronomic timing locations. You may find that in some instances moving something onto the grid yields easy and desirable results. For example, you hear one snare drum hit from the drummer that sounds late. You locate the snare beat, and you can see that it is beyond the gridline for the beat where it should be located. You separate the snare-drum beat in question from the start of its attack to the end of it—actually you have to move all the drum tracks (as a group) where that snare drum was played because the snare sound leaks into all the other mics as well. You then select that piece of audio and move it so that the approximate center of the snare-drum attack (transients) is centered on the gridline for the appropriate beat. You then audition the results. You may find that you still need to nudge the snare beat earlier or later from the grid to get it to sit right with the rest of the drums.

There are many more elaborate techniques and tools for adjusting audio timing based on a grid. These techniques evolved out of the MIDI quantizing function that allowed recordists to align the timing of a MIDI performance to a grid automatically. Because each MIDI event was a completely distinct object, and because MIDI data were very simple to manipulate compared to audio recordings, this was quick and easy to do. Today's DAWs and computers

SCREENSHOT 4.25

Snare-drum hit lined up with the appropriate beat gridline

allow us to quantize audio much in the same ways that we do with MIDI. To do this, we must first divide the audio into individual events. There are programs that analyze audio based on transient patterns; these are the leading-edge high-frequency sounds created when an instrument is struck, plucked, bowed, or blown. The program then divides the audio into segments (regions) based on what it has analyzed, intending to yield the beginning of each individual event. This can be relatively simple with recordings with very strong transients (drums and percussion) and almost impossible with slow and/or weak transients (vocals and strings). There are user parameters that can be helpful in differentiating events based on transient qualities. As these programs have become more sophisticated and users more adept, it is often possible to create audio that can be quantized to a grid relatively quickly. Many DAWs come with timing analysis and adjustment programs as a feature (such as Beat Detective, Beat Mapping, etc.).

When using grids, you have a variety of options that may produce more natural-sounding results. As with MIDI quantizing, it is possible to adjust audio elements to a grid but allow for varying degrees of less than perfect placement. You may move the audio a defined percentage closer to its grid location (e.g., a quantizing "strength" of 75 percent moves events 75 percent of the way toward the exact grid location). You can also work with groove templates that establish various rhythmic "feels" that are based on variations from perfect timing. You can use groove templates designed by others, use those derived from other performances, or create a groove template based on one of the performances in your recording, and use it to adjust the timing of other performances. For example, you can use one of the timing programs to analyze your drum track and map the variations in performance from the metronomic grid. You can then use this tempo map to "groove" other per-

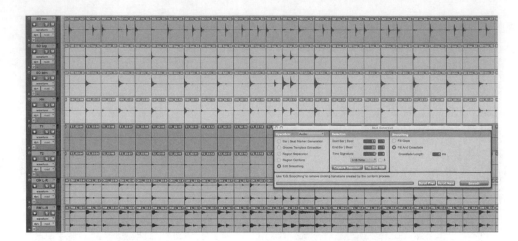

SCREENSHOT 4.26

Bits of a drum performance quantized using Beat Detective

formances (e.g., the bass track) to the idiosyncrasies of the drum track. If you choose to go down these roads, the possibilities are endless—endlessly creative and endlessly time-consuming, too!

Adjusting pitch

More recent innovations in DAW functionality have greatly expanded the recordist's ability to adjust pitch. These are used most frequently to adjust intonation—understood as the degree of pitch accuracy—but they can also be used to shift in half and whole steps and to change key signature (transposing). The ability to pitch-shift a musical sound, without affecting its speed, came early in the development of digital audio and was a great advancement from the direct connection between pitch and speed in analog audio (to raise pitch, the recording had to be speeded up—the "chipmunk effect"—and vice versa; lower pitch could only be created using a slower playback speed). Now, we can adjust small changes in pitch to improve intonation by selecting a piece of audio and using a transpose function to raise or lower the pitch by a user- definable amount without affecting the playback speed of the audio. This moves pitch in much smaller increments than true note or key transpositions—often shifting only a few cents (there are 100 cents in a musical half step). This can be difficult for fixing performances, especially because pitch often wavers relative to the note rather than being consistently sharp or flat throughout. Even when theoretically possible, pitch adjustment requires a very good ear and a lot of experience or a lot of tries to successfully correct intonation this way.

The development of the now-famous Auto-Tune program changed all this by providing a means of adjusting pitch that was completely variable, allowing for different adjustments in pitch over the course of one performance or even one note. Auto-Tune provides a graphic readout to show the user how the performance differed from "correct" or "perfect" pitch, and the audio can be adjusted graphically or in an automatic mode. In the graphic mode, you redefine the pitch of the performance by redrawing the graphic representation of pitch. The automatic mode adjusts pitch according to various parameters and can (sometimes) correct whole performances in real time (this may or may not work all of the time, depending on the exact nature of the original performance). Auto-Tune—and now its many successors with similar capabilities—allows detailed pitch adjusting far beyond anything previously available. Its primary limitation is that it can only adjust single-note performances—it can't differentiate between two or more notes played simultaneously and adjust them independently (though at the time of this writing this polyphonic capability has been released in a new version of Melodyne—an alternative pitch-fixing program).

To use the graphic mode of pitch correction, you have several routing possibilities. You can copy the piece of audio you wish to adjust onto a new audio track, put Auto-Tune or whatever program you're using in as a plug-in (insert) on that track, and route it back to the original track using an internal buss. Place the original track in record ready and make sure you are in "input only" mode rather than auto-switching (covered in section 5.3). When you play the segment, the plug-in will read the pitch of the performance and you can make adjustments within the program as desired, hearing the results through the original channel. When you are happy with the adjustments you've made, simply activate recording and the adjusted material will be recorded onto your original track. You may want to adjust the timing of the new recording to correct the small amount of delay (latency) created by the pitch-correction software.

You can also make these corrections off-line, auditioning the material in the plug-in directly from the track and then processing it directly back onto the original track. This requires an off-line processing capability (such as audio-

147

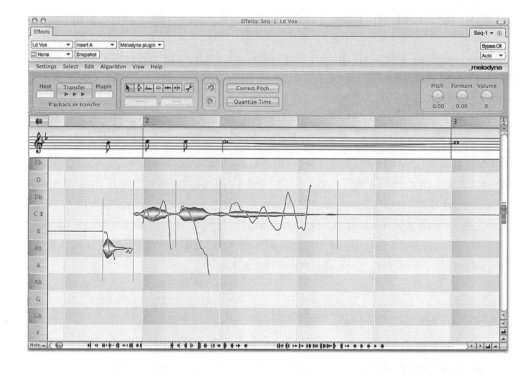

SCREENSHOT 4.27

Melodyne pitch and time correcting software

suite processing in Pro Tools). You will need to check to see if this function also causes a small amount of delay in your DAW.

New techniques for pitch correction are being added to programs regularly and also offered by third parties. Elastic pitch in Pro Tools now offers the ability to adjust pitch in real time without having to render new audio files (you can render them later if you want to save on computer-processing power). The ability to adjust intonation using one or more of these programs has become a part of the recording process. While some artists use it extensively and some very rarely (and a few never), operation of pitch-correcting tools is a necessary skill for virtually every professional recordist.

Adjusting by ear or by sight

Along with these expanded capabilities of adjusting timing and pitch has come a basic conflict concerning whether adjustments should be made and the extent to which things should be adjusted. Part of the conflict comes from the visual nature of the tools we use to make these adjustments versus the aural (sound) nature of the material being adjusted. When looking at waveforms of two different performances in the same piece of music, you can see how well they line up with each other—at least it seems that you can see that relationship. Waveforms can be deceptive in appearance, depending on attack and frequency characteristics, but the visual cue as to rhythmic relationships is generally pretty reliable. This is similar with pitch correction in a plug-in's graphic pitch mode. You can see how far the note strays from the "correct" pitch and you can adjust it by sight. Again, there may be some problems with this depending on the nature of the program material, but it is generally quite reliable. We can adjust thousands of elements in performances, both timing and pitch, completely by sight. We can also make these adjustments automatically using auto mode for pitch shifting and various forms of quantizing (automatic rhythm alignment)—a whole other creative approach, or can of worms, depending on the circumstances and your point of view.

But should we use the visual cues for making decisions about adjusting timing or pitch? The simple answer is no; adjustments should be made and accepted based on the way things sound, not on the way they look. I often tell the artists I'm working with, "If you can't hear it, don't fix it" though the advice is not always followed. That said, sometimes visual cues can make the process of time and pitch adjustment much faster and simpler. If you feel something isn't right and you want to adjust it, using the visual aid of waveform position or graphic pitch readout can make the task easier.

Time compression and expansion

Another function that is used frequently in contemporary editing is time compression and expansion. This is the reverse of the new pitch-adjusting software that changes pitch without changing length. With time compression and expansion, you change the length of a piece of audio, making it either shorter or longer, without changing the pitch. This has become especially valuable and useful in music that uses preexisting audio and when the recordist wishes to conform the timing of these various elements to each other.

Compressing or expanding loops

The most common use for time compression and expansion is to adjust drum and percussion loops to conform to a particular tempo. The use of loops in contemporary music has become very common, and this is partly due to the fact that it is now quite easy to make various loops play at the same tempo. The basic operating procedure for setting any loop to a specific tempo varies in different DAWs. Many DAWs now have multiple working procedures for time compression and expansion, and there are a variety of third-party plug-ins and programs that make working with loops very simple.

The first thing to be sure of is that the loop you're planning to use is looping "correctly." That is to say, when looping back from the end point to the beginning, make sure the transition sounds seamless and rhythmically comfortable. You will certainly need to do this if you are creating the loops yourself, but even commercial loops sometimes require adjustment (adding or subtracting time and or small fade-ins/fade-outs) in order for them to loop comfortably. Once you have created an audio region that is looping properly, you can then adjust its tempo in a variety of ways.

There are programs—some within certain DAWs and some from third parties—that allow you to select a region and assign a new tempo to it. The program then creates a new piece of audio that has been either compressed or expanded to the tempo you have entered. In order to do this you must know (or be able to figure out) the tempo of the original audio so you can instruct the program to change from x tempo to y tempo. While pretty straightforward, there are several programs that do this same thing using shortcuts that make the process even faster and simpler. You may be able to set the tempo for your file, go into grid mode (using bars and beats as your time basis), and then take any piece of audio and place the beginning at the start of a bar and use a trimming tool to place the ending at the desired end point (perhaps exactly one bar long, or two bars or whatever). When you release the trimming tool, the program will create a new piece of audio that has been either compressed or expanded to fit exactly the selected amount of time.

Further advancements in time compression and expansion now provide these capabilities without having to render new audio files. The program analyzes the material and compresses or stretches it as directed. Because it doesn't actually render a new file, it works much more quickly than the traditional techniques. You may have the option of rendering your work later, once you've settled on the various expansion and compression adjustments that you want

SCREENSHOT 4.28

A time compression/expansion menu

to make, in order to relieve the computer's processing power of analyzing each element during playback.

Compressing or expanding melodic material

All of the techniques described above in regard to drum and percussion loops also applies to melodic material. Often, melodic loops, such as a two-bar bass line, are used along with rhythmic loops and their times can be adjusted to a tempo using any of the techniques described above. Sometimes melodic material is expanded for different reasons. You may find a particular note to have been played shorter than you wish—perhaps it stops a quarter note short of the next note and you want it to sustain to the next note. You could expand the note in question by the small amount needed for it to last until the next note.

Quality issues may be more pronounced in compressing or expanding melodic material. The delicate timbres of acoustic instruments may be most noticeably altered when compressed or expanded. The algorithms used for

SCREENSHOT 4.29

Before and after expansion to fill a space

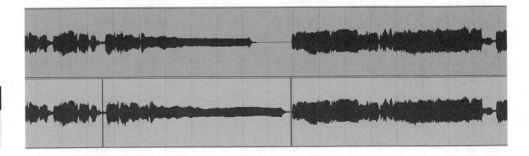

compression and expansion have become increasingly sophisticated. Revised and newer programs are capable of greater alterations in even the most delicate audio material with fewer and fewer undesirable artifacts.

Global compression or expansion

The ability to easily adjust the overall tempo of the many elements in a typical recording project is one of the very few things that were lost in the move from analog to digital. While it is true that both time and pitch are shifted when a tape recorder is speeded up or slowed down, it was a welcome capability in many situations. Sometimes things just sounded better a little faster and a little higher in pitch (or slower and lower) than where they were recorded. The varispeed control on an analog tape recorder has still not been completely replicated by DAW developers, but they are getting much closer to similar capabilities. they can also separate the alterations in time from those of pitch, providing even greater flexibility. Compression and expansion programs sometimes offer different settings for different kinds of material, and in some instances they are capable of changing the length of all of the individual tracks within a project or altering final mixes, without noticeable side effects.

Strip silence

Another innovative editing tool within many DAWs is a function called *strip silence*. The strip silence function is akin to what is traditionally done with a noise gate, but it does so with much greater control and operates off-line rather than in real time. Like a noise gate, strip silence provides a means of differentiating between desired material and noise or leakage by detecting the louder elements. Strip silence "strips," or removes, the quieter elements rather than "gating" them, but the effect is the same as a hard gate. The term *strip silence* is a little confusing because you're not usually stripping silence; you're stripping low-level noise and turning it into silence.

Strip silence provides a set of parameters, with the primary one being the threshold (just like a noise gate). The threshold is set in dB and determines the level above which material is retained and below which material is stripped into silence. Along with the threshold, you set the minimum length of time for each element (to avoid very short spikes or random noise elements, if desired). You can also set an attack buffer (region start pad), which allows you to retain the rising transients at the beginning of a sound whose level exceeds the threshold rather than simply starting the sound once it has reached the threshold. A release time (region end pad) can also be set to allow for the natural decay of a sound, even though it falls below the threshold.

In practice, strip silence is most useful on drums, percussion, and other material made of relatively short percussive sounds, although it can also be used on material of mixed sustain such as guitar tracks, where you might want to eliminate a lot of amp noise between the guitar parts. The most typical usage would be on kick, snare, or tom-tom tracks within a recording of a full drum set. Sometimes leakage from other drums onto these tracks may add undesirable elements to the overall drum sound.

The great advantage of strip silence over real-time gating is its ability to adjust for anomalies, such as a snare-drum hit that might fall below the general threshold of noise on the snare-drum track (a roll that starts quietly and crescendos in volume, for example). The following screenshot shows a snare track that is ready to be stripped, then stripped, then adjusted to include the low-level snare elements in the roll. It is shown on three different tracks here to follow the process, though, of course, only the final, processed snare drum would be playing.

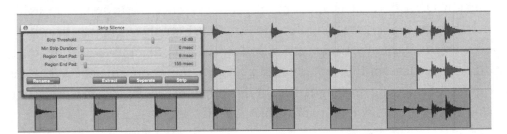

SCREENSHOT 4.30

A snare-drum track before processing with strip silence, after, and finally adjusted for low-level elements

In regard to tom-tom tracks, it is almost always desirable to strip silence. This is because the positioning of the toms means that there is likely to be a lot of leakage into those microphones, and yet the toms themselves may be played rather rarely. However, it is often easier to manually "clean" the tom tracks rather than bothering with the strip silence function. To do this you would simply navigate to each place the toms are played, select the region, and separate it, leaving a little buffer before and some release time after the tom hit. The material before and after the tom hit can be muted or cut. The effect is the same as what would happen with strip silence, but for a limited number of tom hits this would be faster.

Miracle edits

Using combinations of the above-mentioned techniques (and others that will no doubt be arriving soon to various DAWs), it is possible to do some rather miraculous things when it comes to editing. By exploring different possible edit points and different sizes and shapes of cross-fades, you can massage into

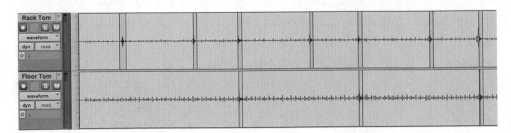

SCREENSHOT 4.31

Manually "cleaned" tom tracks

shape the edits that might at first seem problematic. Adding the ability to gain change, pitch shift, and/or time compress or expand can sometimes allow for seemingly "miracle" edits. After doing a lot editing, using all the tools at hand, you will learn to foresee your options and choose the most likely tactic for successful edits. Unless you're really pressed for time, don't give up too quickly on a difficult edit—you may find that you will create some miracle edits of your own!

Chapter 5

Three Fundamentals
Techniques Every Recordist Needs to Know

This chapter covers essential technical and procedural practices that are part of almost every recording setup: inserts, sends and returns, and auto-switching. These are signal-path basics that often pose the greatest problems for many beginning to intermediate recordists. These three fundamentals are not obvious parts of the mixer or recorder, but are crucial signal-path operations used in almost every recording session.

Proper routing for digital-signal processing (DSP, such as EQ, compression, delay, reverb) is one of the most basic practices in audio recording, yet it is often done improperly and in ways that make the recordist's job more confusing and complex than need be. There are two fundamental techniques for using signal processing: the insert model; and the send and return model. I cover them here as the first two of these three fundamentals. The third fundamental—auto-switching—describes an important option in the monitoring capabilities of every DAW and is discussed later in the chapter.

5.1 Inserts/Plug-ins

Proper routing begins by employing the most efficient signal-path model for each type of signal processor. In chapter 2, I covered all of the basic types of signal processors and I introduced the idea of plug-ins, which is the format for using signal-processing tools in the DAW. You'll remember that the plug-in is often the digital equivalent of the effects box from the analog world of hardware processing. The simplest way to use a plug-in is as an insert, and it is the proper way to use many, but not all, of the signal-processing tools.

Individual channel inserts

An insert is a means of making a particular processing tool a part of the audio channel. The easiest way to understand an insert might be to go back to the way we access EQ in an analog mixer. In almost every analog mixer, there is EQ circuitry built into each channel. Thus, as the signal flows through the channel path, it passes through the EQ. That is to say, equalization circuitry is physically inserted into and made a part of the channel in the mixer. You probably just thought of the EQ as part of the channel, not as at insert, but *it is the insert model of routing that makes the EQ part of the channel.* In the virtual mixer of a DAW, there are multiple positions to insert plug-ins, each one making any inserted processor part of the channel.

Just as EQ is normally put into use as an insert, the same is true for the general category of signal-processor tools called *dynamics.* Processors that control dynamics generally reshape the audio of each individual sound, creating new contours in the fundamental gain structure of the processed audio. The insert model allows dynamics processors such as compressors, limiters, expanders, and gates to completely integrate their effect into the channel output. Using EQ and/or compression on inserts of individual channels is a very common method of shaping sound as part of the mixing process, as described in section 6.2.

Because inserts are effectively a part of the channel, when you are using more than one processor on a single sound source, the specifics of the insert signal path become an important concern. For example, consider the common technique of using an EQ and a compressor on a single channel. Two processors inserted on the same channel must be placed in sequence—that is, one insert must follow the other in the signal path. Therefore, there is the potential for interaction between the two processors. For example, when EQ and compression are in sequence, the action of one of the processors may affect the other. What happens if the compressor follows the EQ in the signal path? The compressor's functions are dependent on the threshold setting that controls the actions of the compressor based on the level of the

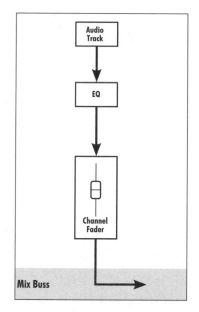

DIAGRAM 5.1

Insert routing for an EQ plug-in

155

SCREENSHOT 5.1

An EQ plug-in inserted directly into the first-position insert of a virtual mixing console

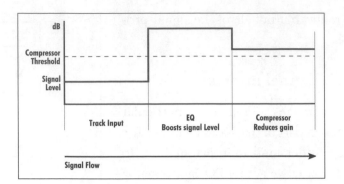

DIAGRAM 5.2

EQ feeding a compressor

incoming signal. If the signal level that feeds the compressor is increased or decreased (while the threshold is constant), then more or less compression will be applied to the signal. But boosting or dipping frequencies using EQ affects the signal level. *So, if the compressor follows the EQ in the insert path, changes in the EQ settings will affect the actions of the compressor.* This may cause unwanted effects.

Despite the possible problems created by placing a compressor after an EQ, there are times where you may choose this signal path. You may want the EQ to influence how the compressor responds. For example, if you are adding a lot of low end to a particular sound, and you want the compressor to control the dynamics based on this added low-end content, then the compressor needs to follow the EQ.

If the EQ follows the compressor in the signal path, the compressor is unaffected by changes in the EQ setting. Changes in the compressor settings won't affect the EQ because the effects of EQ are constant, regardless of changes in input level. For this reason, placing the EQ after the compressor is the more common routing for using these two processors on a single channel.

It is simple to reorder the insert sequence in most DAWs by dragging the insert into a new position. As you build a sequence of inserts on an individual track, it may be necessary to change the order so as to control the interaction between the processors.

Inserts on groups and on the stereo buss

Inserts are also used on groups and stereo buss (master) channels. In these cases, you are applying DSP on multiple tracks; but again, you are integrating the processing directly, using insert routing. You may want the same EQ or the same compressor on a group of tracks—drums, backing vocals, or whatever. While the effect is different from individual track processing, it may be desirable (for example, group compression tends to blend elements). It is also

SCREENSHOT 5.2

An EQ follows the compressor in a typical insert series

SCREENSHOT 5.3

Multiple drum channels grouped and bussed to a stereo auxiliary channel with a compressor on the insert of the aux channel

more efficient in terms of computer-processing power to use groups to do this rather than using individual processors on each channel. Group compression on drums is quite common.

Similarly, compression or EQ (or other effects) may be used on the overall mix by placing them on the master or sub-master fader insert. In chapter 6 (mixing) and chapter 7 (mastering), I explore the specifics of using DSP on groups and on the mix buss.

The graphic interface used to control processors takes advantage of the computer's flexibility and helps to maintain the best use of the monitor screen's real estate. This means that when a processor is placed on an insert, it is generally shown as a small box in the insert section of the virtual mixing board. When the box is clicked with the mouse, the full control panel of the processor is revealed and parameter changes can be made. The parameter control panel can be put away when not being used, so as to maintain a clear working space for other functions. A typical EQ control panel is shown on the following page.

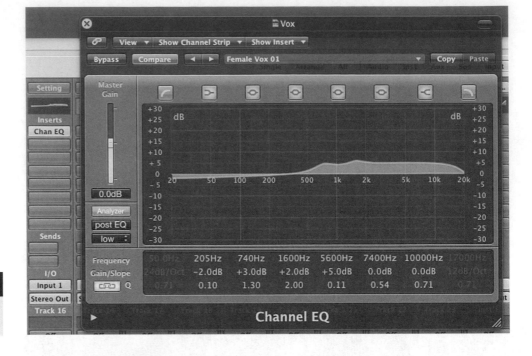

SCREENSHOT 5.4

A six-band EQ control panel

WHAT NOT TO DO

Don't always follow the "rules!"

This is a reminder that audio recording is a creative endeavor, and as with all creative endeavors, rules are made to be broken (sometimes). There are good reasons for the standard operating procedures, and most of the time we are best off if we follow them, but there are always instances where breaking the rules might yield desirable results. That's why I keep using the words typically or generally in my explanations; these suggestions are not meant to be absolute. For example, using EQ or compression on the send and return model may be worth trying, and it provides a different kind of flexibility that you may like. In general, the model that puts EQ and dynamics on channel inserts is going to work best—but nothing is to be considered sacred. You never know what unorthodox experimentation might yield! However, any experimentation is going to work best if it is done with knowledge of what rules are being broken and what kind of effect is being sought. Random experimentation that isn't based on a solid understanding of fundamentals tends to waste a lot of time and yield random results.

The input and output connections for a software plug-in is handled automatically when it is inserted into one of the insert positions on the virtual mixer. Hardware inserts (on mixing consoles, guitar amps, etc.) require a physical input and output to get to and from the piece of hardware (processing unit, reverb, EQ, etc.) that's being inserted. These connections need to be made with cables. These I/Os are sometimes labeled "insert in" and "insert out" and sometimes "insert send" and "insert return." In this case, the terms "send" and "return" mean the same as "output" and "input." This is a slightly different use of the terms from the send and return model for the use of software DSP plug-ins that I describe in the following section.

5.2 Sends and Returns

One of the most common and most challenging signal-path models for using signal-processing tools (plug-ins) is the send and return model. I introduced the idea of sends and auxiliary inputs (used for returns) in the previous section on mixing boards (section 2.4), and delved further into the use of sends in the discussion of headphone mixes (section 3.2). The complete send and return model is probably the most complex kind of signal routing that is still a fundamental part of basic engineering practice. Sends and returns form the routing model that is the alternative to using direct-channel inserts for plug-ins, which was covered in the previous section. In brief, rather than inserting the plug-in directly into the channel, you use an auxiliary input channel and insert the plug-in there, accessing it through the mixer's send capabilities. I show this routing model in detail, but first it helps to understand the most frequent uses for the send and return model.

Sends and returns rather than direct-channel inserts

Generally, it is reverbs and delay—the time-based effects first discussed in section 2.7—that are accessed using sends and returns. The key reasons are that the send and return model allows you the *share* these effects among many audio channels and provides greater flexibility in operation. The logic of this is pretty straightforward: time-based effects simulate environments (rooms, concert halls, the Grand Canyon, etc.) and you may well want different audio elements to share acoustic environments (you may want all guitars to sound like they were played in the same room, for example). Because the EQ and dynamics effects are specific to the sound (this guitar brighter, another guitar warmer, etc.) the direct-channel insert on each individual instrument is generally the best approach for EQ and dynamics processing.

Send and return signal path

It makes it easier to remember how to set up a send and return system if you keep the logic of what you're trying to accomplish in mind. You want to be able to access one effect (a reverb, for example) from many different audio channels. In order to do this, you must place the effect on an auxiliary input channel (or aux track). The aux track is always accessible for input, unlike an audio channel that only receives signal when it is in the record mode. Once you've created an aux track and inserted a reverb (or other signal-processing plug-in), you want to be able to send audio from any audio track to that reverb. Each audio track has many auxiliary sends, so you need to make sure that you are using the correct send to get the audio signal over to the reverb on the aux track. As previously discussed regarding aux sends (section 2.4), you have the choice between external routing (through the hardware interface) and internal routing (through the internal bussing system). Because you are operating with internal processors (plug-ins), you want to use the internal buss system for your routing. So, you start by setting the input of the aux track to a buss, and if this is the first buss you are using in this particular session, you might as well start with buss 1. This means that any audio sent over buss 1 will arrive at the input of the aux track and get fed into the reverb.

In order to send audio from a given audio track, you must create a send for that track and assign it a buss routing. To access the effect that is receiving signal on buss 1, you must create a send that is sending on buss 1. Having done that, you set the level of the send for each individual track and you have created a send and return model that allows you to access that particular effect from any audio track via buss 1.

Besides providing access to the effect (plug-in) from any audio track, the send and return model provides considerable flexibility. The overall return level of the effect is variable (more or less total reverb, for example), but by adjusting the level of the send from each track, you can vary the amount of effect on each track independently. The routing model for two audio channels being sent to the same reverb, but with different amounts of reverb added to each track, may be described like this.

- *Audio track 1 with a send routed to buss 1 and the send level set to 0.0 dB (unity gain).*
- *Audio track 2 with a send routed to buss 1 and the send level set to -5.0 dB.*
- *Aux track with a reverb inserted and set to receive on buss 1.*

As the output of the aux track is raised or lowered, there will be more or less overall reverb added to both the audio channels, but there will always be 5 dB less reverb on audio track 2 than on audio track 1 (unless the send levels are altered).

By using the send and return model, you have balanced the original audio track (the "dry" signal) with the effect (the "wet" signal). This process of balancing audio and effect is sometimes accomplished by inserting the effect directly on the audio channel (the insert model) and then balancing the two using a dry/wet control on the plug-in. Using a send and return model allows for easier balancing of dry and wet (the two are controlled separately with faders rather that interacting with the single dry/wet control), while at the same time providing the added flexibility of use on multiple tracks.

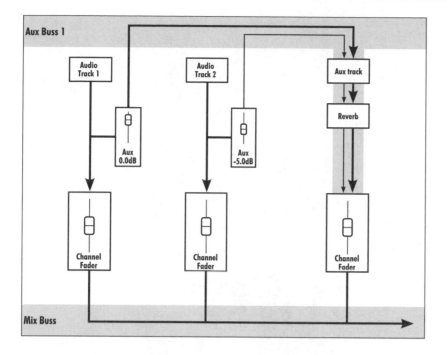

DIAGRAM 5.3

Send to reverb

Send and return model and panning

The send and return model also provides more flexibility for changes in panning between the dry signal and effect. In the example below, one audio channel is shown with a send going (via buss 1) to an auxiliary track, which is receiving the send on buss 1. There is a reverb inserted on the aux channel. The original audio is panned 50 percent left and the reverb is panned 75 percent left. This can be helpful in creating the subtle panning relationships that combine to produce the overall stereo field.

Expanding the send and return model using stereo effects requires managing stereo sends and returns. One frequent model maintains the mono send going from the audio channel, but a stereo effect is created by using a mono in/ stereo out (mono/stereo) plug-in. This was discussed in section 2.7, when reverbs and delays were introduced and I noted the common practice of feeding a mono signal into a reverb and letting the DSP create a stereo reverb effect. This is much like what occurs in nature when a single sound source (voice, guitar, horn, or whatever) is affected by the room acoustics and received by our two ears. It's our two ears, receiving slightly different versions of the effects of room acoustics, that create our sense of stereo, even though the original sound was mono (single sound source). Reverb plug-ins simulate this effect in their mono-to-stereo mode.

True stereo effects require stereo sends, and they allow the panning from the original-source audio to be reflected in the effect (a stereo reverb, for example). As in the example below, the original audio (which is a single track and thus a mono source) is sent via a stereo send and the send is panned 75 percent to the left). The stereo reverb receives the panning information and the amount

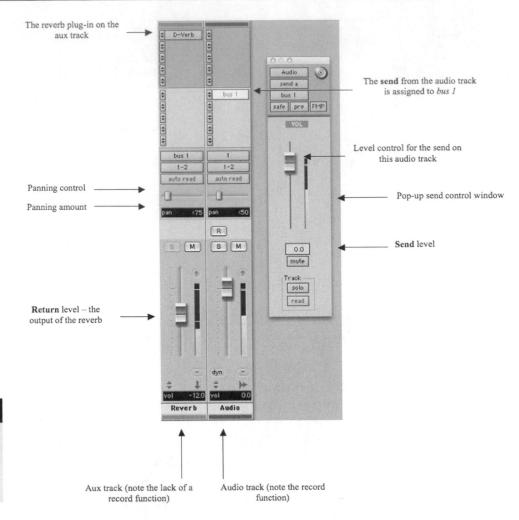

The reverb plug-in on the aux track

The **send** from the audio track is assigned to *bus 1*

Level control for the send on this audio track

Panning control

Panning amount

Pop-up send control window

Send level

Return level – the output of the reverb

SCREENSHOT 5.5

A send and return setup showing a variation in panning between the audio channel and the reverb return

Aux track (note the lack of a record function)

Audio track (note the record function)

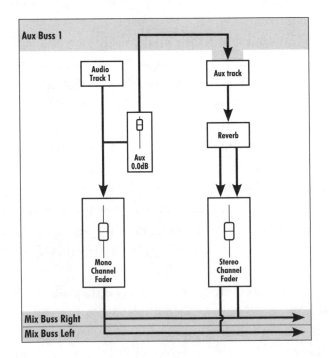

DIAGRAM 5.4

Mono aux to stereo reverb

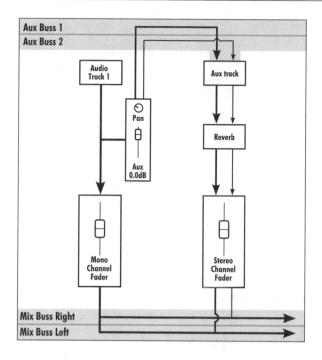

DIAGRAM 5.5

Stereo aux send to stereo reverb

of reverb is balanced according to the panning of the send. This is particularly useful in instances such as sending an entire stereo program to a reverb (a completely mixed song containing many elements, for example), and you want the reverb to retain as much of the left/right panning field as possible.

It should be noted that not all reverbs or other time-based delays offer true stereo functionality even in their "stereo" mode. You can check this by setting up a send and return model such as the one in Screenshot 5.6 and see if the reverb return follows the send panning. If it doesn't, the plug-in is not operating in true stereo mode but, rather, blending the left and right outputs to maintain a balanced stereo output (as it does in the mono in/stereo out operating mode).

In Screenshot 5.6, where a mono send (buss 1) is feeding a reverb set to the "mono/stereo" mode, note that the stereo return is not identical left to right—at the moment captured, the right channel is slightly louder. This is because, in simulating the kind of stereo spread created

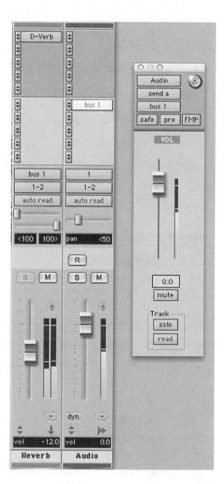

SCREENSHOT 5.6

Mono aux send to stereo reverb

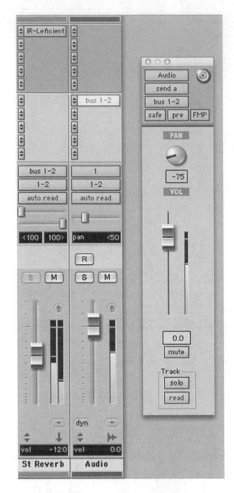

SCREENSHOT 5.7

Stereo aux send to stereo reverb

by room ambiences arriving at different times to each ear, there are going to be continuous but minor variations in the left and right channels.

In Screenshot 5.7, where a stereo send (busses 1 and 2) is feeding a stereo reverb (inputs set to busses 1 and 2), note that the send is panned 75 percent to the left, and as a result, the reverb return is considerably louder on the left side. If another audio track were sent to this reverb with the panning set far to the right, the reverb for that audio would appear primarily on the right-hand channel of the reverb return.

Send and return and CPU usage

One final note on sends and returns: Besides all of the benefits of using this model that have been covered above, the ability to use one effect on many tracks adds the benefit of saving on computing power. Whether your plug-ins are being powered by the host computer CPU or through an external card or interface, plug-ins—especially reverb plug-ins—can gobble up computer processing power, so sharing effects among tracks can greatly aid in maximizing the efficient use of your system.

WHAT NOT TO DO

Reverbs and delays on inserts.
Typically it is not a good idea to use individual channel inserts for reverbs or medium to long delays. This is partly because it is often desirable to share delays or reverbs between two or more tracks, which requires the send and return model, but even if the effect (reverb or delay) is being used for only one audio track, the send and return model provides easier use and more flexibility, as described above. Still, it is a good idea to know how to use a reverb on a channel insert and be able to make adjustments with the wet/dry control in case you have run out of sends.

5.3 Auto-switching (Auto-input)

Auto-switching (same as auto-input) refers to changes in the monitoring during the course of normal punch-in recording. *Punching-in* refers to rerecording parts of a previously recorded performance. *Monitoring* refers to what you are listening to during playback and recording. Certain signal path procedures, such as auto-switching or using sends and returns, are very common yet difficult to fully understand. Again, it is most helpful to begin with the logic of what you are trying to do before you look at the more technical aspect of signal path.

Input-only mode

In a lot of music production, punching-in is used extensively after the initial recording. You may punch-in and replace a portion of a track or you may punch-in somewhere in the middle and record all the way to the end of the track. In any event, the process of punching-in is dependent on the musician's ability to hear (monitor) in an appropriate manner. This means that the musician needs to be able to hear what was previously recorded on the track up until the time the punch-in is made and recording begins. So the monitoring must be switched while the music is playing—switched from playback (what was previously recorded) to input (what is being recorded). The evolution of this kind of switching ability on analog tape recorders marked a major change in capabilities. The original monitoring default situation, prior to the advent of auto-switching, was what is referred to today as "input-only mode." In this mode, a track that is armed (in record ready) is always monitoring input regardless of whether it is playing back or recording. Playback is not available until the track is taken out of record ready.

In order to complete an effective punch-in, it is necessary for the recorder to be able to be switched from playback to record while running. It would not be possible to do an effective punch-in while in input-only mode because the performer may not be able to tell where he or she was in the arrangement of the music. It was not an easy technical development for an analog tape recorder, but eventually the electronics were developed and the ability to punch-in was created. As shown later, this was not easy for the computer to accomplish either, but first the details on punch-ins.

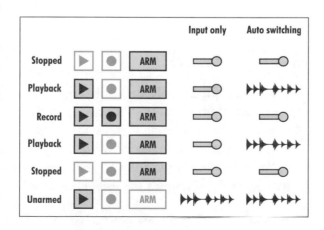

DIAGRAM 5.6

Input-only versus auto-switching

Punch-ins and auto-switching

Let's say there's a singer in the iso booth and you're about to fix (rerecord) a few vocal lines. As you're preparing to do this, you want to be reviewing the plan with the singer. This means that you need to be in communication with the singer, and that means that you need to be monitoring his or her input. By placing the track into record ready the recorder automatically switches the monitoring status of that track from playback to input (while stopped). Once you're ready for the punch-in, you will start playback. If the recorder is not in auto-switching (or auto-input) mode, the singer's track will continue to monitor input while the recorder is running (input only). That means that the singer can hear him or herself but not the pre-recorded vocal and he or she won't be able to tell where the entrance for the punch-in is. In auto-switching mode, when playback is started, the singer's track is automatically switched from input to playback, even though it is in record ready. This allows the singer to hear the already recorded vocal. When it comes time for the punch-in, the engineer activates recording and the track starts to record and also starts monitoring input. Go out of record (punch-out), and playback is monitored again (as long as the recorder is running). Stop running the recorder, and the singer's track reverts to input (and two-way communication via talkback is available again). The gist of the matter is this: in auto-switching, the recorder is automatically switching between input and playback according to the demands of a typical punch-in recording. The following diagram indicates the differences in the monitoring status of input-only mode and auto-switching.

Note that the input-only model is sometimes referred to as "audition" mode because it allows the user to audition whatever is to be recorded, without actually recording. That's because you can play the recorder and be listening to the musician sing or play as long as the new track is in record ready and input-only mode. You cannot hear anything that may have already been recorded on that track, so it is not a useful mode for punching-in, but this *might* (see below) be convenient for such activities as setting levels or warming up.

WHAT NOT TO DO

Don't use input-only or audition mode.
This may seem rather odd advice, but in the age of computer-based, nondestructive recording there is little reason to use input-only or audition mode. As explained in the following, the computer environment lends itself to "always being in record" whenever a musician is playing to a track, and this generally eliminates the usefulness of input-only mode.

Let's say you are setting up a vocalist and you need to have the person sing to the track so you can set the record level and the singer can check the headphone mix. The likelihood is that you'll be adjusting the level as he or she sings, which probably prevents you from using anything that is recorded, and they're just warming up anyway. Often singers will say something like, "I just want to try it once—don't record this." So if the recording is going to be unusable anyway, and/or the singer doesn't want the track recorded, shouldn't you use audition mode? I say no! One of the beauties of DAW recording is the undo function. I suggest that you remain in auto-switching mode and simply go into record from the start in order to be hearing input at all times. You are recording, but the effect is the same as being in audition or input-only mode from a monitoring point of view (you're always hearing input when you're recording). When the level testing or trial run is over, you can easily hit "undo record" and that recording is gone, just as if you were in audition mode. But on some occasions, after a supposed audition or test run, I have had singers or other musicians ask, "Did you record that?" You just never know when you might get something good—and with the DAW there's no risk of losing something already recorded, as there was with analog tape. Sometimes people play or sing particularly well when they don't think they're being recorded—and first takes can have a magic that is unreproducible!

Sometimes a musician will play or sing something I particularly like during a trial or warm-up pass. I might say, "I really liked what you played during the bridge [or wherever] in that warm-up." In the past, the musician might reply, "I have no idea what I played in that part. Did you record it?" If I had been in audition mode, I would not have been able to play what they had done. Now, if I have recorded it, I can go back and play it for the musician so the person has a reference. With nondestructive recording (and with the price of hard drives so low that storage really isn't an issue), there is no reason not to *always* be recording, even if you delete it later or have responded "Okay" when a musician asks not to be recorded. (If a musician has asked not be recorded, and if he or she doesn't ask if you happened to record that bit, and if you don't tell the singer that you did record it, the right thing to do is to eliminate that recording before moving on). Saving practice runs or any number of alternate takes is easy using virtual tracks, covered in section 4.2.

How auto-switching works in a DAW

Finally, a note about the way auto-switching is accomplished in a DAW. As I mentioned, this was a technical challenge that had to be overcome in the world of analog tape recorders, and it turned out to be a technical challenge for the DAWs as well. The problem for the DAW was that it is not easy for a com-

167

puter to start recording. Streaming 24-bit audio onto a hard drive at 44,100 samples (or more) per second is pretty demanding. As a result, it takes at least a few milliseconds for the computer to begin a recording. You may notice this when you go into record from stop—there is a slight delay before the recorder actually starts up and starts recording (more or less of a delay depending on how fast your computer is, how many tracks are in record, how many playback tracks and plug-ins are in use that are making demands on the CPU, and how efficiently the software is that you're using). Regardless, any discernable delay is unacceptable in a punch-in situation. The recorder needs to respond to the record command immediately. The solution in the DAW is both ingenious and beneficial in unexpected ways.

In order to provide immediate punch-in capabilities, a DAW actually starts recording on any track in record ready as soon as playback is started. This is why you may notice a slight delay on startup if one or more tracks are in record ready, even though you haven't instructed the recorder to start recording yet. The DAW is recording on those record-ready tracks from startup, but it is "pretending" not to be recording! That is to say, it is monitoring playback on those record-ready tracks just as it should be in auto-switching mode prior to being placed into record, even though it is recording on that track at the same time. Unlike an analog tape recorder, the DAW can record *and* play back on the same track at the same time because it uses random access storage—it isn't limited by a physical tape track. So, the DAW is recording, pretending not to be recording, and as soon as you tell it to record, it switches to input and places the new audio in the timeline, appearing to act just as it would have on an analog tape recorder track. The same is true when you punch-out; the DAW continues to record, but the monitoring switches to playback. This allows for instantaneous punching because the DAW isn't actually punching-in, it isn't really going into record; it already was in record and it is simply switching the monitoring from playback to input. The supplemental benefit is that all the stuff before and after the actual punch was recorded as well.

Actually, the ability to uncover or trim back material from before or after the punch can be both a blessing and a curse. It's a blessing because sometimes you may have been late with a punch and you can retrieve the bit that you missed. Or the musician might say, "I think I played a great lick right before the punch; can we hear that?" and in fact, you can hear it and keep it if you want to by uncovering it on the track's timeline. The curse is the way in which this might encourage sloppy punch-in and punch-out habits. While it's true that if you punch late you haven't actually missed the point at which you were supposed to punch-in (it's been recorded and is easily retrievable), the musician couldn't hear what he or she played or sang at the point he or she was supposed to enter because playback was still being monitored until the punch was made. This can be distracting for the musician. When (I must admit) on occasion I have made a late punch, the musician will often ask, "Did you get the beginning of that?" They couldn't hear it, so they didn't know if was actually recorded. Many musicians now know enough about DAW operation to recognize that the beginning had been recorded—but it's still distracting. Careful, accurate punching is still an important part of good studio practice.

Chapter 6

Mixing
The Most Creative and the Most Challenging Stage

I call *mixing* "the most creative and the most challenging stage" because there are endless variables to mixing and much less in terms of the concrete guidelines I've been presenting in regard to making good recordings (mic techniques, etc.). Mixing requires imagination and vision in order for you to achieve your sonic goal for the final mix—this is very creative work. But there's a lot of detail work that needs to be done to serve the larger vision, and there are a lot of technical elements that affect your ability to get from your recorded material to your goal for the final mix. These are the challenges.

Sometimes I hear mixes of music and my immediate response is, "What were they thinking?" Some mixes sound so wrong to me that I am at loss to understand how the recordist arrived at what it is that I'm hearing. On the other hand, I sometimes focus on the mix of a piece of music that I've heard many times and realize how truly odd the mix is and how different it is from what I would have likely done had I been the mixer—yet I have accepted and enjoyed the music (and the mix) without noticing its details. Both cases remind me how subjective mixing is. For the most part, we can assume that the listener does not consciously notice the details of the mix (how loud the vocal is or how affected the guitar sound), but we can also assume that these details affect the impact of the music on the listener—possibly even to the point of making the difference between the listener's liking or disliking the recording.

The following is intended to detail the way the DAW tools are used in the mixing process, examine the various elements that should be considered while mixing, and raise the creative issues that each recordist will answer in his or her own way. It is organized along the more practical guidelines—what you need to do in order to mix, how you build your mix, and how you finish your mix—but the more subjective and creative challenges arise within each part of the process.

6.1 Mixing Requirements

What do you need in order to effectively mix a project? There's no simple answer, but first you must ask both what is meant by *effectively* and what is meant by the *project* at hand. Being an effective mixer requires a certain amount of experience, a critical ear, and usually a healthy willingness to collaborate. Mixing is a skill as well as a creative endeavor, and there's no substitute for time spent mixing to develop that skill. Mixing also requires a good listening environment and an appropriate set of tools to manipulate sound. What constitutes these technical requirements may vary considerably among recordists working in different styles of music. Having the luxury of a home system or good access to a commercial facility, along with projects to work on, will allow you to go through the trial-and-error process necessary to develop effective mixing skills—guided by the good advice from this book, of course.

As to the project, the nature of the recording and the music you are mixing will greatly influence your ability to mix effectively. Musical genres have many conventions in terms of how mixes sound; and even if your goal is to defy those conventions, you will likely have limited success mixing styles of music that you are not very familiar with. The number of sonic elements in the musical piece is also important to the mixing skill set. There can be masterful mixes of solo piano recordings, but that is quite a different task from mixing a hip-hop track with tons of loops, percussion, samples, instruments, rappers, vocalists, and background singers. Different projects suggest different sets of tools and require different kinds of experience with mixing in order for you to achieve outstanding results.

Ultimately, your greatest asset in mixing is the same as your greatest asset in all other elements of the recording process—your ear! The more experienced and developed your ear, the better your chances for effective mixing of any kind of project. If I were hiring a mixer, I would opt for an ear that I trust far above any considerations of quality of gear being used (though both a great ear and great gear is really what you want).

What is mixing and remixing?

Let's establish exactly what is meant by the term *mixing*. As the word suggests, mixing is the combining of audio elements. While mixing in some form has been an essential part of recording from the beginning, it was initially accomplished by the placement of musicians and microphones as the music was being recorded. If the singer wasn't loud enough in the mix, he or she was moved closer to the mic.. It was with the advent of multitrack recording that the contemporary process of mixing began.

Because many distinct elements are recorded on separate tracks in the typical DAW environment, you must ultimately "mix" these to create a final version of the music. Typically, mixing involves setting the level and panning position; and considering the tonality, dynamics, ambience, and other effects of each separately recorded element. A new stereo file that incorporates all of these elements is created and used for burning to CD, posting to the Internet, and so on. You might sometimes be creating a 5.1 surround mix, or even 7.1 surround, or some other configuration—but stereo is still the predominant delivery format.

Remixing used to simply mean doing the mix again; and because of the power of the DAW, recordists find themselves redoing mixes more frequently than ever before. But the word *remix* has come to have its own, separate meaning. Remixes are reimaginations of a piece of music, often using completely new elements and eliminating other elements that were used in the initial mixed version. Remixes for specific functions—such as club play—are common, but remixes simply as creative exercises have also found a significant role in popular music. Beyond remixing are mashups and other newfound ways of recombining music elements. All of these are extensions of the basic mixing process, and mixing is what I cover here.

The mixing environment: The room and playback system

I have already discussed room acoustics and monitoring systems at the beginning of chapter 2, and that information pertains to the mix environment as well. In fact, control-room and speaker considerations that are important to recording become even more critical in the mixing process. I've made recordings in some pretty funky listening environments, and sometimes I simply rely on experience: "It doesn't sound very good in here—and I don't trust these speakers or this control room—but it sounds good in the recording room and I know the mics are working properly and positioned correctly so I'm going to assume that the recording sounds good." These kinds of situations have worked out for me with recordings, but they won't work out when it comes to mixing.

A sonic environment and playback system that you can trust is critical to mixing. Near-field monitors reduce the effects of room acoustics, but they do not eliminate them. Your room and your speakers must be reasonably neutral. This means that frequency buildup and reflections should be kept to a minimum through good room acoustic management, and your speakers need to be studio monitors that have at least reasonably flat response across the spectrum. All speakers have different qualities, and no speakers are truly flat, so finding the right mixing speaker is usually a process. Research at various discussion group sites, such as www.gearslutz.com, can be useful and give you a lot of ideas about available studio monitors. You may have access to a recording-equipment supply store that has monitors set up that you can audition, though those environments may be quite different from your setup, so the situation isn't ideal. Of course, budget will probably be a major factor, as well. Once you've settled on a good candidate through research, and, if possible, some auditioning or studio experience with a particular speaker model, try to buy them from a dealer that will allow returns, so that when you get them to your studio/home studio you have an option if they just don't seem right in your environment.

Ultimately, a good-sounding room and accurate speakers need to be combined with experience for you to create reliably good mixes. Getting used to your room and your speakers requires some time and some trial and error. Learning to listen as a mixer must be supported by confidence in what you're listening to, so don't shortchange your environment or your playback system. There is more on making your mixes translate to all listening environments at the end of this chapter.

How mixing relates to composing, arranging, and performing

Because mixing involves the ultimate way that a musical recording is going to sound, it shares many of the functions of composition (or songwriting), music arranging, and musical performance. In some fundamental ways, it is impossible to separate the mixing process from the writing, arranging, and performing processes; they all interact to form our ultimate experience of the musical recording. As a result, it isn't possible to completely distinguish the effects of the mixing process from these other musical activities. A beautifully composed, arranged, and performed piece of music will be much easier to mix than one with awkward composing, poor arranging, or inconsistent performances.

One example is mixing a song in which there are two different guitar parts and a piano part, all played in the same register as the vocal melody. No matter how you mix these elements, they are going to be competing for the same frequencies. Level and panning strategies—key to mixing—can create some sense of separation between these parts, but nothing a mixer can do will completely solve the overloaded frequency range caused by the arrangement. The situation is similar with a performance that feels uncomfortable rhythmically or out of tune. Performance problems such as these will always make the mix sound unfinished. And a composition in which the melody jumps awkwardly from one theme to another can never sound settled, under any mixing strategy.

The above situations are true except to the extent that the mixer actually alters the composition, arrangement, or performance. As discussed in the chapter on editing, recordists have powerful tools for altering all the elements of a recording, and more pronounced alterations have become common in contemporary recording work. Arrangements, performances, and even compositions are routinely altered as part of the recording/editing/mixing process. We can alter the rhythm and pitch of performances, we can mute or move elements, and we can reorder pieces to change arrangements and compositions.

Two questions arise: Who has the authority to undertake such transformations? and When are they to be done? There is no simple answer to either question. The authority may be centralized in one person—artist, performer, producer, recordist, or a combination of these—but it is more likely spread among all of them, without clear dividing lines. Good collaborative relationships allow ideas that change compositions, arrangements, or performances and can be suggested at any time during the process. They can be tried and then accepted or rejected by a consensus, though one person will need to have the final say if there is disagreement. And, while there's often an immediate consensus about a change—that is, all agree, "That sounds better!"—there can be healthy, and even frequent, disagreement without harming the working relationship if all are working with the spirit of creative experimentation.

The second question—"When are they to be done?"—is generally answered as "At any point in the entire process." This means that editing, fixing, moving, and so on might get done right at the same time as things get recorded, or in dedicated editing/fixing sessions, or during mixing. Which brings me back to the question, What is mixing? I recently received an e-mail asking if I was interested in a mixing project. The inquiry said that they have budgeted a certain amount to mix five songs. The budget works for me, if—and this is a big if—by "mixing" they are not expecting any editing or fixing as well. If I'm working on an hourly basis, or on my own, then the task of mixing may well get blurred with those of editing and fixing. Even though composing, arranging, and performing matters may have a strong relationship to mixing, they are separate from the fundamental task of mixing.

Mixing tools

Mixing tools, beyond the room and the playback system discussed previously, encompass a broad world of systems and processors. The equipment starts, of course, with your computer and your particular DAW, though every major DAW system is well equipped to handle the basics of mixing. Before I get too far with mixing tools, however, I have to consider one of the major ongoing debates in regard to mixing: should you mix entirely within your DAW, using only digital processing available within the computer (mixing in the box), or should you supplement the DAW with analog equipment (mixing out of the box)?

Mixing in or out of the box?

The notion of mixing "in the box" is simple: everything you do as a part of your mix occurs within your DAW (the computer is the box). Mixing "out of the box" can take myriad forms, from using just one or two analog processors to supplementing a mix that's done primarily in the box, to mixing with an analog console and all analog processing gear (often with external digital processing gear, as well). In this book, I limit the discussion to mixing within the box. I'm not arguing that this is the best way to be mixing, but this approach has some distinct advantages in regard to budget and work flow, and it has become increasingly common at all levels of production, including big-budget projects.

Beyond budget, the advantages to mixing in the box include ease of setup and outstanding automation and recall systems (discussed later in this chapter). The primary disadvantage is that you eliminate your access to analog processing gear, which some people prefer. Some people also believe that analog summing (combining of tracks) is superior to the digital summing within a DAW. While there continues to be considerable debate about the relative merits of analog and digital processing and summing, everyone agrees that the digital options have been tremendously improved in the last several years and there are more digital options than ever before. There's no simple answer, but the fact is that a great many projects, including some high-profile projects, are being mixed in the box—including several of my own Grammy-nominated projects.

Processing gear (plug-ins)

Along with setting levels and pan positions, it is audio processing that occupies most of the recordist's attention in the mixing process. The tools of DSP (digital signal processing) include the EQs, dynamics, and ambience processors discussed in the second half of chapter 2. These tools play a critical role in mixing, as you will see in the following section, when I discuss building a mix. Each DAW comes with plug-in versions of most of these tools, but there are an enormous number of third-party developers that supply additional tools for every DAW. Some supply capabilities that are not included with the DAW and some supply higher quality versions of the same basic tools. Obtaining these plug-ins can be a near endless process of acquisition (and expense!). What do you need to mix effectively? As you might expect, there is no simple answer to that question.

Theoretically, you don't need anything more than the tools that come with your DAW. More important than any plug-in is the ear and creative vision that drive the mixing process. That said, not having some high-quality processors of nearly every kind can be a distinct disadvantage in trying to create satisfying mixes. I remember very well the first time I got access to an SSL mixer (one of the highest quality analog consoles). As I was working, I started thinking, *This is why my drums have never sounded the way I want them to—I didn't have the necessary tools!* It's true that certain qualities to sound are just not available unless you have the right tools—with either the right capabilities, or the right level of quality, or both.

So, again, what do you need to mix effectively? As much gear as you have the ear and the experience to use effectively—and can reasonably afford! It's not

175

always easy to know what that means—and sometimes gaining the ear and the experience first requires having access to the tools in order to learn—but often your system will grow and develop naturally with your experience. And the income from your work will provide the opportunity for growth; I still use part of the income from big projects to expand my processing arsenal. There is more about specific tools in the following section on building a mix.

6.2 Building a Mix

Building a mix is an apt metaphor for the mixing process because mixing is a form of construction. Really, it's a reconstruction, taking all of the recordings that have already been constructed for the particular piece of music to be mixed and reconstructing them into their final form. The following addresses both the strategies and the processes involved in building a mix.

While mixing provides endless opportunities for creativity, there needs to be a balance between art and artifice. The art of mixing encompasses all mixing strategies, both artful and artificial. According to the dictionary, *artifice* is "an artful strategy," but it is also sometimes understood to be a trick. *Artificial* in mixing may refer to sounds and effects that aren't natural, that wouldn't occur in natural acoustic environments. The art of mixing must employ artifice, but it does so somewhere on the continuum between artful strategies that employ only natural acoustical effects and those that defy natural acoustics and include any number of audio "tricks" that fall well outside anything possible in nature. I worked on one mixing project where the artist definitely wanted to limit my choices to "sounds found in nature"—a perfectly fine strategy for mixing a lot of music. On the other hand, some mixing requires a lot of "artificial" effects and unnatural sonic environments, and these can still sound very musical. Some sense of where your project is going to fall along this scale between art and artifice is a valuable starting point for building your mix.

Approaches to listening and listening levels

How we listen is an important part of effectively building a mix. I have had musicians tell me that they have trouble listening to the balance between frequencies (from the lows to the highs) because their ear keeps focusing on the musical content. Some engineers miss musical relationships, like the interaction of counterpoint, because they're used to concentrating on sound rather than musical ideas. A good mixer needs to be able to listen sonically and musically. Sometimes we need to focus our ear on the way things sound, ignoring musical relationships, and sometimes we need to consider the musical functions before we decide about sound and placement issues. Often we need to balance the sonic and the musical contents at the same time.

I have dedicated a whole section of the final chapter of this book to listening levels during recording session—it's an important topic that deserves significant attention. Much of what is covered in that section is applicable to the mixing process, but in addition to that material I want to emphasize two points in regard to listening levels while mixing. The first is that listening at a variety of levels, from soft to loud, is a valuable part of referencing your mix. Second, ear fatigue is the enemy of mixing—it's the enemy of all audio work, of course, but especially mixing because of the subtle nature of the critical relationships being manipulated. Referencing your mixes loud is valuable as an occasional part of the process, but most of your mixing should be done at moderate levels. Peak volume readings of about 85 dB SPL represents a good standard for much of your listening while mixing and will allow you to work long hours without ear fatigue (a decibel reader, available from Radio Shack and other electronic supply stores, is a good investment).

In regard to listening at various levels, you need to take into account the Fletcher-Munson curve (and its later refinements that I discuss in section 2.5) that describes the way the ear's ability to hear different frequencies changes at different listening levels. This explains why it is just as important to not listen too quietly or too loudly when mixing. Loud listening will cause ear fatigue, but quiet listening will cause the ear to misjudge the relationships in the frequency spectrum because you don't hear high or low frequencies as well during low-level listening. But for this same reason, low-level listening can cue you to volume relationships that may be missed during moderate and high-level listening. The elements that you want in the front of your mix (vocals or solos, for example) should really pop out during low-level listening; if they don't, they might not be loud enough in the mix or they might require further EQ work.

Subtle background sounds, such as reverbs, are sometimes easier to judge with pretty loud listening. After working at a moderate volume for a while, give yourself a short period of loud listening to reveal some relationships that were not so obvious before, such as an excess of delay or reverb. Use your listening level to monitor various elements of your mix: moderate-level mixing for the general balance of all mix elements, low-level mixing for the level relationships between primary elements, and (relatively) high-level listening to check the relationship of quiet elements within your mix.

Preparing your file: Tracks, grouping, and routing

When you are ready to mix and all (or most) of the recording and editing is done, it is worthwhile spending a bit of time preparing your file for mixing. Part of organizing your files means creating a logical layout for your tracks. Often, during the recording and editing process, tracks get created or moved around to serve whatever is being done at the moment. A guitar track might get put next to the kick-drum track to check timing and a vocal track might get moved next to the piano track to make critical monitoring changes during a take. When mixing, it's nice to have the tracks laid out in some logical manner. For a typi-

177

cal band recording, I organize my tracks as follows, moving from left to right on the mixer: drums, percussion, bass, guitars, keyboards, vocals, background vocals. Of course, your recording may have more, less, or other elements, but you simply make a progression that makes sense to you.

Part of organizing your tracks may involve getting rid of tracks that you're not using. Many DAWs allow you to "hide" tracks so that they're not visible in the mixer or edit views, but still available if you change your mind later and want to include them in your mix. You should also be able to disable or deactivate those tracks so that they are not using any computer resources while they're on hold. Once you have an organized track list that contains only tracks you're planning to use in your mix, you're ready to consider some essential grouping and routing options.

Channel groups

It's likely that during the recording process you created some channel groups and possibly subgroups to make working easier. We encountered the notion of grouping in the chapter on editing. A group is simply a means of linking channels together so that you can control all of the tracks as a unit. Editing, changing the volume, or copying and pasting multiple parts are much simpler and more efficient when done as a group. For example, if you have multiple drum tracks and you haven't already made a drum group, you will certainly want one for mixing. In general, groups are very valuable in the mixing process, and you will want to go through your tracks and make groups for all the basic relationships: a drum group, a percussion group, a background vocal group, and so on, depending on the elements in your recording. You can disable any group while you make changes to one or more of the individual elements separately and then re-enable the group for overall group changes.

You may have groups within groups, smaller groups that are also a part of a larger group. A typical example would be the tom-tom tracks group, or the overhead tracks group within the larger drum group. DAWs have some means of showing groups within groups: in Pro Tools, the larger group is categorized by letter (a group, b group, etc.) and when a smaller group appear within a larger group, and the larger group is activated, member tracks from the smaller group are identified with a capital letter and member tracks that aren't in any other groups are identified with a lowercase letter. In the screenshot on the following page, the drum group is the a group. Because the toms and the OH (overheads) are also grouped separately, they are shown with a capital A while the tracks not in another group, such as the kick and snare, are shown with a lowercase a.

SCREENSHOT 6.1

Multiple groups within Pro Tools

Submixes, subgroups

The terminology is not consistent when it comes to making subgroups or sub-mixes, but the practice is very common. By routing multiple tracks to an aux track (typically a stereo aux to maintain the stereo position of the individual tracks), you can use the aux track to apply processing and automation to a group of multiple tracks. In the example on the following page, six background vocal tracks have been routed, using buss 5–6 to a stereo aux. This submix or subgroup channel is being used to apply EQ and compression to all six tracks at once, and to send them all to a reverb (using buss 7–8), as well. You can also automate the level of the tracks together. This can save on processing power, as well as making your work go quicker.

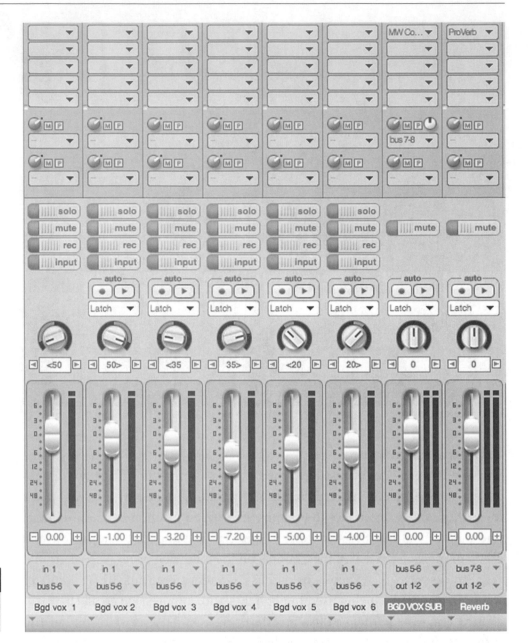

SCREENSHOT 6.2

Multiple tracks routed to a
stereo aux with processing

Master fader

There can be only one true master fader in a session, but the terminology can be confusing because sometimes what are technically sub-master faders may be identified as master faders. All tracks feed the master fader, and generally the stereo outputs of the master fader are the pair that feed the playback system (amplifier and speakers).

The master fader can be used for stereo buss processing. If you place a plug-in on the master fader, that DSP will be applied to your entire mix. This can be useful for overall buss compression, EQ, or other effects. (Note: the stereo feed from your DAW is sometimes referred as the "2 buss" or just the "buss.")

There is a problem with fade-outs when using dynamics processing (compressors, limiters, expanders, etc.) on your master fader. Because the processors are fed by the master output, the processing is affected when creating an overall fade (such as the fade-out at the end of a song). As all the tracks fade, the send to the dynamics processor will drop below the processing threshold. Although the track is fading, the music's intensity is not meant to be affected, so you don't want the dynamics processor to stop doing its work. The way to avoid this is to set up a master auxiliary track—you may want to label this "SUB," as it is a master submix. If you feed all your tracks to the SUB using a stereo buss, and then feed the SUB to the master fader, you can place your buss processors on the SUB; and then, when you create a fade on the master fader, the overall mix will continue to be processed (via the SUB plug-ins) as the track fades.

SCREENSHOT 6.3

All channels routed to a sub-master and then to the master fader

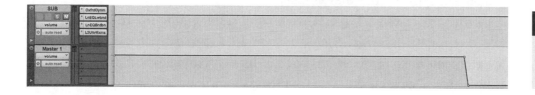

SCREENSHOT 6.4

A master fader fade-out after the sub-master processing

Mixing: Basic operations

As with any construction project, there are many possible routes to get from the beginning to the final form; but because effective mixing generally involves a whole series of steps and resteps, the exact sequence of events is not necessarily critical. Mixing involves drilling down to great detail while at the same time it requires a consistent focus on the overall sound being created. The "micro" is managing every part of each track's mixing parameters, including the level, panning, EQ, dynamics processing, effects, room ambiences, reverbs, short delays, and long delays, that may combine to create the sound of each element. At the same time, you must not lose focus on the "macro," which involves considering each individual sound in the context of every other sound that is part of the mix.

In this section, I consider each of these mix parameters as part of building a mix. Both micro and macro points of view are included in the discussion, as well as reflections on the working process. All of these elements have already been discussed as part of our general understanding of the recording process, but here the focus is on the mix, where greater detail and a more creative point of view are required. *The goal of creative mixing is to find the right sound and the right place for each element to best serve the creative vision.* Many factors combine to give each element its proper sound and place.

Level and gain structure (balance)

The number one task of mixing is to establish the relative levels of all the elements in your mix—which are louder and which are quieter. However, as you begin to mix, you also need to be aware of your overall gain structure. Once all the elements are in play, you will want your overall gain—your two-buss level as reflected on the meters of your master fader—to be at a comfortable level. Too much gain will overload the system and cause distortion, and too little gain decreases resolution and control.

You will want to start by playing all your tracks together, setting a quick balance among elements, to see what your overall gain structure looks like, and to imagine a creative strategy for how you will eventually position all the elements. You can adjust all the tracks together to set your overall gain, allowing a fair amount of headroom, as levels are likely to increase with the addition of EQ. At the loudest part of your rough mix, all of your tracks together shouldn't peak over -6 dB on your master fader.

An important part of creative mixing is imagining the relative levels between elements in terms of *foreground* and *background*. Unless you have very few elements in your mix, it isn't possible for everything to be in the foreground. How you treat elements in terms of processing will be affected by their position relative to foreground and background. (You may remember that I discussed recording techniques in these same terms—how you choose to record elements may also be influenced by their ultimate position as foreground or background in the mix.)

As you begin to mix, the first element you consider exists in a kind of vacuum, as you have no other elements to balance it against. Having established an overall gain structure means you can start with the first element at the level it is already set, and that becomes the baseline as you add elements. In a traditional band recording, the first element mixers consider is often the drums—and the first element from the drums is often the kick drum—but some mixers prefer to start with the bass. Different mixers take different approaches, but because you will be returning many times to each element in a mix, it isn't critical which element you choose to start with. I return to the question of how you might order the introduction of elements into your mix, and ultimately how you might settle on relative levels, after considering the other major parts of the mixing process.

Panning

Creative use of panning is one of the most frequently underutilized tools in the mixer's toolbox. It's useful to remember that the word *panning* comes from *panorama*, which refers to an unobstructed and wide view; and creating a wide and elegant aural panorama is one goal of all creative mixing. The complete panning spectrum runs from hard left to hard right, and the creative mixer will make the most of this entire field.

I covered the basics of panning in chapter 2, so here I focus on panning strategies for mixing. The first strategy is to have a strategy—that is, you want an overall plan for panning elements before you start addressing individual tracks. Certain panning approaches may remain constant. Drums may be panned according to their physical setup, with the kick and snare tracks centered, the hi-hat track to one side, the tom-tom tracks spread from one side to the other depending on the number of toms, and the overhead mics split in hard left/right stereo. Drum panning can adhere to either the drummer's perspective or the audience's perspective and either is acceptable as long as it is consistent. (Don't pan the hi-hat based on the drummer's perspective and the tom-toms based on the audience's perspective.) I was a drummer for many years, so I usually pan the drums using the drummer's perspective because that's what sounds most natural to me, but if I'm mixing a live recording, I'll use the audience's perspective because that's the way the live audience was hearing the drums. Bass and lead vocals are usually center-panned along with the kick and snare (though it's perfectly fine to stray from this convention if you find a compelling reason to do so).

Beyond these generally accepted practices, panning is wide open to creative approaches. Getting the macro of panning established for your mix means considering each element in the mix and placing it in the panning spectrum. You might start with four basic positions (seven total positions)—center, soft left or right, medium left or right, and hard left or right—and place every element in one of these positions. Your decision will be based on the number of elements, their relationship, and your vision of how they will best fit together across the stereo field. For example, a tambourine track may belong in any one of these seven places, but the part it plays (simple or complex), its relationship to the position of the hi-hat, its interaction with other rhythmic elements such as the snare drum or a rhythm guitar, its relationship to other high-frequency elements such as a shaker, its history in the style of music, and so on might all affect your decision. Four tracks of background vocals may be panned in a multitude of ways, including spreading them evenly left to right, spreading them across either the left or right panning spectrum, and lumping them together at one spot in the panning spectrum. Your decision may be influenced by the relationship of the four parts (which are high and which are low), by the relationship of the parts to the lead vocal, by the existence of other elements in the track that may have similar function such as a horn section, and so on.

There are an enormous number of considerations that you might take into account in any panning strategy. There is no substitute for experimentation and creative thinking while making panning decisions, but here are some further guidelines.

1. Don't be afraid to abandon an initial panning strategy and start again from scratch.
2. After you've applied your basic strategy for panning all the elements, continue to experiment with slight changes in positioning to find the best possible position for each element.
3. Use the entire panning spectrum. If there are very many elements in your mix, it is almost always the case that one element should be panned hard left and one element hard right. Don't leave the far ends of the panning spectrum unexplored.

WHAT NOT TO DO

Panning stereo tracks

Just because something was recorded (or sampled) in stereo, that doesn't mean that you have to use its full stereo capability in your mix. When you create a stereo track, it defaults to placing the two panning controls set to hard left and hard right. Sometimes you will want to leave them set this way, but often you will want to adjust the stereo balance within a stereo recording. For example, even though the piano is recorded in stereo (using two microphones), there may be a lot of elements in your mix and the piano will be heard better if it occupies a smaller piece of the stereo image and doesn't compete across the entire stereo spectrum. You may want to set the one panning control soft right and the other medium right—keeping the piano on the right side but allowing it to be spread a bit across the spectrum on the right. Or instead, you might want to set both panning controls to hard left and let the piano have its own place at the far left end of the spectrum. The two tracks are still providing complementary information to fill out the piano sound, even if they are panned to the same place, making them sound like a mono recording. Too many elements spread out in wide stereo will often make a mix sound indistinct and congested.

4. Remember that altering panning changes volume. There is a power curve to panning controls, which means that sounds increase in volume as they move farther left or right (the difference between center position and far left or right is between 3 and 6 dB, depending on the system). Consult your DAW manual, but your ear is best source for setting volume regardless of specs.

Auto-panning is another powerful panning tool that can be effective (or distracting) and has become much more versatile in the DAW world than it was in the analog world. *Auto-panning* refers to "automatic" movement in pan position as the music plays. I will explore auto-panning in the following section on automation.

Equalization (frequency range)

As previously discussed in chapter 2, EQ represents the most powerful and important of all signal-processing gear. EQ is an essential part of the mixing process. However, I am reminded of a discussion I had with a colleague shortly after having my first experiences mixing on an SSL console. He said, "That SSL EQ is powerful and can be a great tool, but it can also destroy a mix." Indeed, EQ can be your best friend or your worst enemy. Used wisely, it can transform mixes into works with greater clarity and impact; and used poorly, it can make mixes sink in a morass of shrillness and/or mud.

There are two essential considerations to keep in mind as you EQ elements for your mixes. The first is what kind of frequency shaping with EQ is going to make this element *sound best*, enhancing the sound of the recording. The second is what kind of frequency shaping with EQ is going to make this sound *fit best* with all the other elements in my mix. Typically, these two considerations will have some things in common and others in conflict. Your job as a mixer is to make the best compromise between "sounds best" and "fits best." Sometimes these two things are really completely complementary, but that is usually only the case in mixes involving very few elements. On a solo piano recording, you can ignore "fits best" and only consider "sounds best," but on a mix involving 15 different instruments, there will need to be a lot of "fits best" considerations that override "sounds best."

A typical example of the "sounds best" versus "fits best" EQ-ing conflict would be in regard to an acoustic guitar recording. Acoustic guitar is a full-frequency instrument that often has very rich overtones throughout the frequency range. A well-recorded acoustic guitar may sound best with no EQ at all, or with a slight amount of high-midrange frequency, high-frequency, and/or low-frequency boost to accentuate the overtones and make the instrument speak, sparkle, and resonate most fully. The fullness of an acoustic guitar is wonderful for solo guitar or in small ensembles, but it is often problematic when the instrument needs to fit in with a larger group or in a rock-type setting. The rich low end of the guitar tends to get muddied up with the bass and other low-frequency sounds. In a mix with drums, bass, electric guitar, vocals, and possibly many other elements, that full-frequency acoustic recording takes up way too much space. In a dense mix, it is likely that you will want to severely cut frequencies from the acoustic guitar, especially in the lows and low-mids, and you may want to accentuate the higher frequencies beyond your normal "sounds best" sensibility in order to get the acoustic to cut through in the mix—the guitar must fit in and making its presence known without competing with too many frequencies from other elements (panning plays an important role in this equation as well, as discussed above).

One might well ask, "How do I know what 'sounds best' and what 'fits best'?" Here, there is no easy answer; in fact, there is no one answer or best answer. Certainly, there are some general criteria that most (but not all) recordists would agree on, but these are themselves somewhat vague. "Sounds best" is rich in pleasing and musical overtones. "Sounds best" is well balanced through all the frequency ranges that are appropriate to that particular instrument. "Sounds best" is warm and present. "Fits best" is focused on the frequencies where there is the most space for this particular element. "Fits best" sounds like it belongs in this environment. "Fits best" sits in a mix with a clear identity and place. While many might agree on these descriptions, exactly what kind of EQ-ing might be employed to achieve them could differ pretty radically from one recordist to another.

I have been surprised by the proliferation of "presets" for EQ-ing various instruments that are found as a part of many EQ plug-ins now. You may even get (or you may be asked to buy) EQ presets from well-known recordists for certain EQ plug-ins. I find this odd because each particular recording of any given instrument, and each particular use of that instrument within a particular recording, is best served by an individual approach to EQ-ing that element. That said, it is true that approaches to EQ-ing certain instruments may be relatively consistent within a specific genre of music, so perhaps these presets are useful in pointing people in the right direction. Perhaps. But they also might have a negative effect in making people think that there is a "right way" to EQ a snare drum or an acoustic guitar, or that all they need to do is apply the preset EQ for each element and their mix will be EQ'd in the optimal way. My advice is, sure, go ahead and explore the presets, but *use your ear* and don't be afraid to make changes to the preset or of even taking a completely different approach. I have given some advice on using EQ in chapter 2, but you will not find any packaged formulas for EQ-ing here. You must explore on your own.

Dynamics processing

Dynamics processing plays a major role in mixing. Most of the time, the emphasis is on compression and limiting, as opposed to expanding and gating. This is evident in the section on the basics of dynamics processing in chapter 2, where most of the discussion focuses on compression and limiting. As with EQ, dynamics processing can be your friend or your enemy. Effective use of dynamics requires the technical mastery of the tools and the development of listening skills in the service of your creativity.

Compression has two distinct functions in mixing. One is the subtle control of volume dynamics that evens out performances and helps them retain their presence throughout a mix. This first function of compression is generally pretty transparent; the goal is for the dynamics control to *leave the sound as unaffected as possible* in any way other than shrinking the dynamic range and thereby leveling out the performance. The second is the use of compression to *create a variety of obvious effects*. The most noteworthy effect from certain kinds of compression is the addition of impact through a concentration of the audio energy. This is most frequently heard on drum tracks in many genres of contemporary music.

Using compression for the subtle control of dynamics can be an enormous aid in getting elements to sit comfortably in mixes. Featured elements such as lead vocals and bass are particularly susceptible to problems from too great a dynamic range. The basic argument for using compressors is laid out in section 2.6, where I introduced the functions and operations of dynamics processors; elements that have less dynamic range can be heard more consistently when competing with a lot of other sounds. As a general rule, the greater the number of elements in a recording, the more help can come from compressing them. In many contemporary recordings most elements are compressed, and there is frequently overall compression applied to elements in subgroups (such as drums), as well. There may also be additional compression on the overall mix. One well-known producer has said, "Compression is the sound of rock and roll."

My overall creative vision for the sound of the mix, along with the density of the mix and the relative position of each element, dictates how aggressively I use compression in any given mix. In relatively spacious recordings without a lot of elements, I rarely go above a 3:1 ratio and 4 or 5 dB of compression on the loudest sounds. On a dense mix, I might use ratios as high as 6:1 or higher and hit 7 or 8 dB of compression at the maximum levels. In dense mixes, I might use a bit of limiting as well as compression on some elements to tame the peak levels.

I use a bit of buss compression (overall compression on the entire mix) on most mixes as well. Gentle buss compression acts as a kind of glue that helps blend all the tracks together, although too much glue can make mush of the tracks. Aggressive buss compression can be used as an effect—to add impact to mixes. The difference between gentle and aggressive buss compression has to do with ratio and threshold—higher ratios and lower thresholds ramp up the aggression—but processors also have characteristics that are the result of many other elements in their design. Many compressor plug-ins have settings that simulate a wide range of compressor types from their analog antecedents. Mixing is the place to explore all kinds of compressor types and functions, from the most gentle and transparent to those with the most "personality."

There is one type of control over dynamic range that is not really a part of the mixing process and that is brick-wall limiting—it belongs to the mastering process covered in the next chapter. But because this process has such a profound effect on the sound of mixes, and because it will be applied moderately to heavily most of the time in mastering, you need to integrate it into your mixing practice as well. I cover the basic idea of how to integrate this into your mixing process in the final section of this chapter on delivering mixes and I cover it more thoroughly in the following chapter on mastering.

Mixing: Creating ambience and dimension

Certain mixing processors can add ambience and dimension to your recording. These processors are the delays and reverbs covered under FX ("effects") in section 2.7. Most FX processing of this type is done as part of the mixing process, although you might use delays as an integral part of a sound when recording (chorusing on a guitar, for example), and you might use some reverb for monitoring your vocal (meaning you add reverb to the vocal for listening purposes, but you do not actually record that reverb as a part of the vocal recording).

Waiting until the mix to add these kinds of effects allows you to create a unified *ambient* environment for your final audio presentation. The combination of delays and reverbs creates a kind of delay pool that, though made up of individual effects on each element, also combines to create a sound stage that you want to consider as a whole. As you build your sonic landscape (or sound stage), both musical and technical considerations come into play. You may wish to construct a naturalistic environment—one that sounds true to a real-world setting, such as a nightclub or a concert hall. Contemporary popular music tends more toward unnatural environments, in that many different kinds of ambience are used within one mix, even though it wouldn't be physically possible for all the elements to be in those environments at the same time. Some mixes combine many different effects but limit them to the kinds of reverbs and delays that are found in natural environments such as rooms, theaters, and concert halls. Other mixes incorporate unnatural delay effects, such as "gated reverbs" with abrupt cut-offs, and ping-ponging delays that bounce back and forth between left and right speakers. Whatever your approach to the environment that you are creating, it is the construction of a sound stage that is one of the most creative parts of the entire process of mixing.

Using delays in mixing

I covered the basics of short, medium, and long delays in section 2.7. Here, I discuss some of the fundamental ways that they are used to enhance elements during the mix. Short delays can be used to thicken, to add interest, and to expand the stereo field of a sound. Medium delays can open up a sound while reinforcing the rhythm. Long delays can also reinforce rhythm, they can call attention to a sound, and they can be used for special effects.

Short delays are often used to thicken sounds. The classic "chorus" effect thickens elements in the way that vocal choruses are used to create thickness with many voices. Sometimes the short delays that create the chorusing effect are used without the modulation that is characteristic of the chorusing effect. This is generally referred to as a doubling effect, and it may be created with straight delays or it may be created with micro-pitch shifting to further thicken the sound without modulation (usually shifted in pitch either up and/or down 6 to 9 cents). These kinds of effects can be used on virtually any kind of audio, though they are generally not effective on short drum and percussion sounds. They can sound good on rhythm and lead instruments, as well as vocals. Of course, thickening is a two-edge sword—it can enhance and add interest to almost any element, but too much of it in a mix makes the mix too thick and blurs the sound. You must pick the elements that will benefit the most from short delay effects, and this will vary from mix to mix and in relation to different genres. For example, punk rock may not call for too much thickening with short delays (though flanging on the vocal can be very effective and appropriate to the genre), whereas electronica might benefit from quite a lot of short delay effects, creating a wall of thick, lush ambience.

Short delays can also be used to spread elements across the stereo field. If a sound is split evenly between right and left, it will sound center. It is mono if there is no difference between the sound in the left and the right channels. If you introduce a short delay on either side, the sound will suddenly acquire a stereo spread (anywhere from 3 to 30 ms delay would be typical). Although that application can be useful, it is somewhat artificial sounding. More subtle variations on using short delays involve less radical panning options, such as having the original signal soft right and the slightly delayed signal mid-right, just spreading the sound slightly across the right side. Two or more short delays, with slightly different delay times and panning positions, can yield endless possibilities for thickening and spreading sound across the stereo spectrum.

One classic short-delay application involves two delayed and pitch-shifted signals—perhaps one delayed 15 and one delayed 25 ms, with one pitch-shifted up 7 cents and one pitch-shifted down 7 cents, and then split hard left and hard right. The original, unaffected signal is centered. The two delayed and effected signals can be pretty quiet and still provide thickening and stereo spread to the original signal. You can also collapse the two signals a bit (bring them in from hard left and right to closer to center) if you want a less audible effect. This type of effect is used fairly commonly on vocals, lead guitar, and other upfront sounds.

Medium delays provide a sense of space by simulating medium to large environments. Medium delays in the 125 to 175 ms range are often referred to

189

as *slapback.* A very audible version of this effect can be heard on many Elvis Presley recordings, and this effect has become somewhat identified with his vocal sound. The advantage to slapback delays is that they provide a sense of space without the complex and potentially cloudy effect of reverb—though they may also be used in conjunction with reverb, as a further enhancement rather than as a replacement. Although they can be used to broaden the stereo spread, they are generally panned to the same location as the direct signal to provide a more subtle effect. You can use feedback (multiple repeats) on a slapback delay, but generally one slap provides a cleaner sound. The level of slapback delay can vary from very rather obvious (the Elvis effect) to rather subtle, where you can't really hear the delay but you notice a change in the depth of the sound if the effect is removed.

You can set the delay time for a slapback effect by ear, but you might want to set it based on the tempo of the piece of music you are mixing. Using "in time" delays—delay times that are based on the musical subdivisions of the tempo—generally support musical propulsion, while delays that are contrary to the beat can diminish the rhythmic energy. Most delay plug-ins have options for setting delay times based on beat divisions (quarter notes, eighth notes, etc.). Of course, the plug-in must "know" what the tempo is in order to do that, so you need to have the file referenced to the correct tempo. Even if your music wasn't recorded to a set tempo, you can usually determine the approximate tempo using various tap tempo tools that allow you to tap on one key of your computer keyboard in time with the music and get a read-out of the tempo (check your DAW for this "tap tempo" function).

Long delays can really open up a sound and can also be used for all kinds of special effects. It is especially important to use musical timing when setting long delays, as they can really confuse the rhythm if they are not in time. When used as an effect to suggest a very large space, it is typical to use some feedback, simulating the characteristics of sound bouncing back and forth in a large space (15 to 30% would be a typical range for feedback). As with slapback effects, normally the long delay would be panned to the same position as the direct signal. The volume of long delays can range from a subtle effect that is only audible at high volumes to an obvious repeating effect that is easily heard. With such a strong effect that is creating new and distinct rhythmic patterns, it is generally used rather sparsely.

Long delays are commonly used for special effects such as obvious and audible repeats, stutters, and cascading sounds. Such effects can be playful and fun, and they can add elements that become integral parts of an arrangement. To some extent, however, the ease of editing in a DAW has replaced the need to use long delays to create some of these effects. We can copy and paste, using a musical grid, and create repeating effects that can be more easily controlled than those made with a delay. In any event, repeats occupy an important role in the creation and mixing of popular music.

Using reverbs in mixing

Reverbs are the principal tool used to create (or recreate) ambience when mixing. As more thoroughly explained in section 2.7, reverbs simulate or actually reproduce the effects of real-world environments. When used creatively, reverbs provide tools for mixes of great depth and interest. When used without sufficient planning and careful listening, reverbs can be a primary source of problems that produce a lack of clarity in mixes.

First, keep in mind that reverbs cover the entire range of room acoustics, from closets to bathrooms, nightclubs, concert halls, and outdoor arenas. Most reverb plug-ins organize their sounds by type of space (rooms, clubs, theatres, concert halls, etc.) and by type of reverb simulation (plates, springs, chambers etc.). There are two primary qualities to reverbs: length and timbre. Length is expressed in seconds and can run from .1 to 7 seconds or longer, but most reverbs are in the .3- to 3-second range. Timbre of reverbs ranges from warm (concert halls) to bright (plate simulations) with rooms, chambers, theaters, and the like varying depending on the nature of each individual space.

WHAT NOT TO DO

Tweaking reverb presets

With the huge range of reverbs available, it is usually possible to find the ambience that you want without having to do much in the way of tweaking the sound. If the preset you choose doesn't sound like what you're looking for, don't spend time trying to tweak it into shape. Go for another preset that gets you closer to what you want to use as a starting point.

My number one rule for selecting reverbs is: Don't use a longer reverb when a shorter reverb will do. Often, the goal of creating an ambience for an element is satisfied with a relatively short reverb, such as a room with a length from .3 to 1 second. These short reverbs create depth and interest without washing a lot of sound over an extended period of time. If you have a variety of room reverbs available, from small to large and from warm (wood rooms) to well-balanced (standard rooms), to bright (tile rooms), you can use these to create much of your overall ambiance pool.

Short reverbs (such as rooms) are often the best choice for any element that has very much rhythmic interest. The more rhythmically active a part is, the more it will get clouded by longer reverbs. Long-sustaining elements can be treated with longer reverbs to give them a lot of depth without smearing the sonic landscape as much, and sometimes a single lead instrument or voice can be enhanced by a longer reverb. When using multiple reverbs, the combined effect must be considered—another argument for using shorter reverbs.

Reverbs do not have the same distinct kind of timing quality as delays have because they decay slowly, but tempo should be a consideration in reverb selection. You can use tempo timing as you do with delays to set certain kinds of reverbs. Gated reverbs (and some rooms) have a pretty steep decay, and you can set their length to a quarter note or a half note to good effect. Because of the more typical slow decay, timing most reverbs is best done with the ear, listening to how the trailing off of the decay fits into the overall rhythm of the piece. As you adjust the length of the reverb you will begin to hear what length seems to allow the decay of the reverb to become a part of the rhythm. The longer the reverb, the more difficult it is to have it interact with the music rhythmically, but the less important it is because the slow decay of long reverbs will tend to blend the reverb in without disrupting the rhythm.

I generally don't share reverbs, which means that each element in the mix gets its own distinct reverb. I may use the same reverb plug-in multiple times, but with different settings that recall different spaces and reverb types. Nonetheless, I use reverbs on the send and return model, rather than on the direct channel insert, because it allows for easier fine-tuning and for panning variations. In a typical mix I use different reverb settings (rooms, halls, plates, etc.) on the drums, the percussion, the piano, the organ, the rhythm guitar, the lead guitar, the horn section, the background vocals, and the lead vocal. I often use more than one reverb on some elements, such as drums and lead vocals, and blend them. Of course, not every mix has all these elements, and some mixes have other elements, but the principle is that each element may benefit from its own ambience. The individual sound can be tweaked separately, and you will have the opportunity to create a more distinctive sound and place in the mix for each element.

It might seem tempting to send many things, or everything, to the same reverb so they "sound like they're all in the same room together," but in doing so you may create a muddy ambience pool, with elements competing for the detailed reflections that reverbs are capable of. In some instances, this may be the right approach—perhaps on a live recording—but in general we are able to create more distinctive and interesting recordings by combining many reverbs, each one suited and balanced for the each specific element. You may have to limit your number of reverb plug-ins because of limits to your computer's DSP power, in which case you need to be creative to get the most out of your limited resources; but most contemporary computers have enough CPU power to drive as many plug-ins as you need, even for the most complex mixes.

Panning reverb returns

Panning reverb returns is an important part of creative reverb use. There are three input/output configurations for implementing reverbs: mono in/mono out, mono in/stereo out, and stereo in/stereo out. Exploring these configurations, along with the more detailed possibilities with reverb panning, is an important part of the mix process.

Mono in/mono out reverbs are handy when you want to place the reverb return directly behind the direct signal in the panning scheme (e.g., guitar panned 37% left and mono reverb return panned 37% left). You can also use these mono reverb returns to push the ambience farther to the edges of the panning spectrum (e.g., guitar panned 75% left and mono reverb return panned 100% left).

Try to avoid too many instances of the most common configuration—mono in/stereo out, with the stereo outputs (returns) split hard left and right. This spreads the reverb return across the whole panning spectrum, and more than a couple reverbs in this configuration can blur a mix rather quickly. Rather than having the returns fully panned, you can use this configuration to spread the reverb a bit over the spectrum (e.g., guitar panned 60% left and the two reverb returns panned 40% left and 80% left). You might spread the return even farther but still avoid using the entire spectrum (e.g., guitar panned 35% left and the two reverb returns panned 70% left and 20% right). Because the stereo outputs often have considerable phase differences in order to create a spacious sound, it can create problems if they are panned too closely together or to the same position. For this reason, it's best to use a mono in/mono out configuration or just one channel of the stereo return when a single point reverb return is desired.

Reverb configurations that have stereo inputs use varying strategies for feeding those inputs to the reverberation algorithms and generating stereo returns. Many reverbs sum the inputs to mono at some stage in the processing, so that the return remains equal in both channels no matter what panning strategy is used to feed signal into the input. True stereo reverbs maintain the stereo position of the signal's input in the reverb's output. That means that if you feed a signal to the left input of the reverb only, then the reverb for that signal will be returned only on the left channel.

True stereo reverbs can be very useful in mixes with multiple channels of one type of element. For example, if you have six tracks of background singers, you can feed them all to a stereo submix by using a stereo send to a stereo aux track, and then feed the stereo submix to a true stereo reverb. This will put the same reverb on all of the singers' voices, while maintaining the panning position of each voice within the reverb return, helping to create a distinct position for each voice while blending them in the same reverb.

Advanced techniques with delays and reverbs

There are many more advanced techniques for using delays and reverbs than I have space to cover here, but I will mention a few and encourage you to use your ear and imagination to find more. To begin, you can combine any number of the techniques described above to create more complex ambiences. It would not be uncommon for a vocal to have some kind of short delay/doubling effect, a slap delay, a room reverb, and a hall reverb—all used rather subtly but com-

193

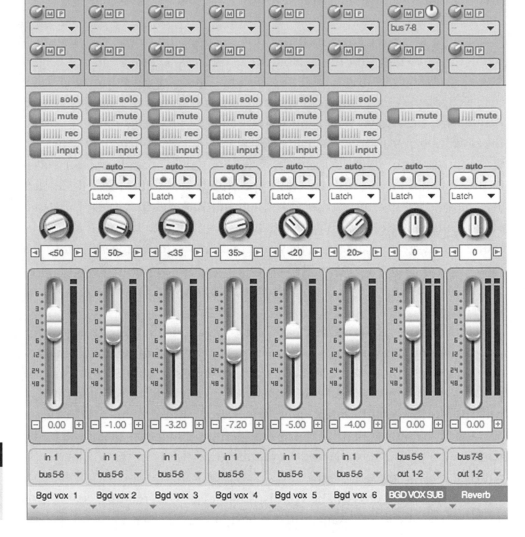

SCREENSHOT 6.5

Backing vocals routed to a stereo aux and then to a stereo reverb

bined to create a complex ambience. A solo saxophone might have a long delay and a medium reverb. A lead guitar might have a slap delay and long reverb, or it might have a doubling effect, a long delay, and short reverb. There are endless possibilities for combining effects.

When combining delays and reverbs, you can apply your effects either in parallel or serial. *In parallel* means that each effect is independent of the other, and this is the most common configuration when combining delays and re-verbs. *Serial* effects feed from one to the next. A typical serial usage might be a signal that is sent to a long delay and then the delay is sent to a reverb, so that the delayed signal is softened and spread by the reverb.

As explained in section 2.7, delay and reverb effects are typically used in a send and return configuration, with the send being post-fader so that the level of the effect follows the level of the direct signal. By sending to an effect pre-fader, you can create unusual ambient results. Pre-fader sends to reverbs allow you to use the sound of the reverb only, without any of the direct signal, and that can create some eerie and unusual effects (screenshot 6.7). The output fader of the audio channel can be set to zero, but the signal still feeds the reverb because the send is set to pre-fader.

By sending a direct signal to a long delay, and then sending from the delay pre-fader to a reverb (with the delay channel output set to zero), you can create a reverb that follows the direct signal after a long delay. This same effect could be created using a long pre-delay setting on a reverb plug-in, but reverbs do not necessarily provide pre-delay lengths that would be equivalent to a normal quarter note or longer.

You can duplicate a track in your DAW and then radically EQ, heavily limit, or otherwise process the duplicated track and send that processed sound to a reverb or delay pre-fader. In this way, you create unusual effects without having to use the more radically altered source track as part of your mix. These more extreme-sounding effects may be combined with the more normally processed direct sounds for subtle but unusual results.

SCREENSHOT 6.6

Serial routing from a delay to a reverb

195

As you can tell from the above examples, the creative way of accessing and combining effects is limited only by your imagination. Exploring routing possibilities is a big part of accessing these more advanced processing techniques. The flexibility of DAW routing, and the variety and easy access to so many DSP effects, provides tremendous opportunities for new approaches to creating sonic landscapes.

Mixing: Procedures

How do you proceed through the mixing process from beginning to end? There is no standard answer to this question. Different recordists apply different procedures; even the same recordist will use different procedures in different instances. Nonetheless, I offer some general advice on how you might effectively

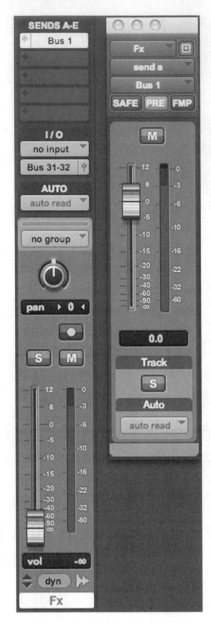

SCREENSHOT 6.7

Creating "reverb only" effects by using pre-fader sends

move through the mixing process. I would expect you to adapt this to your own working process.

Setting levels: Building and sustaining interest

Setting levels for each individual element is the primary activity of mixing. The goal with levels is to build and sustain interest over the entire musical timeline. Effective setting of levels can be approached with a variety of techniques, but one general practice that I have found particularly useful is to build the primary elements of your mix first, and then add the parts that interact with those primary elements. In a typical rock mix, that would mean setting levels for drums, bass, and one or two rhythm instruments (guitars and/or keyboards) and then the lead vocal. You don't have to work in this order, though recordists often do. It's much easier to get a proper relationship between the lead vocal and the rhythm section without other elements confusing the balance. By getting these primary instruments into reasonable balance, you have a framework within which to add other elements. The proper levels for lead guitar or other solo instruments, background vocals, horns, and so on all need to be set in relationship to the lead vocal and the rhythm section.

Of course, what is meant by "proper" is certainly subjective—but what is proper for you and the music you are mixing is aided by this procedure, regardless of how that may translate into the specific levels you set.

Another important tip for setting levels is to vary your playback volume. The ear processes sounds different at different volumes, as discussed in section 2.5, and therefore your mixes sound different to you (and everyone else), depending on the volume that you are listening at. To properly balance levels, you need to evaluate your mixes while listening, from very quiet to quite loud. As previously noted, most work can be done effectively at moderate listening levels, but a quiet listen can be especially helpful in setting the most important level relationships. This is because your ear filters out much of the higher and lower frequencies at low volumes, revealing the fundamental level relationships among prominent elements. Sometimes you can miss a simple problem at normal listening level—for example, the snare drum is too quiet or too loud—and a quick check at a quiet level makes this obvious. On the other end of the spectrum, you can miss details in low-level sounds when listening at moderate levels and a louder listen can reveal these details, such as murkiness in the reverb pool or clipping on an effects send, as well as extraneous noises or sounds (like quiet pops from edits that were poorly cross-faded).

Headphone listening is also valuable for revealing low-level problems. But, a note of caution here: don't revise basic mix decisions such as level relationships based on headphone listening. Despite the popularity of iPods and the prevalence of earbud listening, your best chance at getting mixes that will translate across all playback systems is through moderate listening levels on studio monitors that you are very familiar with. There are too many variable listening possibilities—from the huge variety of home stereo listening environments and speaker setups, to cars, to computer playback systems, to TVs, to blasters, to headphones, to earbuds—to possibly check mixes in all environments. Use alternative playback levels and systems to gain more information, but in the final analysis you must trust your studio monitors at moderate listening levels.

The three-dimensional mix

One primary goal in mixing is to achieve the best possible three-dimensional mix. It is up to you to define what is best, but one way to do that is to consider your mix as a three-dimensional object (variations on this approach have been used by others in describing mixing methodologies). The three dimensions are height, width, and depth. In mixing, the notion of *height* has two possible meanings. The obvious one is level. You can imagine the relative volume levels of each element as relative height relationships—the louder the element, the higher it is—and, as already noted, the first job of mixing is setting the level for each element. Height, however, can also be considered in terms of frequency range. You can think of the frequency range on a vertical scale—ranging from lows to highs—with the higher frequencies viewed as higher in height. A proper height relationship might be considered to be a balance in the frequency ranges from low to high. Listening for balance throughout the frequency range is an important part of the mixing/listening process. Although you can use a spectrum analyzer to check frequency balance, I recommend this only for gathering a very limited amount of information. An analyzer might reveal problems in areas that your speakers don't reproduce well (very low or very high frequencies), but they might also lead you to make unwise decisions by showing frequency bulges or deficits that are a natural part of the program material you are working on or the style of mixing that you wish to create. For most decisions regarding frequency balance, your ear is a much better guide than a spectrum analyzer.

Width in mixing is defined by the panning spectrum from left to right. As I have pointed out, panning represents one of the most powerful tools in creating effective mixes. It helps to think of panning as width, and as a three-dimensional mix as a goal, because it encourages you to use your entire spectrum from left to right. Small variations in panning can dramatically alter the sense of space within a mix.

Depth is the subtlest and most potentially artful and creative part of creating a three-dimensional mix. As with height, depth may be thought of in two different ways. Depth can be created just by volume relationships between elements. The development of foreground and background elements through volume relationships, as discussed earlier in this chapter, is one way to create the sense of depth in your mixes. The other is the delay pool made from all the delays and reverbs that you are using. As discussed, these delay elements can also have a significant effect on panning and the sense of width in your mixes.

Mixes as three-dimensional entities is really just another way of thinking about all of the practices already covered in this chapter. However, it provides a concise way to view and evaluate your mixes, and it gives you a visual metaphor for imagining your mix. While this visual metaphor can be helpful—and we live in a culture that is heavily oriented toward seeing over the hearing—I cannot stress enough that, in the end, you must use your ear. All that really matters, to quote Ray Charles again, is: "What does it sound like?"

198

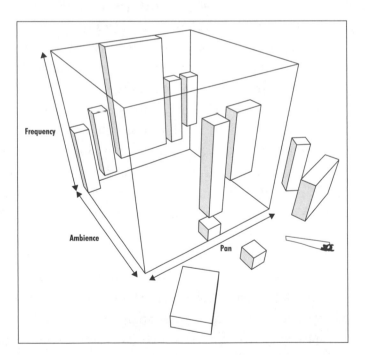

DIAGRAM 6.1

Three-dimensional mixing model

Revise, revise, revise

Here is a final bit of general advice on building mixes. Everything I have discussed in this chapter is subject to constant revision as you mix. You have to do some things first and other things later to build a mix, and I've made suggestions on strategies for doing this, but you also have the option of returning to anything you've done previously. Thus, EQ and compressor settings, panning positions, reverb choices and amounts, not to mention just basic level placement, should all be subject to review and revision as a mix progresses.

For this reason, it is valuable to save mixes under different names once you think the mix is getting close to completion. I use a numbering hierarchy; for example, if the song title were "Blackbird," I'd start with a file named *Blackbird Mix 1*. When that mix seemed close, or if I wanted to try a different tact and was planning on altering a bunch of elements, I would save my mix as *Blackbird Mix 2* before proceeding. If I stop work for the day, when I open the mix the next day to continue working, I would name it *Blackbird Mix 3*. If I decide to make an edit—let's say I wanted to try cutting out the third verse—I would save that mix as *Blackbird Mix 3 Edit*. Once I am convinced I want to keep the edit, I would go back to a simple numbering hierarchy, but I would always be able to easily find the last mix I did before I made the edit. Keeping track of mixes by using a naming structure is especially useful when working with other people, so that you can identify mixes as the process continues. I discuss collaboration on mixes more thoroughly in the last section of this chapter.

6.3 Automation and Recall

Automation and recall capabilities have been greatly expanded within the DAW environment. *Automation* refers to the ability to alter settings in real time as a mix plays. *Recall* refers to the ability to remember and restore all the settings in a mix. The ease with which a computer can handle data management has resulted in the ability to automate virtually every parameter in a mix. The nature of computer files means that if you have done all your mixing in the box (as discussed above, under "Mixing Tools"), you can have complete, accurate recall of your mixes in the few moments it takes to open the file.

The extent of automation capability can be either a blessing (greatly increased creative options) or a curse (you can get lost in the endless number of possibilities). The ease, speed, and accuracy of the automation functions are only a blessing. As I discuss automation in mixing, I focus on the practical side of things, but I also touch on some of the creative capabilities that are open to the recordist as a result of automation in a DAW.

Online versus off-line automation

Many of the capabilities of DAW automation will become clear as I explore the differences between online and off-line automation. *Online automa*tion refers to changes made in real time. That means that faders or rotary knobs or other controllers are moved as the music plays and the automation system remembers whatever moves are made. This operates on the recording model; movements are "recorded" as they are made, and then played back on subsequent replays. DAWs usually use the term *write* for the act of recording, writing automation data as controllers are moved and then reading them upon playback. The process often resembles recording in that the automation function needs to be armed and the "write ready" mode often consists of a flashing red light, just like the "record ready" mode for audio recording. Online automation follows the automation model established by the high-end analog recording consoles with integrated computers.

Off-line automation refers to changes made independent of playback, usually utilizing a graphic interface. Off-line automation functions similarly to the editing process and generally uses many of the audio editing tools in slightly altered fashion. Although the automation is controlled off-line, there can be immediate playback auditioning of the changes made. Some analog consoles have limited off-line functions, but the DAW has vastly expanded the capabilities of this approach to automation.

Before delving into the specifics of these two systems, I explore the pros and cons of each. Online automation has the advantage of real-time input that allows the recordist to be responding to aural information, and it has a tactical component that means you can use the fine motor control in your finger for automation moves. Online automation has the disadvantages of being dependent on physical response time, which can be difficult when trying to do things such as raise the volume of one word in a continuous vocal line. To take advantage of the finger's motor control, online automation also requires a hardware interface for your DAW. Moving controllers with the mouse does not provide nearly enough fine control for most of the kinds of changes made during the automation process.

Off-line automation has the advantage of exceeding fine control over both the position and amount of controller changes—for example, raising the volume of one word in a vocal line by exactly 1.2 dB is very easy with off-line automation. Off-line automation also has the advantage of certain kinds of automation moves, such as time-based auto-panning, that are impossible using online automation. (I explore these in more detail in the section "Details of Off-line Automation," below.) Off-line automation has the disadvantage of not having a physical component (finger movement) and of being a completely different process for those used to working online.

I spent many years using the automation systems on SSL consoles, which had taken analog/digital online automation systems to new heights of functionality and user friendliness. Nonetheless, I now do all of my automation off-line in Pro Tools. The ability to have precise control of parameters has proved too big an advantage, even over the familiarity of the online model. Some recordists find that they prefer to control certain functions online—fades, for example— but most functions are faster and more accurately done off-line (and many are impossible online). Many recordists do not have a hardware interface for their DAW, and the constraints of mouse movement mean that they will naturally use off-line automation; but many of those with access to physical controllers are still tending toward off-line automation for most functions.

Details of online automation

The basic "write/read" functionality of online automation is enhanced in many ways, though the details vary among DAWs. In most systems, you begin with a write pass, during which you create some of the basic automation moves that you want to hear. Once you've made one basic write pass with online automation, you probably will work in one of various updating modes. A typical update mode might be called "touch." In touch mode, the previous automation is read until you move (touch) a fader or other controller, and then new automation begins to be written. There may be two types of touch mode—in Pro Tools, touch mode retains all automation written after you release the controller you touched to begin rewriting, and the latch mode erases all the automation past the point of the touch update. The choice of which of these to use depends on whether you are updating a section in the middle of some established automation (touch) or working across a timeline from beginning to end (latch).

Another common online automation mode is "trim," which updates already written automation. If you had a bunch of automation moves on the lead vocal of a song's chorus, for example, but decided the whole thing needed to be a little louder, you would use the trim mode to increase the volume (trim up) the entire section. The trim function would change the overall volume while retaining the previous automation moves.

Details and further functionality of online automation will vary in different DAWs and with different hardware controllers. If you have access to physical controllers, I recommend that you familiarize yourself with their use, but that you also explore off-line automation for increased automation accuracy and functionality.

Details of off-line automation

Off-line automation, using a graphic interface, allows for very fine control of automation data and the opportunity for some unique automation effects. Off-line graphic automation uses a horizontal line to represent a scale of values: the higher the line on the graph, the greater the value of the parameter setting. For volume, the horizontal line represents the fader setting—all the way up is the maximum fader level (+12 dB on many systems) and all the way down is 0 dB (equivalent to off). The following screenshot shows some volume automation created by raising and lowering certain parts of a vocal take. The line represents volume, with greater volume (output fader position) indicated when the line is higher and less volume when lower. In the background, you can still see the waveform of the vocal, allowing you to pinpoint the places that you wish to raise or lower volume. Although the actual movement of the volume by raising or lowering the line on the graph is done off-line (the music or program material is not playing), you can immediately audition the results by having the curser placed just in front of the passage being automated and playing back the results.

201

SCREENSHOT 6.8

Volume automation on a
vocal track

As mentioned previously, the big advantage to this kind of off-line automation control is the ability to easily select the exact portion of audio that you wish to control and then to make very precise changes in parameters. Most systems allow control to 1/10 of a dB (.1 dB increments), and this allows for very fine tuning. After using this technique for a while, you begin to become familiar with the likely results from certain degrees of parameter changes. I have a good idea of what a 1 dB or 2 dB (or 1.5 dB!) change in volume is going to sound like, so I can often make exactly the right automation move for what I want to hear on the first try. In any event, I can easily revise a move by whatever increment I want in order to achieve the result I want. Some systems show both the new absolute level as you move a portion of the vertical line and the change in level. In the following screenshot, you can see the readout is showing the original level (-2 dB) and then in parenthesis is the new level (-.8 dB) and the change in level (1.2 dB). The change in level is preceded by a triangle, which is the Greek symbol for change (delta).

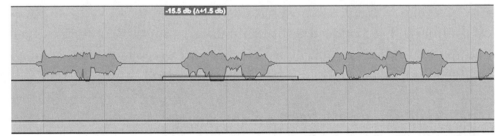

SCREENSHOT 6.9

Off-line automation
readout

Level changes in auxiliary sends can also be created off-line, allowing for easy implementation of special effects, such as a repeat echo on one word within a vocal line. By accessing the effects send level in the graphic automation mode, you can take a send that is set to 0 dB (so no effect is heard) to whatever level you wish in order to create the special effect. Because the graphic representation of the program material is seen in the background, it is easy to isolate the effect send on something like one word.

Breakpoints indicate the spots where the graphic line moves in position. In Screenshots 6.8 to 6.10, all the movement between the breakpoints is linear.

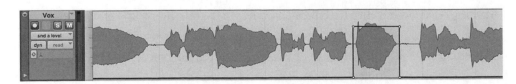

SCREENSHOT 6.10

Automating a send so that
one word goes to an effect

Online automation will create nonlinear data, which is reflected in the graphic readout by multiple breakpoints. Many DAWs provide tools that allow you to draw nonlinear or free-hand automation data off-line as well. To prevent over-taxing the computer's CPU, you might be able to thin the nonlinear automation data, as shown in Screenshot 6.11.

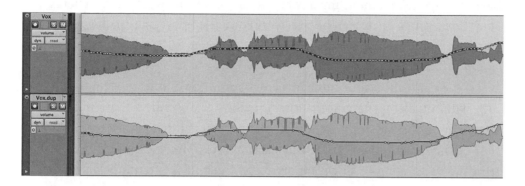

SCREENSHOT 6.11

Nonlinear automation data as written, below as thinned

203

These same tools might be configured in various other graphic arrangements, such as triangles or rectangles. The graphic shapes are typically used in one of the editing grid modes. Grids set in musical time—for example, a quarter-note or an eighth-note grid—allow for some great special effects done in musical time. The following screenshot shows two different panning effects, the first using a triangular shape to create smooth movements between hard right and hard left, and the second using a rectangular shape to jump from right to left and back again. The general effect is often referred to as *auto-panning*, as it is the automatic and regular changes in panning position.

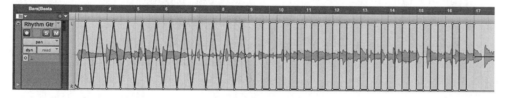

SCREENSHOT 6.12

Variations in "auto-panning" type effects using off-line panning automation

The following effect uses the same triangle-based automation editing tool on off-line volume rather than for panning. This creates a tremolo effect in musical time (tremolo is created through cyclical changes in volume).

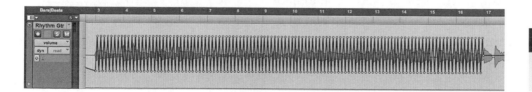

SCREENSHOT 6.13

A tremolo effect using off-line volume automation

Advanced automation techniques

Automation is created using the tools I have discussed, but it can become complex when many elements are combined and manipulated in great detail. You can create elaborate graphic automation that alters changes on every word in a vocal, and you can automate volume, panning, sends, and plug-in parameters on every track. Automating plug-in parameters offers a near endless number of possible real-time changes through automation, but it also threatens to create complexity with little audible advantage. The depth of possibilities though automation provides wonderful creative opportunities, but they need to be balanced against maintaining a coherent vision of the overall sound being created. Sometimes mixes can be overworked to the point that the bigger picture is lost in the details, so the mix doesn't hold together. *Sometimes simple mixes sound the best.*

One convenient technique involves trimming volume on elements in your mix without using the automation functions. I described the trim function above, in discussing online automation, and you can trim sections of automation off-line, using the graphic interface, as well. However, when you wish to trim the volume up or down on an entire track, it is often quicker and more convenient to use the output function of one of your plug-ins. Some DAWs provide a separate trim plug-in for just this purpose. By raising or lowering the output on a plug-in, you effectively trim up or down that track, retaining all of the volume automation already written for that track. Compressor outputs are often good candidates, but it could be a dedicated trim plug-in or one of many other options, depending on what plug-ins you already are using on the track you wish to trim. In the analog world, we used to call this "fooling the automation" because it allowed global volume changes to a track without the time-consuming job of trimming an entire track in real time (as was necessary on most automation systems within analog consoles). It's easier and quicker to trim off-line now, using the graphic interface, but "fooling the automation" with plug-in outputs is still a convenient way to make adjustments.

Although it should be clear from the above discussions, and it will certainly be clear once you start working with automation, any automating that is done in one mode will be reflected in the other mode. That is, online automation moves show up in the off-line graphic automation mode, and off-line automation moves create the same real-time effects, such as fader movement, that online automation creates. Advanced automation practices may involve use of both modes of operation to create the automation data you want. For example, you might write a piece of automation online for the creative engagement of working as the music plays, and then make small changes to details in off-line mode where you are able to fine-tune all the parameters. As you gain familiarity with your automation system, you can explore the best ways to achieve your creative vision.

Recall

Recall refers to the ability to recall all the parameters of a mix. This includes automation, panning, plug-ins and their settings, and anything else you have done to create your final mix. This used to be a very difficult, if not impossible, process when using analog equipment. Eventually, elaborate computer-assisted analog consoles were developed that could remember the position of every fader and knob on the console and could display those graphically. Nonetheless, an operator had to reset each parameter on the console by hand. In addition, someone (usually an assistant engineer) had to log all of the hardware outboard gear that was used, what the signal path was, and what the setting was for each parameter on each piece of gear—and all of these had to be reset by hand. This was a long and tedious project, and as you might imagine with so many settings involved, not always successful.

While the debate continues over in-the-box mixing (mixing entirely within the DAW) versus use of some gear outside of the DAW, in regard to recall, in-the-box mixing provides the ultimate in convenience and reliability. In the time it takes to open a session file (less that one minute), you can re-call complete and perfectly accurate mixes. Many of us have come to rely on this capability, especially as remote mixing has become more common. Remote mixing—sometimes called *unattended mixing*—refers to working with clients in other locations by sending mixes over the Internet and taking feedback and making revisions after the client has had an opportunity to review the mix (see the Appendix for information on some of the formats commonly used for shar-ing mixes). DAW recall has opened up the possibilities for these kinds of mix-ing strategies that rely on easy, accurate recall at the click of a mouse!

6.4 Mix Collaboration, Communication, and Delivery

In the end, mixing is almost always a collaborative process. What used to be a bunch of people with their hands on faders, trying to make mix moves in real-time because there was no automation, has become mixes of enormous complexity recalled and replayed effortlessly. And what used to be groups of recordists and artists working late into the night, trying to get a mix done be-fore the next recording group came in and broke down the console in order to start a new session, has become a series of mixes and responses often sent via the Internet from remote locations and sometimes going on for weeks. In between are any number of combinations of collaboration and communication used to complete a mix. It's not possible to cover them all, but I discuss some collaborative possibilities to consider and some ways of talking about mixes as they progress.

Delivery of mixes has also come a long way from the ¼-inch 15 IPS tape master. While delivery formats have always been in flux, contemporary digi-tal file formats offer a large number of possibilities. Fortunately, there is much less of a compatibility problem than when a particular piece of hardware was required for each possible delivery format, as DAWs can usually handle most digital audio files. A larger question remains about the best way to deliver your mix for mastering, and I begin that discussion here, before delving into it more deeply in the following chapter on mastering.

Mixing collaboration and communication

You can't separate working together on mixing with communicating about mixes, as the ability to talk about mixes is required in order to collaborate on them. Mixing collaboration now comes in many forms, both technical and interpersonal, and happens both in close contact and remotely. Working with others remotely means using some medium for communication (phone, texting, e-mail, etc.). This can have some advantages—having to put mix notes into writing can make revisions easier and clearer for the recordist, though sometimes the written word can be as obscure as the spoken one ("Please make this mix more purple").

Having the language for communicating about mixing is largely a matter of having built a vocabulary for talking about mix and sound issues. Some things are easy and straightforward—"I think the vocal needs to be louder"—though this leaves the question of how much louder still an open matter. "I think the vocal needs to be a lot louder" or "a little louder" helps clarify things, but the exact degree of change that is going to satisfy the request is still a matter of trial and error. Working in collaboration is another reason I like off-line automation. I can adjust the vocal up 2 dB, and if my collaborator says that's too much, I can say I'll split the difference (up 1 dB) and we can work from there, knowing exactly what changes have been made and adjusting in definable degrees.

Mix issues other than questions of volume start to create a greater need for a shared vocabulary. Questions regarding frequencies, as controlled by EQ, have inspired a huge vocabulary of descriptive words, some more easily understood than others. Words that rely on the scale from low to high frequencies are more easily understood and interpreted. These include *bass, middle, treble*, or *bottom* and *top*. Other words that are used pretty frequently are suggestive but less precise and thus open to more interpretation—words such as *boom, rumble, thump, fatter, warmer, honk, thinner, whack, presence, crunch, brighter, edge, brilliance, sibilance*, and *air*. These might be pretty easy to interpret, especially if they are used often among frequent collaborators, but they may also mean very different things to different people. Other words, such as the sometimes inevitable color references or highly subjective terms such as "magical," really give the recordist almost nothing to go on.

The most precise language for EQ is specific frequency references, and with the proliferation of engineering skills among musicians and other contributors to the mixing process, these are becoming more frequently used. Suggestions such as "I think it needs a little boost around 8 K" or "Perhaps we could thin this sound a bit around 300" (meaning dipping at 300 Hz) are becoming increasingly common in mix collaborations. The recordist may still need to adjust somewhat from the suggested frequency—it's impossible to know exactly what the effects of any given frequency adjustment are going to be without listening—but this language is certainly the most precise and the easiest to respond to.

Communications about ambience and effects can be more obscure. A request for a sound that is "bigger" probably refers to a desire for increased ambience—but not necessarily. Again, suggestions that a more "mysterious" or "unusual" mix is desired leave the recordist without a good idea of how to proceed. With the widespread use of recording gear, however, specific suggestions and references are more common. A guitarist may well suggest, "How about some long delay on the lead guitar?" The guitarist may even be more specific: "Can we try a quarter note delay on the guitar?" The more exact nature of the delay (overall level, amount of feedback, etc.) may be left to the recordist or may continue to be part of collaboration as an ongoing discussion of details.

Some terms can suggest changes in mix ambience pretty clearly. Certainly "wetter" and "dryer" are accepted terms describing relative amounts of reverb and/or delay, though how to implement a request for a wetter vocal or a wetter mix still leaves a lot of options open to the recordist. Similarly, terms such as "closer" or "farther" generally can be interpreted as references to types or degrees of ambience, though again the way to accomplish such changes can vary widely.

It is very helpful for a recordist to have a variety of terms available to try to help the collaborators clarify what it is they want out of a mix. Sometimes, when a person is struggling with what he or she wants out of the sound of their vocal, for example, the person can be greatly aided by being asked if it should sound more "present" or "closer" or perhaps "bigger" or "richer." This can give the collaborator a term that you might then have a chance of interpreting technically, as opposed to something like, "Could you change the way the vocal sounds?" Of course, you can, but how? Don't rely on your collaborators to clearly express their interests; develop the vocabulary to help them (and you) create mixes that you all love.

Finally, when working remotely, make sure you are listening to and collaborating on the same mix! I have had confusion with artists over elements in a mix, only to discover that we were not referencing the same mix. This is why I number and/or date the CDs I give to artists. I can then refer that information back to a specific mix file so that changes are made from the correct starting point.

Delivering mixes

The best way to deliver mixes depends on answers to a couple of key of questions: To whom are you delivering them? and For what purpose? The mix format must be appropriate for the person who is receiving the mix. Often, you will need to deliver mixes in a variety of formats to different participants in the process. In a commercial project, you may need to deliver one mix to the artist, one mix to the record company, one mix to the Webmaster, and one mix to the mastering house. To a large extent, questions surrounding the mastering become an important part of how you deliver your mixes. This is true whether or not your project is going to undergo a formal mastering process. If your project is not going to be mastered beyond your final mix, then you will need to incorporate at least some of the standard processing for mastering as a part of your mix. If it is going to be mastered, you will probably want to deliver a separate mix format to everyone involved in the project other than the mastering house and two different formats to the mastering house.

I cover most of these topics in the following chapter on mastering and also in the Appendix. As a part of this chapter on mixing, however, I want to alert you to the fact that you will need to have a good understanding of the mastering process in order to finish your mixes properly, whether or not they are going on for final mastering. As I mentioned in the above section on uses of compression in mixing, there is a type of compression that has become an essential part of the mastering process, and that is brick-wall limiting. This is discussed more thoroughly in the following chapter on mastering, but for now know that brick-wall limiting has a profound effect on mixes. For this reason, you will probably want to use it prior to finishing your mixes, so you have a better idea of what they are going to sound like after mastering. You will also probably want to use it on all mixes (including rough mixes) that you give to the people you are working with, so that what they hear will sound more like what the final recording is going to sound like. In most cases, the only time I create a mix without brick-wall limiting is when I make the file that is going to be used for mastering, so that the limiting can be applied as a part of mastering instead. Even then, I also supply the mastering house with a brick-wall version, so they can hear what the artist has been hearing and something close to the way I imagine my mix will sound after the mastering process restores the limiting that I have removed for their working file.

Taking multiple mixes

We used to record multiple versions of a mix, simply as a matter of course. Because it was so difficult or impossible to recreate a mix once the studio was reconfigured for another session, we would try to anticipate changes that we might want to consider. The most common variations on mixes were ones with different lead vocal levels. We'd take a mix and then a "vocal up" mix in case we wanted a louder vocal. We might also take a "vocal down" mix, or two mixes with different "vocal up" levels, or a "drums up" mix, and so on. The problem, of course, was that there were an endless number of possible options, and the time and materials it took to run alternative mixes started to defeat the purpose.

If you are mixing in the box, then the only reason to take multiple mixes is to have different possibilities to review. Otherwise, it is usually most efficient to make one mix for review and then simply open the file and make revisions as desired. Even if you are supplementing your mix with some outboard gear, if most of the work is done in your DAW, it might be fairly easy to log the settings on a few external pieces, so as to allow for pretty simple recall. Many recordists and artists have come to depend on ease of recall as a means of providing opportunities to live with mixes for a while, or to work remotely, with easy revisions being an essential part of mixing collaborations.

Chapter 7

Mastering
One Last Session

I am calling this chapter on mastering "One Last Session" because mastering is typically the last part of the process that starts with recording or assembling audio and ends with providing audio destined for the end user: CD, Internet download, Internet streaming, game audio, DVD, and so on. Mastering also is typically done in one session, unlike the recording, editing, and mixing processes that frequently take place over multiple sessions. However, depending on the size of the project, and the degree of scrutiny of all the details, mastering can require several sessions or at least several rounds of revisions. While the following chapter is hardly intended to be exhaustive, it provides a basis for understanding and undertaking the mastering process. As you progress through the various stages of creating audio programs, it is important to be familiar with each previous stage before undertaking the next one. For this reason, a good mastering engineer has a strong basis in recording, editing, and mixing.

7.1 What, Why, How, and Where

What is mastering? Why do we need to do it? How might you accomplish it? And what is needed in terms of a facility in order to effectively master a project? There are no simple answers to these questions, but first you must ask both what "effectively" is and what the "project" is at hand. To master effectively requires a certain amount of gear/software, experience, a critical ear, and usually a healthy willingness to collaborate. Mastering is a skill, and there's no substitute for time spent mastering to develop that skill. Having the luxury of a home system, and having projects to work on, will allow you to go through the trial-and-error process necessary to develop mastering skills—guided by the good advice from this book, of course.

The nature of the music in the project, as well as the recording and mixing already done, will greatly affect your ability to master effectively. Musical genres have many conventions in terms of how final masters generally sound, and even if your goal is to defy those conventions, you will have limited success mastering styles of music that you are not very familiar with. The number of elements in the final audio program is also important to the mastering skill set. There can be beautiful masters made from solo piano recordings, but that is quite a different task from mastering a compilation of large ensemble recordings from a variety of sources. Different projects will suggest different sets of tools, and different kinds of approaches to mastering. Ultimately, however, *your greatest asset with mastering is the same as your greatest asset with all other elements in the recording process—it's your ear!* The more experienced and developed your ear, the better your chances for effective mastering of any kind of project. Finally, if you notice a marked similarity between this introductory paragraph and the one for the previous chapter on mixing, it is because the overviews for these two parts of the recording skill set are remarkably similar.

What is mastering?

Let's establish exactly what is meant by the term *mastering*. As the term suggests, mastering is the creation of a final "master" version of your audio program. This final version is what is usually delivered to the manufacturer to replicate as CDs or for other forms of duplication or dissemination, such as audio placed on the Internet for streaming or downloading, or loaded onto a DVD as audio to accompany video, or placed into a game as audio to accompany game play. Typically, a mastering session involves working with the final mix or mixes that, in combination, form the complete audio program for any particular project.

Why master?

The goal of mastering is to create the best final version possible, and to put that version into the correct format for its final destination or destinations. The "best" version possible is, of course, a subjective process that requires creative decisions and may vary considerably depending on who is doing the mastering. It is also very much dependent on what happened before, in the recording and mixing of the audio, as these will have been completed before mastering begins. The fundamental task of mastering is to make all the audio elements work together in their final delivery configuration. I cover the creative process in the following sections on the "how to" of mastering.

Creating the correct format is the other part of mastering, and this is purely technical. Different audio applications require different file formats, and their creation may require particular media (CD-Rs, DVD-Rs, hard drives, lacquers, etc.). I discuss delivery formats at the end of this chapter.

How do you master? The basics

In order to make the master that has been creatively and technically optimized for final delivery, there are a variety of typical tasks. Generally, the most essential job in mastering is to set final levels for all of the elements. Beyond this, it is the job of mastering to balance the sonic characteristics of all the elements so that they fit well together. Finally, it is a part of mastering to put all the elements together exactly as they are meant to be in their final delivery—sequencing and creating the spaces between all the songs on a CD, for example. I cover these level, sonic characteristics, and sequencing considerations separately. There may be other tasks in mastering as well, many of which I cover in the section on advanced mastering techniques.

Level

There are two basic aspects to setting levels in mastering—absolute level and relative level—and they interact, so they need to be considered as one process. *Absolute level* refers to the volume of the particular audio element (such as each individual song on a CD) and *relative level* refers to how loud the element sounds relative to the other elements in the project. I use the model of mastering a CD made up of a variety of songs in the following discussion, but you could be mastering any number of different kinds of audio for different projects. Just substitute "audio element" for "song" in the following if you're working on something other than a traditional CD.

Because of the dynamic range of audio, trying to balance the volume from song to song is a subjective process. *The key to level balancing in mastering is to focus on the loudest part of each song.* The goal is to give the listener a consistent experience when listening to the entire CD. If the loudest part of each song is balanced with the other songs, then the listener will never feel like a particular song on the CD has suddenly gotten louder. When the loudest part of each song on the CD is relatively balanced, the quieter sections will vary depending on the dynamics of the song, but this is the nature of musical dynamics and it doesn't usually present a problem.

Brickwall limiting

Absolute volume is the volume relative to digital zero. Digital audio has a binary code for volume (along with everything else), and the maximum volume is digital zero. Contemporary mastering tools include a brickwall limiter that allows the recordist to push the program material up against the digital volume ceiling. Brickwall limiting increases the absolute volume of your program material, and therefore affects the relative volume between songs.

To understand brickwall limiting, you might begin with the processing known as *peak normalization*. To normalize a piece of audio means to find the loudest sample (peak) and to raise the volume of the entire audio piece to a given maximum volume. While this may be digital zero, it is usually recommended that you stop just short of digital zero to prevent misreadings by the CD player that may result in distortion. The typical normalization (and brickwall) ceiling is -.2 dB (2/10ths of a dB below digital zero). Normalizing raises the volume of every sample equally, placing the loudest sample at whatever limit you set (e.g., -.2 dB). Because the overall volume of each sample is raised the same amount, it doesn't change the dynamics of the audio piece.

Brickwall limiting takes the idea of normalization and extends it into limiting. Instead of just placing the one loudest sample at -.2 dB and everything else in the same relative volume position, brickwall limiting allows you to push all the samples above a user-set threshold up to the ceiling. It does this by setting a "brick wall" at the ceiling point (-.2 dB, for example). As the threshold lowers, more and more samples are lifted up to the brickwall volume limit. The lower the threshold, the greater the number of samples that are lifted to the ceiling of the brick wall. In the following screenshot, the threshold is set to create about 3 dB of brickwall limiting at the moment that the screenshot is captured.

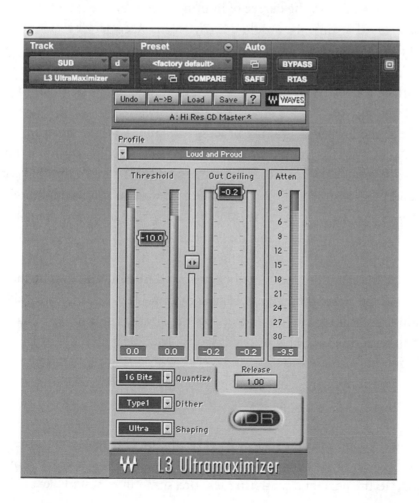

SCREENSHOT 7.1

A brickwall limiter

Theoretically, a song that has considerable brickwall limiting isn't any louder than a song that has been normalized to the same limit, in the sense that there aren't any samples in the brickwall-limited version that are louder than the one loudest sample in the normalized version. However, the brickwall-limited version may sound considerably louder because so many more of the samples are reaching the volume ceiling.

Over time, the extent of brickwall limiting has increased in a sort of escalating "volume war" to make one CD sound louder than another. There has also been considerable debate about the effects of brickwall limiting and the decrease in dynamic range that is created by the process. Some go so far as to argue that brickwall limiting has effectively killed popular music by flattening musical dynamics to such an extent as to make music unpleasant to listen to. It is true that consumers tend to listen to CDs many fewer times than they did in the past, but the extent to which this is the result of brickwall limiting (versus the natural results of a less patient society), we can't really know.

Balancing levels

Balancing the levels in mastering a popular music CD is usually accomplished by adjusting the threshold on the brickwall limiter. This means that relative levels are controlled by the degree of limiting used—by the extent to which the song is pressed against the absolute level. This is necessary because, once you have started to use the brickwall limiting process, the only way to make a song louder is to increase the brickwall limit. If you try to simply raise the volume after hitting the brickwall ceiling, you will get digital distortion (audio pushed beyond digital zero).

Once the brickwall-limiting process is begun, you will generally raise or lower a song's overall volume with the limiter's threshold control. While you can lower overall volumes rather than lowering the extent of limiting with the threshold control, this will often produce undesirable results. If the ceiling of song 1 is set to -.2 dB, with many samples hitting that limit, and song 2 sounds louder than song 1 with the same threshold setting on the brickwall limiter, you may be tempted to reduce the ceiling of song 2. If you set the ceiling (output) to -1.2 dB, for example, song 2 will often sound unnaturally quieter than song 1. The effect of raising the threshold of song 2, to decrease the extent of brickwall limiting, will usually produce a more desirable result in level balancing. Exceptions to this are likely to result from program material that is sonically very different. If you have a full-band record with one or two songs that are just acoustic guitar and voice, for example, you may find that you do need to lower the overall level of the acoustic songs to prevent their sounding louder than the band tracks.

The best approach to achieve level balancing is repeated listening, focusing on the loudest sections in each song. DAWs allow you to easily jump from one song to the next, and mastering sessions sometimes sound like a jumble of snippets as you jump from song to song, listening to short segments of each. It often takes many rounds of listening and making very small adjustments before you begin to feel as if the overall level of each song is well balanced against the others.

Sonic characteristics

By sonic characteristics, I refer to the qualities of the sound that might be adjusted with your typical DSP tools. These would be EQ, compression, and ambience. EQ adjustments in mastering are common, though usually rather subtle, whereas additional compression or expansion (outside of the brickwall limiting discussed above) is less common, and adding ambience, such as added reverb or delay, is quite rare. Nonetheless, all these tools and many others—including fades or editing—are sometimes part of the mastering process.

Wanting to adjust the sonic characteristics of songs may involve two distinct goals. The first is to make each song sound as good as possible. The second is to give the songs a sonic consistency from the beginning of the CD to the end. The first goal should be approached cautiously, with the assumption that the mixer has made the song sound the way everyone involved in the production wanted. I try not to second-guess the production process that has come for mastering. I might add a very small amount of EQ, or even compression or reverb, based purely on the sound of the individual song, but I need to feel strongly that the song would be improved. Otherwise I accept the mixes and I focus on the second goal.

Sonic consistency generally means that the frequency balance from song to song sounds uniform. If one song has a stronger low end or a brighter top than the following song, one will suffer by comparison. In these cases, EQ adjustments are not made so an individual song sounds "better" but, rather, to balance the frequencies from one song to the next. Of course, the decision whether to dip the low end or the high end of one, or boost the lows or highs in the other, is part of the creative process. I often listen to all the tracks on the CD and try to find one that I feel has the best overall frequency balance, and I use that as my model. I will then EQ other songs to match the frequency balance of my model song as best as possible. Again, as song keys and arrangements vary, this can be a highly subjective endeavor, but it may serve as a good working model.

I find that it is helpful to work with the songs in the same sequence as they will appear on the CD. Ultimately, all the songs should work together in any order, but sometimes knowing the final sequence can help guide both level and frequency adjustments.

Sequencing and spreads

In a typical CD mastering session, creating the final sequence of songs and the time between songs (spreads) is usually the last step. You may actually burn your CD-R master straight from your DAW, in which case sequencing and spreads

215

will be handled in the same program as all the other mastering functions; but often I prepare all the files in the DAW, create the master files for whatever format is required, and then do the final sequencing and spreads (assembling) in a separate program.

Deciding on the sequence of the songs for a CD is an art in itself. Flow, energy, and commercial concerns are part of the decision-making process. Fortunately, the ease of burning CDs at home means that the creative team can try out a variety of sequences either before mastering or as part of the mastering process. Changing the sequence is simple and CD-Rs are very inexpensive, so if you aren't sure of your sequence, it's worth trying out numerous possibilities.

Spreads between songs can be deceptive because they depend a lot on the volume of playback. If some of the songs fade, or even have a short tail of reverb or other ambience at the end, the apparent time before the next song depends on how much of that fade or tail is heard, and that depends on how loud the music is. Quiet listening will make the spread seem longer and loud listening will make them seem shorter. Moderate listening levels are the best compromise for setting spreads.

One technique for setting spreads is to play the end of each song and have one person—whoever is most responsible for setting the spreads—indicate the moment he or she thinks that the next song should enter. The person might tap on a table, say "Now," or whatever. You can assemble the master, song by song, in this way. Or you might just place a default time (usually 2 seconds) between each song. Then, once the master is assembled, listen to each spread and adjust according to taste. Some burning programs have the ability to play a user-defined amount of time at the end of each song and the beginning of the next, essentially playing each spread for you in sequence. It's best to listen to all of the spreads, making notes about each one as you go; conversation during the listening process means you will likely miss hearing the next spread play. You can then adjust the spreads that felt as if they needed more or less time and listen again until you're satisfied.

Creating and delivering your master

There are a lot of technical requirements for making a proper CD-R master, but fortunately most of them, such as file format and P&Q codes, are taken care of automatically by your CD-burning program. Some burning programs still offer a choice between TAO (track-at-once) and DAO (disc-at-once) burning protocol. CD-R masters must be burned using DAO protocol, but that is the default for most programs.

There are options for what information is added to the audio program, and in the digital age this has become increasingly important. CDs can code the song title and artist name to every song by using a CD-burning program capable of adding CD text. You should make sure that your master has that information encoded, so that it will appear on CD players and computer programs that read those data and radio stations that transmit them. CDs can also have an ISRC (International Standard Recording Code) identifier included for each song. This code that provides ownership information, so that tracks can be digitally traced for royalty collection, administration, and antipiracy problems. You have to register to get these codes—they used to be free, but now there is a charge to get your codes. Search ISRC code registration on the Internet for more information.

Once your CD-burning program has everything sequenced as you want it—the protocol set to DAO, with the proper spreads and all the text and coding information correctly entered—you are ready to burn your master to a CD-R and send it off for manufacture. There seem to be endless debates as to what CD-R medium is best (which manufacturer, which color, etc.) and what speed masters should be burned at. There has been a lot of testing done, and the up-shot is that it really depends on your burner. No one medium is better and no one burning speed is best. In fact, tests show that sometimes faster burn speeds result in CD-Rs with few error readings. Most of the time, pretty much any CD-R, burned at any speed, will create a master with error rates well below the danger level. If you find a particular brand of CD-R that seems to work well with your burner, and you are getting good results at a particular burn speed, then you might just want to stick with that. You might want to try different brands of CD-R and different burn speeds, and do some listening tests to settle on a way to create your masters with your system.

Once the master is burned you will need to listen to it before sending it for manufacture. It does no harm to a CD-R to play it, as long as it's handled care-fully, by the edges. Occasionally there are problems with a blank CD-R or with a burn, and there can be audible pops or distortion on a particular burn. You want to listen carefully to the master to make sure it doesn't have any of these unforeseen problems before sending it to the manufacturer.

Most professional burning programs also create a printout that shows the track list, the time between tracks, index times, cross-fades, and so on. Manu-facturing plants like to have a copy of this printout to confirm what they are seeing when they analyze your master, but most plants will accept your master without the printout. Be sure to burn a duplicate master for yourself so you can compare it to the manufactured CDs that are sent to you later by the plant. You should not be able to hear anything more than the very slightest difference be-tween your burned CD master and the completed CDs from the plant.

In regard to digital delivery formats other than the CD-R, see the Appen-dix.

How do you master? Advanced techniques

Mastering may encompass a variety of tasks beyond the basics covered above, though most mastering sessions don't get much more complicated than what I've described. Certain things, such as editing, are usually considered part of

```
○ ○ ○                              📄 Name the Day!.txt
(Note: Items are separated by tabs.)

Name the Day!   11 Tracks   41:46:15
All times are minutes:seconds:frames (1 sec = 75 frames)


Start Offsets:    0 CD Sectors
Stop Offsets:     0 CD Sectors
Track 1 Start Offset:   0 CD Sectors
UPC/EAN Code:     0000000000000


      Start at         Title                      Length      Stop at      Pause         ISRC


1     00:02:00         Breakin' Free              04:15:10    04:17:10     00:02:00    1   USBP11013401    •
      00:00:00         -0:02:00   Index 0 Pregap
      00:02:00         00:00:00   Index 1 Audio Start

2     04:17:40         Name the Day               03:34:36    07:52:01     00:00:30    1   USBP11013402    •
      04:17:10         -0:00:30   Index 0 Pregap
      04:17:40         00:00:00   Index 1 Audio Start

3     07:54:01         Do You Really Want That Woman  03:39:61  11:33:62   00:01:45    1   USBP11013403    •
      07:52:01         -0:01:45   Index 0 Pregap
      07:54:01         00:00:00   Index 1 Audio Start

4     11:34:37         Heartbreak With a Hammer   04:06:74    15:41:36     00:00:50    1   USBP11013404    •
      11:33:62         -0:00:50   Index 0 Pregap
      11:34:37         00:00:00   Index 1 Audio Start

5     15:43:36         Tuff Girl                  03:05:24    18:48:60     00:02:00    1   USBP11013405    •
      15:41:36         -0:02:00   Index 0 Pregap
      15:43:36         00:00:00   Index 1 Audio Start

6     18:50:60         I Said Too Much            05:07:27    23:58:12     00:00:40    1   USBP11013406    •
      18:48:60         -0:00:40   Index 0 Pregap
      18:50:60         00:00:00   Index 1 Audio Start

7     24:00:12         Home In Your Heart         02:33:24    26:33:36     00:01:50    1   USBP11013407    •
      23:58:12         -0:01:50   Index 0 Pregap
      24:00:12         00:00:00   Index 1 Audio Start

8     26:35:36         Save A Little Love         03:39:51    30:15:12     00:01:30    1   USBP11013408    •
      26:33:36         -0:01:30   Index 0 Pregap
      26:35:36         00:00:00   Index 1 Audio Start

9     30:17:12         You Know                   03:03:33    33:20:45     00:02:00    1   USBP11013409    •
      30:15:12         -0:02:00   Index 0 Pregap
      30:17:12         00:00:00   Index 1 Audio Start

10    33:22:45         Why Not Me                 04:36:38    37:59:08     00:02:10    1   USBP11013410    •
      33:20:45         -0:02:10   Index 0 Pregap
      33:22:45         00:00:00   Index 1 Audio Start

11    38:01:08         Funky Feelin'              03:47:07    41:48:15     00:00:40    1   USBP11013411    •
      37:59:08         -0:00:45   Index 0 Pregap
      38:01:08         00:00:00   Index 1 Audio Start
```

SCREENSHOT 7.2

A printout from a master created in the program Jam

the recording or mixing process, but they sometimes end up getting done at mastering sessions. I have received files in which the ending fade of songs was saved for mastering, but that is the exception rather than the rule.

In some instances, sections of songs may be treated differently in mastering. Most common would be something like an acoustic guitar introduction that sounds a bit too quiet or too loud prior to the entrance of the full band. The brickwall limiting or other mastering processing may have changed the relationship between the two elements enough to require some adjustment. In that case, the intro might be raised or lowered in volume. Manipulating individual sections of songs is certainly possible, and I know of mastering sessions where a lot of volume and EQ changes were made to songs on a section-by-section basis. An example would be, say, a little high-frequency boost on the choruses and a little level boost on the bridge. But this starts getting very close to remixing, and if there are a lot of section-by-section changes, or if you're not getting what your really want by trying to work this way, you will need to go back to the mixing stage and have the changes made there. I have found that on projects that I both mixed and mastered, I have occasionally gone back to mixes to make changes right in the middle of the mastering session; this is a luxury that is made quite easy if all the mixing and mastering is done in the DAW, so that recalling and changing mixes can be very quick.

A recent trend in mastering is called *separation mastering*. This involves delivering *stems* of the final mixes that can be processed individually in mastering. Stems—a term that comes from a common practice in audio delivered for films—refers to submixes of certain elements that can be recombined to create the final mix. In a recent project, I delivered four stereo stems for mastering: drum set minus snare drum, snare drum, all other instruments, and all vocals. The advantage may be twofold: you can control the amount of snare drum more easily, and that is the element that often gets the most suppressed (lowered in level) by brickwall limiting; and you might maintain slightly greater breadth in your stereo image and a bit more clarity because the elements are not as intermingled by the stereo buss processing (typically compression but sometimes additional EQ, analog saturation simulation, etc.). This second advantage may instead be a disadvantage to separation mastering. Stereo processing integrates elements in a mix in a way that might be desirable and that will be diminished by separation mastering. Stereo buss processing, such as compression and analog saturation simulation, may add punch and warmth to the final mix. This stereo buss processing could be added in the mastering stage when the stems are combined, but then mixing becomes increasingly removed from the final sound of the recording, making it more difficult to mix effectively. The differences are fairly subtle, but I have found that, more often than not, I prefer masters made from the stereo mix to those created by the separation mastering technique. Separation mastering also adds time and expense to a project.

In regard to creating the final sequence and spreads, there may be the desire to do some more elaborate transitions between songs. This could include cross-fades where one song begins as the previous song is fading. You may also need to create separate CD track identification number at places where there is no audible break in the music (as in a live music recording). You may also want to include an "invisible track" that occurs at the end of a CD without a track identification number. The ability to create these kinds of advanced sequencing techniques will depend on the ability of your particular CD-burning program and will be something you would want to investigate in acquiring a program to use for mastering purposes.

Where do you master? Mastering environments and tools

Can you do your own mastering? If so, what do you need to do it? There are no simple answers to these questions. What is required for good mastering is as follows:

1. very good playback system in a room that you trust. The system must be flat (within reason) and the room consistent through the

frequency range. The system should extend comfortably through the entire frequency range—which may mean the addition of a properly calibrated subwoofer. Being able to evaluate the low end, especially the lowest frequencies that might not show up anywhere but in a nightclub or other environments that use sub-woofers, is an important part of mastering because material may have been recorded and mixed in environments that don't have that capability.

2. At a minimum, high-quality brickwall limiting and EQ processing. These are critical tools. Other processing gear is valuable, including compression, multiband compression, reverb, and analog saturation simulation software. There are mastering "suites" of plug-ins made by software makers that contain at least the basic tools needed in forms optimized for mastering. Because mastering is done to single files of completed program material (mono, stereo, or surround), there is not a concern about delays (latency) that may be caused by excessive plug-in processing (this can be a problem in mix situations). Some mastering software uses phase-aligning algorithms that make for very high quality processing, but the phase-aligning process means that these plug-ins introduce significant delay. Because the whole program material is being processed at the same time, these delays don't affect alignment with any other audio and these processors can yield outstanding results.

3. A CD-burning program that burns using DAO protocol (usually standard). Preferably you want a program that has cross-fade, CD numbering, indexing, and ISRC-coding capabilities. There are many ways to burn CDs, including some very simple programs built into some computer operating systems. They probably are all capable of creating CD-R masters that would work fine for manufacturing, but you do need to verify that the disc is being burned using the DAO protocol. More elaborate burning programs offer the capabilities that may be essential in many mastering situations (such as text and IRSC coding).

4. The ability to hear audio programming material in ways that allow you to make accurate and creative judgments about the relative levels and sonic qualities of the material you are mastering. This is the result of the ear-training process that requires experience and attention to the essential issues of mastering.

What it is that constitutes an appropriate listening environment for mastering, or the proper software or hardware tools, or the ear and creative capabilities to utilize the gear that you have, is open to interpretation. Some pretty basic combination of the above is enough to get you started, and as with all things audio, experience is the best teacher. Once the master is sent off and approved by the manufacturing plant (or Webmaster or DVD authoring person, etc.), you have fulfilled your responsibilities that may have started when the first sound for the recording was made (or imported or downloaded, etc.). You may be asked to verify that the manufactured product is worthy of approval, but unless the problem is with the master you made, it isn't your responsibility to fix any problems.

The wonderful world of audio is a constantly shifting landscape of creative approaches, working procedures, formats, protocols, listening devices, and delivery methods. Some of the information in this book will be dated almost immediately upon its release, but most of it will reflect the audio creation and delivery terrain for a long time to come. Audio reproduction as a fundamental form of media expression is here to stay.

Chapter **8**

Three Best Practices
Easy Ways to Raise the Level of Your Sessions

There are three aspects to running recording sessions that are often inadequately covered or completely overlooked in recording textbooks, yet these are vital to creative and productive work in the studio. Session flow, talkback operation, and playback volume all contribute in some very obvious—and some not so obvious—ways to getting the most out of a recording session. This chapter explores these three elements from both the technical and the creative points of view.

8.1 Session Flow

The whole idea of "best practices" in running comfortable, creative recording sessions can be contained within the notion *session flow*. How is the session progressing? How is the balance between a relaxed atmosphere and focused work being handled? Are the musicians being given the opportunity to perform at their best? Are the goals being achieved? Is the work getting done efficiently but with enough room for creativity? There are four primary elements of interest in regard to session flow: the verbal, the technical, the musical, and the economic. The *verbal* refers to what is said during a session—what is appropriate conversation, what is constructive feedback, and what might be best left unsaid. The *technical* in this context means understanding how the technical demands of making a good recording may be balanced against the creative demands of making good music. The *musical* requirements of good session flow require an understanding of the fundamentals of music in ways that promote the most efficient and creative recording sessions. And finally, one cannot escape the *eco-*

nomic considerations that almost always form a backdrop to the day's activities in the studio, even in the home studio.

Verbal flow

Conversation during a recording session is vitally important to session flow. To start, let's distinguish between face-to-face conversation and conversation via the talkback system. The comments that follow may also apply to talkback conversations, but I reserve specific observations and advice about talkback for later in this chapter. Also, in many home studios, there is no talkback system because there is no separation between the control room and the recording room.

First, the obvious: *criticism needs to be constructive.* Very general comments like, "You can do that better" are rarely helpful or appropriate. Even specific observations like, "You're rushing the beat" can provoke a defensive reaction, whereas something like, "It feels a little rushed to me" or better still, "Does it feel a little rushed to you?"—which invites the musician's input—helps to maintain a more relaxed atmosphere while addressing issues that may be important to getting the best possible musical performances. Rather than "Your part is too busy," you might invite input by asking, "Do you think your part would work better if it wasn't quite so busy?"

Comments or suggestions such as, "Can you try being more expressive with the lyrics?" get into emotional territory, as opposed to more objective musical feedback. It's much less complicated when you are making an observation such as, "You missed that chord change in the chorus" than when you want to get more or different emotional content from a performer. I recommend going slowly with interactions regarding emotional content. Generally, it is advisable to develop a working relationship and get a feel for a performer's creative process before getting into these sensitive areas. Once you've established a certain level of trust and respect, it may be possible and helpful to push a performer toward a deeper emotional commitment to the performance. This trust can build over the course of a single session, or it may require a few opportunities to work together before you can enter into delicate considerations of expression in performance. Again, it may be best to put these types of suggestions into the form of a question: "Do you think you can bring even more emotion to those verses?"

More of the obvious: *keep extraneous conversation to a minimum.* There is a time to tell a story or make a comment that is unrelated to the work at hand, but those times are pretty rare in the studio. Typical studio etiquette involves a brief preliminary chat before the session actually starts—about personal things or the weather or whatever—but once the work begins, it is important to stay focused on the music. This applies to the musicians as well as the recordist. The most frequent complaint I hear after recording sessions is that one of the participants talked too much. This doesn't necessarily mean the person said too many words, but it does mean the person interrupted the session flow too often with unnecessary and extraneous conversation.

Be mindful of what you say during recording sessions. Positive feedback is a tremendous boon to performers. Some people describe record producers as cheerleaders, and honest enthusiasm can spur performance while creating a positive environment for creativity. If you work professionally, you may find yourself recording music or musicians that you don't feel much of a connection with. You need to find what is positive for you about the music and the performances, so that your enthusiasm can be honest. Lies told in the studio will ultimately be recognized, and dishonest enthusiasm is no better than silence, but *if you can't find something positive to say about virtually any music, then you probably shouldn't be a recordist.* Again, criticism is essential—often it is the core of your job, if you are assuming production responsibilities—but it must be constructive, it must be specific, and it must be balanced with honest enthusiasm.

WHAT NOT TO DO

Don't allow strangers or guests at recording sessions unless you are sure that everyone involved wants them to be there.
Playing and recording music is a very intimate process. It is important to be sure that only those whom everyone involved really wants to be at the session are in the room. Even if it seems like the performer is completely comfortable and relaxed, he or she may be unhappy about the presence of a particular person but not willing to speak up about it (especially in that person's presence). Sometimes it falls to the recordist to ask a person to leave. In any case, carefully monitor who is in the room during recording sessions. If someone new walks into a session in progress, always make some contact with that person and try to ascertain that the person is welcomed by everyone involved.

For many musicians there is considerable anxiety around performing in the recording studio. While encouragement is basic, there are specific techniques that are helpful in putting a performer at ease. The kind of self-consciousness that goes along with anxiety of recording may produce uncomfortable or nervous performances. One of the most surprisingly helpful comments for a struggling, self-conscious performer is, "I can hear you thinking. STOP THINKING!" The humorous element softens the somewhat awkward request for less self-consciousness. Very often performers will recognize that they are "thinking" too much and that they just need to relax and play. *It's no accident that* play *is the term used for making music.*

Along these same lines is the request for a musician, regarding the construction of his or her particular part, to "make it more boneheaded!" This is a comment born of the tendency for musicians to overplay—especially in the studio. Overplaying is usually a symptom of anxiety and self-consciousness. Again, humor eases the request for an altered approach to performance—a request that may be interpreted as criticism. For those of us who work regularly with studio performance, the difference between a self-conscious performance and a comfortable one is usually apparent, though "usually" is an important qualifier and sometimes reading performances is difficult. And, of course, there is much more involved here than a simple distinction between relaxed and overthought; there are considerations regarding musical execution and other subjective elements in judging performance. Nonetheless, a lack of self-consciousness goes a long way toward an outstanding musical performance, and the right feedback from the recordist can do a lot to keep the session flow positive and productive.

WHAT NOT TO DO

Don't be too eager to be sensitive to the performing musician. *While much of healthy session flow revolves around being sensitive to a musician's needs ("Can I get you some water?" or "Are you hearing yourself okay?"), it sometimes sends the wrong message if you are overly attentive. The classic example is asking, "Would you like a break?" too frequently. The intention may be to make sure that the musician is fresh and at his or her best, but the subtext is likely to be, "You're not doing very well, maybe if you took a break you'd do better."*

Technical flow

Technical issues are important (most of this book is dedicated to them!), but it is helpful to keep in mind the true order of importance in regard to session goals. When it comes to the technical part of making a recording, I have one guiding rule: the music always comes first! The primary goal is to encourage great performances, and after that comes the goal of making a great-sounding recording. If one must be sacrificed to the other, certainly it is the technical details that should be sacrificed for the sake of fostering the best possible performance. This dynamic between performance and recording technology frequently comes into play in subtle ways during the course of a session.

How much tweaking of sound before recording begins is one of the issues that most frequently need to be balanced against getting the optimal performance. Here, the proper approach can be complicated and the recordist needs to be sensitive to the musicians and the situation. Let's say you've put a mic in front of a guitar amp and you're getting ready to record some rhythm guitar. You ask the guitarist to play a bit of his or her part, and you listen to the sound that you're capturing. You think it sounds a little thin, so you go and move the mic a few inches farther from the speaker. You come back into the control room and ask the musician to play the part again and you listen. You think it sounds better, but what if you pulled the mic another inch away? Well, maybe it would sound better still, but is the guitar player getting anxious to get started? Is he or she remaining focused on the music or becoming hyper-sensitized to the sound being produced? This is a judgment call on the part of the recordist. Is a slight improvement in the sound worth stretching the patience of the musician? And at some point you have to ask yourself whether the sound would actually be better, especially given how subjective the judgment of sound is. In terms of priorities, the search for the "perfect" sound should be placed well below the state of mind of the performer.

That said, sometimes the reverse may be true. For some musicians (and guitar players are notorious for this), the pursuit of the "perfect" sound is a major part of their pleasure in the studio and it is intimately tied into how they perform. If considerable time and energy is spent exploring the finer details of capturing his or her "sound"—swapping mics to find the "best" one for the job at hand, using multiple mics, fine-tuning the mic placement, and so on, then the musician might feel inspired to perform better. The right balance between tweaking and getting on with the playing requires a subjective judgment, but the primary factor is the state of mind of the musician, not the actual difference made by small tweaks.

Of course, certain technical matters require attention—a significant buzz, a crackly cable, etc.—and there are times when these have to be resolved even

WHAT NOT TO DO

An anecdote regarding technical issues versus performance
Recently I was standing on stage during setup for a performance by a well-known jazz musician. The person responsible for the live sound was setting up microphones on the drums as the drummer was warming up. I saw the sound person stop the drummer and ask him if he could move his ride cymbal up a bit so that a microphone would fit comfortably beneath it. This is an example of a very bad job of balancing technical demands with a musician's comfort. It is not appropriate to ask a musician to adjust his or her setup for the sake of technical convenience. The recordist's (or live sound engineer's) job is to create the most comfortable playing environment possible for the musician, and technical concerns should be addressed accordingly.

if it is inconvenient for the performer. However, finding the balance—knowing when to tweak and when to get started—is a very important part of the record-ist's job. *It is difficult enough to play music; the technical elements should interfere as little as possible.*

Musical flow

It will be difficult to record music effectively if you do not have some basic musical knowledge. Most recordists have some musical background; you need to have an understanding of some music fundamentals, or you will not be able to do a good job with session flow. Knowing the fundamentals of musical rhythm, such as counting, bars and beats, and so on; essential songwriting terminology, such as *verse, chorus, bridge*, and the like; and basic music theory, such as simple scales and chords, is essential to communication in recording sessions. When the performer says he or she wants to punch-in on bar 4 of the verse, you should be able to do that without further instruction. If the musician says "I want to take it from the modulation," you should know where that is. If the band says they want to listen back from the turnaround before the guitar solo on a 12-bar blues, you should know where to start the playback. You don't need to know how to play an instrument, but you do need to know music basics so that you can communicate with the performers. There are a variety of books to assist in this process (see especially *Essentials of Music for Audio Professionals*, by Frank Dorritie).

Besides being able to navigate to appropriate parts of the song based on the musical language, you need to bring some understanding of musical process to the task of making recordings. A key musical element in promoting good session flow is managing run-up time when doing punch-ins. This means knowing the best place to start playback when someone is getting ready to replace one section of a recording (punch-in). If you start playback too far back, the musician may lose his or her focus by the time the punch comes and may play the wrong part, or a singer may lose his or her note, which means s/he doesn't come in singing the correct pitch. If you start too close to the punch-in point, the musician or singer doesn't have enough time to prepare, to find the groove or the pitch reference needed for a good entrance. When I first heard a very experienced background singer comment on how much easier a session had been because I was carefully managing the playback start time, I was surprised. I have since come to realize how much difference this makes in the comfort and performance of musicians, and thus in smooth session flow.

In practical terms, what is the correct amount of run-up time to a punch-in? This varies depending on the tempo and the preference of the musician, but a good guideline for a typical song would be a little more than one complete vocal line or a little more than two complete bars. This allows the musician or singer enough time to get oriented, without losing focus on what he or she intends to do. If a singer can hear a complete vocal line ahead of his or her entrance (which means you must start a few beats before the vocal line entrance for the singer to get oriented), that's usually sufficient time. If a musician can find the beat and then count two bars to his or her entrance, that's also usually enough time. If the tempo is fast or the music complex, sometimes a little more time is necessary—perhaps even two vocal lines or a bit over four bars. Sometime fairly early in the process you might want to ask the musician if you are using a good starting point for punching-in on a part. Some musicians prefer longer or shorter run-up times. The main lesson here is that this is an important concern when it comes to maximizing creativity, and along with a practical understanding of music fundamentals, it is vital to good session flow.

Economic flow

Finally, you can't ignore economics as an essential part of the recording process. Budgets and deadlines may be critical factors, especially when dealing with OPM (other people's money) or with record-company release schedules. On the other hand, recording yourself at your home studio may make economic factors virtually meaningless. I say "virtually" because even recording yourself at home has certain economic consequences. If you never get your recording done, you'll never have the opportunity to see if it has any economic potential! Whatever the level of economic pressure, this does get reflected in creative decision making. All kinds of decisions, from what instruments to use on a song to how much time you take to complete a lead vocal may be affected by budget and timeline. The response to the same vocal take may vary from "Let's do it a few more times and then we'll put together the comp" (as described in section 4.2) to "That was good; we just need to fix one part in the first verse and it will be done." It's great to keep economics from dominating the creative process in the studio, but it's not always possible. Budgets need to be clear, and it is important that economics are kept in mind from the very first day of the project. The best way to keep economic pressures from seriously hampering recording sessions is through plenty of advance planning. From the very beginning, you should guard against allowing a project to fall behind budget without considering the consequences.

8.2 Talkback

As discussed in the preceding section, good communication is key to good session flow, and at the heart of communication in many studio situations is the talkback system. The talkback system provides a way for those in the control room to communicate with those in the recording room. A talkback system involves a microphone that feeds the headphones and/or recording-room speakers when communication is desired.

WHAT NOT TO DO

Don't even use a talkback system if you don't have to! *That is to say, if you can work in the same room with the musicians, so that you can communicate directly, without any talkback system, this is the most comfortable way to work.*

Although *not* using a talkback system provides some distinct advantages, it is often not practical or not possible. That's because bypassing a talkback system comes with the following potential problems:

1. Having a live mic in the same room with the playback speakers, which causes leakage onto the recording and/or feedback
2. Having insufficient space in the control room to accommodate the musicians and their instruments
3. Having fan noise or other external noises in the control room that compromise a live recording

A simple circumstance whereby you can bypass the talkback system is when the recording doesn't involve any live microphones, such as when recording someone playing a synthesizer or recording a guitar or bass guitar using only a direct input (DI). In this case, headphones are not needed and it makes much more sense for everyone to be in the same room, thereby making communication easy. Another example is one in which the mic can be separated from the musician, such as when recording electric guitar with the musician in the control room and the amplifier and mic in a recording room. Sometimes guitarists prefer to be in the same room with their amp (or need to be if they're controlling feedback), but generally the ability to have direct communication, without talkback, makes having the guitarist in the control room the most desirable setup.

But often talkback is necessary. And because communication is at the heart of good session flow, and good session flow is at the heart of a successful session, *proper talkback operation and etiquette are essential!* I address the technical issues regarding setting up a hardware and/or software talkback system first, and then take on some of the often-overlooked issues regarding talkback operation.

Setting up a talkback system

There are many kinds of talkback systems, and they come (or can be built) with a variety of features and options. Generally speaking, if you are using a hardware recording console as part of your setup, you probably have a built-in talkback system. This means that there's a small microphone built into the console that is activated by a talkback button. The button opens the mics routing into the main and/or monitor output, so that anyone who is listening through the mixing console can hear someone who is talking into the microphone. Some consoles have elaborate routing options for the talkback mic, allowing control over which users or which systems (headphones or speakers, for example) receive the feed from the talkback mic. I'm not going to go into all the various console configurations here; you'll have to consult your user's manual for that. I do address the basic kinds of talkback systems that are available, including a look at some of the concerns of special interest if you are not using an outboard mixing console but only your computer and audio interface.

There are two kinds of talkback button operations: momentary and latching. Sometimes you can select between the two. A *momentary* operation means that the button must be held down for the talkback microphone to be active. *Latching* operation means that pressing and releasing the button opens the talkback mic and leaves it open until the button is pressed and released again.

The incoming audio (from a singer's mic, for example) must be managed in some way because of the possibility of a feedback loop when using a talkback system. The feedback loop may be caused by the following: (1) the talkback mic in the control room is switched on by pressing the talkback button and the engineer's voice is carried into the studio and is broadcast through the singer's headphones; (2) the engineer's voice leaks out of the headphones and is picked up by the singer's microphone (which is typically only a few inches from the singer's headphones), then that voice is broadcast through the control-room speakers (set to monitor the signal from the singer's microphone); and (3) the sound of the voice coming through the speakers feeds back into the talkback microphone, creating a loop that runs continuously, building quickly into feedback. It may sound pretty unlikely, but it is a pretty direct path from point A to point B to point C, and is a very common cause of feedback. Here's the abbreviated version of the signal path for the potential feedback loop:

Talkback mic → Singer's phones → Singer's mic → Speakers → Talkback mic (feedback)

In order to prevent feedback, you need to manage what happens to the incoming audio when the talkback microphone is opened. There are three possibilities: muting the incoming audio, dimming the volume of the incoming audio, and leaving the incoming audio unaffected. Each is considered in the following sections.

Momentary systems that mute the incoming audio

This is the classic talkback system, and the one that is most common on hardware mixing consoles. When the talkback button is depressed, the talkback mic is activated and the incoming audio is muted. This prevents any possibility of feedback by cutting the feed from the microphone in the studio to the speakers in the control room. It also means that when the talkback mic button is depressed, the musician in the studio cannot be heard. The challenge for the talkback operator is to switch the talkback mic on and off at the appropriate times—on to talk, off to listen. There is more on dealing with this operation in the following section that discusses talkback operation and etiquette.

Momentary systems or latching systems that dim the incoming audio

The notion of dimming (decreasing the volume), rather than killing the incoming audio, is a relatively new development in talkback systems. The obvious advantage is that two-way conversations can occur because the incoming audio is not completely muted, as it is in the traditional system. The reason for dimming the audio is that it will (one hopes) prevent the feedback loop from developing. If the audio coming through the speakers is soft enough, it will lose enough energy so as to be unable to make the complete loop back through the talkback mic, the headphones, and the singer's mic. This generally works pretty well. As long as the sound is sufficiently dimmed (some systems provide variable dimming) and the headphones don't get too close to the microphone, an open, two-way conversation may be possible. In this circumstance, a latching talkback button is convenient because it means that the operator doesn't have to keep the button depressed during the two-way conversation. The operator must, however, remember to unlatch the talkback once ready to record, to avoid unwanted sounds (talking from the control room, leakage from the speakers, etc.) to be fed into the headphones during recording.

Latching systems that do not affect the incoming audio

A latching system that neither mutes nor dims incoming audio is likely to not really be a system at all, but the result of a typical talkback arrangement created when there is no hardware mixing console or the mixer doesn't have a built-in talkback mic. In this case, you are simply connecting a microphone in the control room and sending its signal out to whoever is on the headphone monitor system. Operation is controlled by muting or unmuting the channel that the mic is plugged into. The problem, of course, is the possibility of creating a feedback loop. This is less of a problem if everyone is on headphones (typical of the one-room home studio setup, where the speakers are muted during recording to prevent leakage into the mic in the control room). A feedback loop is still possible in this circumstance, but less likely because it requires leakage from the operator's headphones back into the talkback mic, rather than from the monitor speakers (which are muted).

Talkback systems of this type, using software only, is less than ideal. Not only is there no muting or dimming of incoming audio, increasing the likelihood of feedback, but also there is no physical button to push, so on/off op-

231

eration is controlled by a mouse click on the channel mute box in the software mixer. This can be awkward and slow, whereas talkback button operation should be easy and quick. Nonetheless, this can be workable if you are careful with the playback volume over the speakers (or if you're all using headphones) and you are quick with the mouse. The nature of the on/off mute control is that it is the same as a latched button operation, and because there is no muting, two-way continuous conversations are possible. There is a software plug-in available from sourceelements.com that provides dimming capabilities for some computer systems and there are dedicated hardware talkback systems available from heartechnologies.com. I would expect expanded options on this front in the days ahead.

WHAT NOT TO DO

Don't turn on the talkback mic when there is a loop that will cause feedback!
Unfortunately, this is easier said than done and all of us who work in this field have, at one time or another, inadvertently activated the talkback and been greeted with feedback that is highly annoying (not to mention potentially damaging) to the musicians wearing headphones at the time. It is appropriate to use extreme caution when first operating the talkback during a session or after making changes in microphones and signal path. Try to check the talkback level before the musicians have put on their headphones (either by putting on the phones yourself and having someone else talk into the talkback or using an assistant as the guinea pig).

Using the talkback button

The heart of the talkback system is the button or switch used to open the signal path from the microphone that permits talkback. What do you need to know about using the talkback button? Believe it or not, *sessions can sink or swim totally based on how effectively that little talkback button is used!* Poor operation of the button can bog sessions down, cause miscommunication, and raise the frustration level so that little or no good work may get done.

There are two primary elements to good talkback operation. The first is knowing when to turn the talkback mic on and off, and the second is the ability to operate the talkback button for conversations among multiple people in the studio and the control room. The first may seem pretty straightforward—*on* when you want to communicate and *off* when you don't—but it isn't always quite that simple. You don't know what people are going to say, and the people in the control room don't always know whether or not you have the talkback button depressed. That means that someone might say something that he or she doesn't want the musician in the recording room to hear, and the remark is accidentally heard. An off-hand remark such as "He never plays anything right all the way through, so we'll just have to edit the pieces together" may be an accurate analysis of the situation, but may not be something the producer wants the musician to hear. As you might imagine, a mistake of this kind can blow a session (or an entire relationship). How do you know what someone else in the control room might be about to say? There's no way to know, but you can try to avoid disasters by making it clear to everyone when the talkback is on and when it isn't. *When you press the talkback button, you may want to say something right away, making it clear that you're in communication with the recording room, and as soon as you think the communication is over, you should let go of the button or switch the latch to off so that the mic is dead.*

Knowing when to turn the talkback on or off can be difficult—and it requires some experience to actually be good at it—but even more of a challenge is managing the talkback when there are multiple participants to the conversation. In some circumstances, such as latched talkback operation, a multiperson conversation may occur without any special maneuvering by the operator, but with the most common kind of hardware system (a momentary system that kills

233

WHAT NOT TO DO

Never let a musician endure silence after a recorded performance. *The best way I can explain the above is to tell a story from early in my career. I was recording a vocalist (and a close friend), and she had just completed a lead vocal take in the studio. At the end of the take, I got involved in a brief discussion with another musician in the control room rather that responding to the singer's performance. When I finally got on the talkback, the singer chewed me out: "Never let me stand here waiting for you after I've just poured my heart out," she said. (Or something to that effect, maybe not using quite such polite language.) This made me realize what a serious mistake I had made. Performing music is very personal and often deeply emotional. If you are sharing in the experience as part of the process, you need to let the performer know that you are paying attention. Ever since that time, after any performance in the studio, I immediately get on the talkback and say something—even if it's just, "That was good; give me a moment while I talk it over with x." Never allow a musician to wonder whether you were even listening, or whether perhaps the performance had been so bad that you were at a loss for words. Even if that's true, you must find some words to reassure the musician that at least you are with the person and going to help him or her in the process of making a good recording.*

the incoming audio), this can be quite demanding. You have to anticipate the conversation as best you can, trying to switch so that each speaker can be heard (button down when the person in the control room is talking, button up when the speaker is in the recording room). One solution is to have multiple talkback buttons. Some studios have a talkback button on a long cable that stretches to anywhere in the control room and can be passed among people when needed. This requires some special wiring, and it doesn't always work out if the speaker isn't experienced in operating a typical talkback—people tend to forget that they can't hear the other speaker until they let the button up. In any event, because communication is such an important part of the recording process, thoughtful operation of the talkback system is critical to good session flow.

8.3 Playback Volume

Controlling the volume of the playback is one of the most critical (and neglected) elements in running a productive recording session. The person controlling the playback volume is affecting the creative process in significant ways, but often even the operator (probably you!) is unaware of the effect the playback volume is having.

The engineer is responsible for the playback volume that everyone hears in the control room (though that might just be you, if you're working by yourself). Regulating playback volume is critical to session flow, to accurate listening for decision making, and to session fatigue. Finding the appropriate playback level requires a sensitivity that can dramatically affect both session flow and musical outcomes. Even if you're not in control of the playback volume, you should still keep these things in mind and request different listening levels when appropriate. Listening levels may need to be adjusted fairly frequently, depending on need. I cover the following six elements in considering playback volume during sessions.

1. Ear fatigue is an important consideration over the course of a session.
2. Quieter levels make pitch and rhythm accuracy easier to detect.
3. Louder levels make very high and very low frequencies easier to hear.
4. Loud levels are important for certain kinds of performances.
5. Controlling volume is an important part of the talkback/conversation matrix.
6. Everything sounds better when it's louder!

Ear fatigue

While mental fatigue (lack of concentration) is the biggest challenge over the course of a long session, ear fatigue ranks a close second—and ear fatigue contributes to mental fatigue, as well. Your ears can take only so much sound over the course of a day. Persistent loud-volume listening will shut down your ear's ability to hear, and eventually everything will start to sound muffled. But before things have gotten to that point, your ears will start to lose some of their ability to hear detail. I'm not going to go into issues about actual ear damage, which can be caused by very loud studio monitoring over extended periods of time, but even moderately loud levels sustained over the course of a day can cause ear fatigue, which really prevents you from being an effective listener.

You can have a SPL (sound pressure level) reader in the studio and be monitoring it for levels, but truthfully, I think we all know what loud is. It is more fun to listen louder, and I address this in the last part of this section, but effective listening requires low-level listening most of the time. Try to train yourself (and those you're working with) to listen at pretty low levels. Knowing when to turn the volume up (again, covered in sections coming up) is also important to workflow, but generally the problem is too much loud level listening.

The key to low-level listening and prevention of ear fatigue is to start the day listening as low as you comfortably can. Your ears are very fresh, and you can listen at a pretty low level and still hear all the detail that you need, in most cases. Over the course of the day, there is going to be a natural tendency for playback volume to creep up, so by starting low you have the best chance of preventing too much high-volume playback.

Quieter levels for detecting pitch and rhythm accuracy

It is a little known fact, but quieter levels can greatly increase the productivity of your recording sessions. *Volume tends to mask performance details.* Problems with both pitch and rhythm tend to be much easier to hear when playback is low in volume. In fact, very low playback—lower than the comfortable listening level for most work—might best allow you to hear inconsistencies in pitch or rhythm. As volume increases, the ear hears more detail in frequencies (see section that follows), and this can distract from hearing small discrepancies in pitch or rhythm

WHAT NOT TO DO

Don't listen very quietly if you have an overly nitpicking artist!
Very low-level listening for checking performance details can backfire if you are working with someone who is overly critical of his or others' performances. If I'm working with someone whom I think is spending too much time trying to correct pitch or rhythm elements, I avoid the low-level listening technique because it can encourage obsessive correction. Although typically I turn the playback down, I have at times turned the playback up a bit when certain artists say, "I think part of that line is out of tune; can we listen again?"

accuracy. Very loud listening levels distract in many ways (and dulls hearing as well), so subtle detail in performance is easily missed during loud playback.

Louder levels for hearing high and low frequencies

Sometimes louder listening levels are necessary. As noted in section 2.5 regarding EQ, equal-loudness contours describe the ways that our ears begin to lose the ability to hear higher and lower frequencies as overall volume decreases. We detailed how this explained use of the smile-curve EQ application and the presence of loudness options on some playback systems. It also explains why we sometimes need to monitor fairly loudly. If you want to hear detail in very high or very low-frequency sounds, you need to monitor at a higher level so that your ear captures the details in the those frequencies. Usually this can be done for a relatively short period of time, as you fine-tune EQ or do critical level balancing. The ear perceives frequencies at different relative volumes depending on the overall listening level (this is described by the equal-loudness contours). To maintain perspective on your recording, you will want to listen at different levels as part of your working process.

Loud levels for certain musicians

There are circumstances when the playback level in the control room needs to satisfy the demands of a performing musician. For example, if you're recording electric guitar with the amp isolated but the guitarist in the control room with you, then the musician is relying on the playback level for his or her performance. This is a different situation from when the playback level serves only the recording process. In these situations, the musician should be allowed to control the level (not literally; you're still operating the knob, but you're asking for feedback on the level until you get it where the musician wants it). This does mean that sometimes the level will be somewhat louder than what you prefer, and this can cause ear fatigue (or worse), but it may be necessary to the process. If you know you're going to be recording something that requires loud playback (rock guitar is a common example), try to schedule that for later in the day so you don't have to do a bunch of sensitive work after having spent a few hours monitoring loud electric guitar.

While fairly loud monitoring may be appropriate in some circumstances, it is *not* appropriate to allow the monitoring volume to get to the uncomfortable level. If the musician keeps asking for it louder, beyond your comfort level, you can ask the musician to wear headphones so that you don't have to monitor that loud. If that doesn't work, you have the right to say that the musician will have to find someone else to run the session if he or she wants it that loud—ultimately, you must protect your ears. It rarely comes to that kind of conflict, and musicians who ask for really loud playback will likely come to their senses if you suggest that you won't be able to work at that volume.

WHAT NOT TO DO

Don't buy in to the argument that certain music has to be listened to loud all the time. *Note that at the beginning of this section regarding loud monitoring levels I say "for certain musicians," not for certain kinds of music. Some may argue that if you're working with heavy metal, or dance-club music, or rap or punk, or whatever, that you need to monitor louder in order to capture the spirit of the music. This just isn't true. More effective work gets done on every kind of music when reasonable monitoring levels are maintained. Sometimes loud listening is necessary, sometimes it's fun (and that's good, too), but it's never appropriate all of the time.*

Controlling volume as part of the talkback /conversation matrix

Clearly, the volume of playback in the control room affects the ability for people in the room to have conversations. This is something you need to be sensitive to as the operator of the playback level. It is often helpful to be listening to playback and talking at the same time, and this requires a tightly controlled playback volume—loud enough to hear the details but quiet enough to be talked over. This may be a different level depending on who's talking. It also may affect the playback duration—that is to say, monitoring conversations also means deciding when playback should be stopped because the conversation has overtaken the listening.

When done with sensitive attention to the situation, this change is often transparent to the other people in the room. They don't even notice that the playback has been turned down or stopped, because they're having a conversation. But it allows that conversation to happen and for the creative process to move forward, as opposed to a situation in which people keep raising their voices to be heard until they have to ask for a lower volume or for you to stop the playback so they can start their conversation over again. This wastes time and causes frustration—both negative outcomes in a recording session.

Everything sounds better when it's louder!

This is generally true (up to a point), and it's part of the constant struggle to be really creative while making recordings. We saw this when it was applied to mid- to high-frequency EQ (section 2.5). Because that kind of EQ adds apparent volume as a part of the frequency boost, there's often an initial response of "That sounds better," which can lead to over EQ-ing. If you want to get more of a kick out of what it is you're recording, turn it up! But, the problems in doing this are many, as just described: ear fatigue, inability to make accurate judgments about pitch and rhythm, and an environment in the control room that makes communication difficult. Loud playback has its place, and at the end of the session you might want to do some pretty loud listening, just for fun. But ultimately, playback level is a tool and it must be used to further the session's goals.

Addendum 1

How to Walk into a Commercial Studio and Be the Engineer

My ascent to the ranks of professional recording engineer was, in brief, as follows. I had been a professional drummer for a few years and had the chance to do a bit of recording as the drummer in various bands I had been in. In 1979, I acquired one of the first Tascam 144 cassette 4-track tape recorders and it changed my life. I started making recordings and learning the intricacies of this amazing little recorder/mixer. Although it isn't quite true that "Everything you need to know about recording you can learn on a cassette 4-track," it is amazing how close to the truth that is. That little machine had output faders, pan controls, EQ, aux sends and returns, and various I/Os on the rear panel, including inserts. With it you could do overdubs, punch-ins, and bounce tracks. It was a miniature version of an entire multitrack recording studio.

I graduated from the cassette 4-track in my living room to an Akai 12-track in my garage. The 12-track was also an all-in-one recorder/mixer that had the expanded capabilities afforded by the extra tracks. I began recording band demos in my garage for next to nothing. One day, one of the bands I was working with said they had cobbled together enough money to go into a commercial studio to do a recording, and they wanted to know if I would come with them and be the engineer/producer. I said yes, though I had never been an engineer at any studio other than the ones in my home. I successfully got through the session and my career as a professional recordist was officially launched.

For many people, including a fair number of those reading this book I would guess, the idea of going into a commercial studio and being the engineer is just too intimidating to consider. Even though you've been running home studios for years, and are really good at making everything work for those "home" recordings, the idea of being the engineer at a studio that has an unfamiliar mixing console or control surface, patch bay, microphones, and outboard gear seems out of reach. I want to encourage you to expand your notion of what you are capable of.

The secret to being an outside, guest, or "independent" engineer at a commercial studio is that you're not expected to necessarily know the intricacies of the particular console at that studio, and you're certainly not expected to do the patching in the patch bay. This is why you are assigned a second or assistant engineer for your session. Commercial studios have to provide someone who

239

knows the ins and outs of their particular setups, including the functions of the console. The assistant is also expected to do all the patching. The person is there to answer your questions and to make sure that everything is working for you.

As a guest engineer, your job is to know what it is that you want to do, not exactly how to do it at the particular studio you are at. You need to know mostly all of the basics that I cover in this book, but none of the specifics of implementation at a particular studio. It's perfectly acceptable for you to ask about the microphone input or the bussing system of the studio's console. Of course, you need to know the general principles behind getting from the mic to the console, and the basics of proper gain structure in doing so, but you can certainly ask for the specifics or ask the assistant to set up one signal path on the console so you can see how the routing works.

It's perfectly fine for you to ask the assistant to suggest a microphone for a particular application. It's not possible for anyone to be familiar with all the microphones available. Even with familiar mics, it's a good idea to find out from the assistant which ones are considered particularly good at that studio, especially for critical recording functions such as vocals.

The main point is this: as a guest engineer at a commercial studio, your job is to know what it is that you want to do from a technical standpoint and the basics of how such a thing is done, without necessarily knowing any of the specifics as to how that is accomplished at the particular studio. If you're accomplished at making your home studio work, then you already know what it is you need to do and you're ready to be a guest engineer at a commercial studio.

Yes, you might require more assistance than a more experienced engineer, but you will be able to make the session happen and fulfill your role. After a few sessions, you will find it rather easy to adapt to a new console or control surface and a new work environment. The principles are always the same—the specifics of signal-path routing always follow the same basic concepts. What's more, the whole notion of what a recording session is—from setup through line tests, to recording and reviewing recordings, to working through all the creative and technical issues that result in getting the work planned for the day done—is the same in the general sense, no matter what studio you're at. And the assistant engineer is there to help you through the details.

The one exception I would make is in regard to the DAW. Pro Tools remains the default standard DAW for commercial recording studios. Just as the 2-inch 24-track tape recorder was the standard previously (and they continue to sit in the corner of the control room or in the machine room of most commercial studios), Pro Tools is now the only piece of technology that is reliably found in almost every commercial studio around the world. For this reason, I highly recommend to any of you who aspire to work in this field commercially that you acquire and learn Pro Tools. You will be expected to know how Pro Tools works in order to be an effective guest engineer at most studios. Asking questions about the console, control surface, patch bay, or studio configuration would be expected of a guest engineer. There are some Pro Tools questions that would be expected as well; resolving the I/O setup between a file that you bring from home or from another studio, and the I/O configuration at the studio you're working at, is something that you may well need the assistant to do for you. But in general, just as you will need to know what has to happen in order to have a successful session, you will need to know how to operate Pro Tools sufficiently to be running the program as part of that session.

Having the confidence to take your sessions to studios outside your home/project studio expands your capabilities enormously, giving you the opportunity to try out new gear and new recording spaces, learn how other studios operate, and meet people in the recording community as colleagues and peers. The first few forays are likely to make you a bit nervous; if you do it with your own band or project you might feel a little less pressured than if you're working for someone else, but I encourage you to take the plunge. In many cases, you will find that you're more ready and more capable that you realize—all that time in your bedroom, living room, or garage really is closely akin to the way recordings are made in all places around the world.

Addendum 2

Researching and Buying Gear
Internet vs. Brick and Mortar

Buying recording gear (and by this I mean both hardware and software) is often an obsessive and confusing endeavor. The Internet is a spectacular resource, but it also removes us from the ability to get in there and muck around with things. What follows may be obvious to those of you with a lot of experience already, but I am responding to a lot of questions that I get from students about the best way to make decisions and, ultimately, to purchase new (or used) gear for their studio.

What Do You Need?

Although this is one of the most common questions I get about gear, it can also one of the most difficult to answer. It's pretty easy to answer this question if it is regarding a particular studio function that you wish to have. Do you need a microphone? If you're going to record vocals, for example, then of course you do. There are basic items that you need to make your studio a studio. But, in fact, there are a lot of different ways of working and of creating different kinds of music; you may not need a microphone at all if you are doing all instrumental, all electronic music.

Do I need a control surface? Do I need a large-diaphragm condenser mic? Do I need an impulse response reverb plug-in? These questions are more difficult to answer. You probably don't absolutely need any of these things in order to get your work done, so it's a question of quality or convenience, and these questions usually don't have clear-cut answers. You may want these things, and they may improve the quality of your recordings or the convenience of your work environment, but there is an endless list of things that can improve the quality of your recordings and make your work easier to do. Where do you draw the line?

Well, budget is the great limiter. You need to be able to afford new gear, or justify it based on the income profile of your studio. Clearly, I can't make these judgments for you, but I can offer a bit of advice on studio upgrade decisions. The first consideration is this: every link in the chain—in the signal path—is critical, so buy gear that is appropriate to the weakest link or upgrade that weakest link. That means that if you have an inexpensive mic preamp and less than high-quality analog-to-digital conversion into the computer, you shouldn't buy a $5,000 microphone. Buy a mid-quality mic—in the $500 to $1,000 range—that will hold up until you upgrade the other elements in the signal path and it becomes the weakest link. Perhaps then you'll be ready for a more expensive mic. If you have some very high quality gear in a signal path with low-quality gear, you are not getting the most benefit from the good stuff.

I often tell people that you get a 5 to 10 percent improvement in quality for double the price. Of course, this is not literally accurate, but it points to the fact that upgrades in quality can often be very expensive without bringing vastly noticeable results. Sometimes the results from individual upgrades can be very apparent. For example, a different kind of microphone that is better suited for certain tasks—say, a good-quality condenser mic when you only had dynamic mics previously—can result in a significant change in the quality of your recordings. If you upgrade each element of your signal path by 10 percent, the difference can be quite apparent, but also quite expensive. In any event, chose your upgrades carefully to maximize the benefits. There is more about the specifics of deciding what to buy in the following section on research.

Research: Try Before You Buy or Rely on Word-of-Mouth?

Is it possible to buy gear successfully based completely on word-of-mouth, without ever trying the gear? Yes, although this is not the most desirable way to buy. Is it okay to buy gear that you've tried out at the store or used in a session at somebody else's studio? Yes, but again, this is not the best way to make buying decisions. Ideally, you use a combination of "word-of-mouth" research and some hands-on experience. I put word-of-mouth in quotes here because the Internet provides the opportunity for getting a lot of written user feedback—not exactly word-of-mouth, but a close equivalent.

The problem with Internet research, as well as recommendations from friends and colleagues, is that not everyone has the same response to gear. What sounds sweet and warm to one person may sound relatively harsh and cold to another. By the same token, your hands-on experience with a piece of gear in an unfamiliar environment, like a store or someone else's studio, may produce a somewhat different response than your reaction to that same gear when you have it in your own studio.

Another problem with Internet research is the sheer bulk of information out there. You can find contradictory opinions about almost anything, and it can be difficult to sort out the valuable information from the casual, and sometimes simply wrong, comments. If you research gear consistently over time, you will probably find some sites and/or reviewers whom you trust. There are moderated discussion groups, free-form discussion groups, blogs, reviews as a part of commercial Web sites where the gear is being sold, and random reviews. Negative reviews can be particularly helpful in balancing what tends to be primarily positive comments—apparently people are more motivated to sing the praises of their new acquisitions than complain about them. This is probably motivated in part by a desire to justify a new purchase. In any event, don't let a few negative reviews scuttle the deal—otherwise, you'll never get *any* new gear—and don't let a few over-the-top raves convince you that you have to have something. Read enough comments and reviews until you feel as if you have a fairly balanced understanding of how people feel about the gear you're researching. Pay attention to how they are using the gear and what their studio environment is to see if it matches your needs and interests.

In some cases, most notably with plug-ins, you have the option of trying before buying. This is the best possible situation because you get hands-on experience in the studio environment where you are most comfortable and where you'll actually end up using the gear. Almost every plug-in company offers free trials of all their plug-ins, either on a time-limited basis or with some of the functionality disabled. These represent your best opportunity for making a purchase that you're going to be happy about. For hardware purchases (but typically not for software), most stores offer a return option, though returning things can be a hassle. This brings us to the final topic in regard to buying gear: where to buy.

Buying: Store versus Internet versus eBay

Where to buy is complicated by several factors, including price, convenience, and return capabilities. There are advantages to buying from your local dealer, most notably ease of return, but it's also positive to support your local recording community and the gear dealers are an important part of that community (though your local store may be a part of a large, national chain). There are a lot of Internet stores that sell gear; some of them also have brick-and-mortar stores. For those not located near physical stores, Internet shopping makes pretty much everything easily available, and many of these dealers have generous return policies, as long as you're willing to deal with the repacking and return shipping chores.

My preference is to shop at my local independent audio gear dealer. I am fortunate to have a very good one in my area. Ideally, the salespeople at your dealer are not paid on commission, and are therefore less motivated to sell you as much gear at the highest price point possible, and are also more likely to take the time to help you find what you really want—and even to save you money where possible—on the understanding that you will become a long-term customer. Nonetheless, I shop the online stores and eBay to see what prices are like before I buy from my local dealer. I won't necessarily demand that they match the lowest price out there, but I don't want to pay a large premium for shopping with my local dealer.

There is a huge amount of audio gear available on eBay, and it is a good place to research prices. It is also a great resource for buying used gear, but that is a specialized market. I do not recommend buying used gear on eBay unless you have a lot of knowledge about the gear you're buying and are an experienced eBay user who feels that you know how to use the system to judge the likely trustworthiness of the seller. To its credit, eBay has made a huge amount of used and vintage gear available to people around the world that would otherwise have had great difficulty in finding it.

To be confident in buying on eBay you need to read and trust the feedback system. You also need to explore the feedback content, as there are some unscrupulous sellers who sell a bunch of cheap items to build up positive feedback and then sell one expensive item that is never delivered. Thus, eBay has done more to guard against fraudulent sellers over the years, but scams still happen. You also need to be able to trust the products because, in general, returns on eBay will be more complicated or impossible, so if that's a concern, you're much better off with a real or virtual store. That said, eBay often has new or nearly new items at the best prices. That's because some items being sold are gifts that people received and never used or that were used very few times and then abandoned, thus selling for well under the price you would find anywhere else. These items may not be returnable, so, again, you have to trust the seller and the product to buy under these circumstances. Also, sometimes the best price for a new item on eBay is more than the price of the item through a normal retailer. Just because it's on eBay, that doesn't mean it's cheaper than from the alternatives.

Buying audio gear is a joy and a disease. New gear can stimulate the creative process, as well as allow for higher quality work, but endless gear research, purchases, and learning curves can become a distraction from making recordings. Plan carefully, shop wisely, and take some breaks from the endless cycle of upgrading.

245

Appendix

Digital Audio Formats, Delivery, and Storage

Of all the sections in this book, this may be the most difficult one to keep up to date. Digital formats are a constantly shifting array of file types, sampling rates, and bit depths. Audio delivery demands fluctuate, depending on the ultimate use for the audio, and the same audio may need to be delivered in a variety of formats for a variety of uses. Digital audio storage options are constantly expanding, but questions of compatibility and longevity remain as potential problems with storage and archiving. The following is certainly not exhaustive, but it provides a primer for both technical and practical considerations at the time of this writing.

Digital Audio Formats—Recording

Audio recording formats differ primarily in their bit rate and sample depth. You may think of digital audio as the computer-language equivalent of taking a picture of audio content. Digital audio formats will vary based on the amount of information contained in each picture (bit depth) and the number of pictures taken per second (sampling rate). CD audio is set to a bit depth of 16 and sampling rate of 44.1 kHz. This means that each "picture," or each sample of audio that is converted into digital code from the original analog sound, contains 16 bits of information. In computer language, "16 bits" refers to 16 ones or zeros, each one counting as one bit. The number of "pictures" or bytes of information used to create CD audio is 44.1 kHz, which means there are 44,100 lines of 16 ones and zeros used to describe each second of digital audio contained on a CD.

Early digital recorders used lower bit depths and sample rates to record audio, but with the advent of the ADAT format, multitrack tape-based systems that were roughly equivalent to the CD standard came to be widely used (16-bit, 48 kHz). Computer-based systems (DAWs) also used something akin to the CD standard, but it was the migration of DAWs to a 24-bit format that was critical to their widespread acceptance as the recording devices of choice. Though the final audio program is often reduced back to 16-bit for CDs, or even lower resolution for mp3s and other formats that use compression to reduce file size, the 24-bit standard allows for much greater detail than 16-bit in the initial recording. Software engineers have found a variety of techniques to take advantage of that detail in the final conversion from 24-bit to lower resolution formats.

Sample rates above 44.1 kHz are available in many DAWs, and recordists vary in their use. The 48 kHz was the digital standard for high-quality audio before the CD standard was accepted, so it remains an option on most DAWs. While 48 kHz offers the benefits of slightly more information per second, it has the disadvantage of requiring complex conversion to get to 44.1 kHz if the final delivery is going to be for CD production. Some engineers chose 48 kHz nonetheless, but I prefer to record as 44.1 kHz to avoid the sample rate conversion when the program material is prepared for CD manufacture.

Sample rates of 88.2 kHz, 96 kHz, 176.4 kHz, and 192 kHz are available with some systems and are used by some recordists all the time and by others for specific projects. The advantage is greater detail, although listening tests seem to indicate a pretty modest improvement—as opposed to the difference between 16-bit and 24-bit audio, which sounds like a dramatic shift in detail to most professional participants in critical listening tests. In general, program material with a lot of very complex harmonics and great dynamic range—such as solo piano, string quartet, and the like—will benefit more from these higher sampling rates than dense material such as found in most popular music. The higher sampling rates also require a lot more processing power for running plug-ins and files with complex automation, and they need twice or four times as much disc space to store the audio. For these reasons, I find most recordists on most projects using the 24-bit, 44.1 kHz audio file format.

Audio files also require a certain amount of nonaudio information, generally contained as header information that precedes the actual bits and bytes of the audio that has been converted from analog to digital. The nature of this header information, and the format used to deliver it, is what differentiates file types such as Wave files and AIFF files. There are many other file protocols, such as red-book audio for CDs and orange-book audio for CD-Rs, and there are other DAW recording formats—mostly legacy formats like the Pro Tools Sound Designer II files—but Wave files and AIFF files dominate the DAW recording landscape. Wave files use the .wav appendix and AIFF files use the .aif appendix. Because Wave files went through a variety of forms, there has been a move to standardize the Wave file format under the name Broadcast Wave Format that uses the .bwf appendix. The main advantage to the Broadcast Wave Format is the inclusion of metadata, including a timecode stamp. The inclusion of the timecode stamp with the audio allows you to import audio from one DAW to another while maintaining the correct audio region locations. Despite the differences, most DAWs can recognize and utilize any of the variations in Wave files.

In general, using .wav or .bwf files for your recordings is the best idea, as it gives you the most widespread compatibility across systems. However,

AIFF files are required in certain delivery situations, such as for many DVD authoring houses, because some popular DVD authoring programs recognize .aif files but not .wav files. Many DAWs can handle mixed file formats (e.g., some .wav files and some .aif files), though not Pro Tools, which requires a single-file format for each session. In any event, almost all of them can convert from one format to another if you need to do this for production or delivery purposes.

Digital Audio Formats—Consumer

The fundamental information regarding digital audio formats for consumers remains bit depth and sampling rate. As described above, CD players use a 16-bit, 44.1 kHz format—or 44,100 16-bit samples every second—to decode the audio program. That's a lot of ones and zeros, but a second is a long time in musical terms (often two or more beats) and sound is complex. Whether or not the CD standard does an adequate job of defining audio detail has long been debated. Certainly, software engineers and recordists have found ways to pack more detail into the CD audio format. In any event, consumer formats with more and less detail proliferate, but it is the format with considerably less detail, the mp3, that threatens to overtake (or already has overtaken) CD audio as the new standard audio format.

The mp3 format uses a variety of sophisticated techniques to try to retain as much fidelity as possible while reducing the file size considerably from the CD standard—typical mp3 files are about 1/10 the size of their CD audio equivalent. Unlike CD audio, mp3s may use a variety of bit rates and sampling rates and can still be read (played) by an mp3 player. The standard for mp3 is a bit rate of 128 kbps and a sampling rate of 44.1 kHz, but there are many lower and some higher resolution options available. There are also a variety of encoding schemes available.

Mp3s became very popular because they allowed audio to be transmitted and downloaded relatively quickly over the Internet. As Internet connections and computers have gotten faster, the options for downloadable audio have increased and we are seeing more and more options for higher quality audio, including audio in the CD format, available for purchase and download.

Commercial audio formats that provide higher resolution files than the CD format have been developed, but none has found much traction in the marketplace. Competition between formats such as DVD-Audio (DVD-A) and Super Audio CD (SACD) hasn't helped higher quality audio find a consumer base. Surround sound (5.1 audio format) has found a large user base for home theater use, but it has yet to attract much interest in audio-only formats. Audio professionals need to be familiar with surround-sound audio-delivery formats (below) if they work on sound for film, video, computer games, or other surround-oriented consumer products.

Digital Audio Delivery

The best method for delivering digital audio depends on its ultimate purpose. Here, I cover delivery for CD mastering, CD manufacturing, Internet applications, film and video applications, and video games. In many instances, it will be necessary for you to talk with the person who will be working with the audio that you are delivering, as different applications require different audio formats even though they may ultimately be put to the same use (e.g., streaming audio over the Internet can use a variety of source file formats, but the particular Webmaster you are delivering to may require a certain format for their application).

Delivery for CD mastering

Although different mastering engineers and mastering houses will want different file formats, depending on the programs they are running, there are two primary considerations for how to deliver your mixed master to the mastering engineer (even if you are the mastering engineer, too). The first is to provide the highest quality file format possible. This generally means maintaining the bit depth and bit rate that you used for your individual files before creating the mixed master. If you recorded at 24-bit, 44.1 kHz (as I usually do), you will want to deliver your mixes in that same format, if possible. If you recorded at 48 kHz or at a higher sampling rate, you will want to maintain that sample rate as long as you've cleared the format with the person who will be doing the mastering. One of the keys to providing the highest quality files is to do as little file conversion as possible prior to the mastering stage. The final CD master will have to be 16-bit, 44.1 kHz, but assuming you started with higher resolution files, conversion to this format should be postponed until the last stage of file processing.

The second requirement is to provide files without any brickwall limiting. Because brickwall limiting has become such a prominent part of final music delivery to the consumer, and because it affects the sound so dramatically, I find that I must complete my mixes using a brickwall limiter so that I can hear the likely effects of its use. However, in mastering I deliver (or use myself, if I'm doing the mastering) my final mix with the brickwall limiter removed so that it can be added back in as the final processor before creation of the mastered mix. If I'm delivering files to a different mastering engineer (not doing it myself), I provide a file without brickwall limiting for use in the mastering, but I also provide a version with brickwall limiting so the mastering engineer can hear what I consider to be the actual sound of the final mix.

Delivery for CD manufacturing

If you are doing the mastering for CD release, the master you deliver will be a CD-R that is an exact version of the way you want the manufactured CD to sound and play. Along with the music, mastered with all the processing and sequencing issues handled just as you want them, the CD-R should contain the metadata that the artist or record company want encoded along with the disk. Typically, this includes the title of the CD, the artist's name, and all of the song titles along with the ISRC codes that I discussed in the chapter on mastering. Some CD-R burning programs allow you to print out a document that contains the critical information regarding the timing and encoding of the burned master. Manufacturing houses like to see this document to confirm what they are reading from the CD-R master, but it is not essential and most manufacturers will accept masters without the printout. It is important that you have given your CD-R master a careful listen to make sure that it doesn't have any flaws that might have come from a poor burning run or a faulty CD-R.

In terms of burning protocols for CD-R masters, there is only one essential and that is that to use the disc-at-once (DAO) burning protocol and not track-at-once (TAO). TAO has become rare, and some burning programs no longer even offer it as an option, but you should check to make sure that you are burning DAO. In terms of what brand of CD-R medium to use and what speed to record at, the opinions vary, but independent lab tests have not shown that recording at slower speeds or using higher priced "premium" CD-Rs produce better results. In fact, in some instances, faster record speeds produce discs with fewer errors. In most cases, almost any CD-R medium and burn speed will produce error rates well below anything near a danger level that would produce any negative results when used for manufacturing. The best advice is to find discs and burn speeds that work well for your burner and use those as your standard.

Delivery for Internet applications

The ultimate file format that will be used for Internet applications may vary widely, but the delivery file is most frequently an mp3 which is then converted or reprocessed as needed by the Webmaster. Protocols for downloading and streaming vary, and the Webmaster may ask for files in a variety of formats as well as mp3s, including mp4's, RealAudio, and/or QuickTime Audio. If you are delivering audio for these kinds of applications, you may need to invest in software that will convert to a variety of formats, or you can ask the Webmaster if they can handle the conversion for you. I always try to deliver the audio in the CD format as well, so that the client has this on file for reference or for use in later applications where higher quality audio can be used.

Many of these Internet file protocols, including mp3s, contain more encoded metadata information than a CD-R. A musical category can be designated, which will enable the music to be sorted and potentially recommended in consumer searches. Information about the original CD release, number of tracks, position of this track in the sequence, whether the CD was a compilation, and so on, can be included with the file, as well as have a link to the artwork if this has been posted at a particular Internet address. I expect digital file formats to continue to add metadata capabilities to further integrate music tracks into the media datastream that is contained on an individual's computer.

Delivery for film and video

Audio for film and video may require synchronization with the visual elements. Obviously, dialogue requires sync, but so do most sound effects and music cues. In order to work effectively to picture, you will need to import a movie file into your DAW. The movie file should be a "window dub," which means that the SMPTE timecode location number has been burned into a small window at the bottom of each frame. Establishing and maintaining sync through the use of timecode is beyond the scope of this book, but a few words about file formats may get you started with understanding the requirements for this kind of delivery.

Audio that accompanies picture may end up in a variety of formats, from VCR tapes to big-screen movie projection, but the most common delivery format right now for picture with sound is DVD. In any event, the file format that will be required will vary depending on which editing and/or authoring program is being used. Surround sound (typically 5.1 surround) is increasingly common for film and video, so you may need to supply both stereo and surround audio files (see below regarding the surround format). You will need to work closely with the other content providers, including the authoring, editing, and packaging people, if you are providing sound that is to accompany visual elements.

Delivery of surround-sound files

Surround comes in various formats, but the dominant format is 5.1 surround, made up of left, right, center, rear left, rear right, and LFE (low-frequency extension) channels. The rear channels are often referred to as the "surround" channels—they feed the "surround" speakers in back or to the sides of the listener. The LFE channel is, in fact, a distinct channel, so there are actually six channels of audio, but because it is not full frequency (carrying only subwoofer information—typically from about 90 Hz and below), it is referred to as the .1 channel of 5.1.

Format requirements for delivery of 5.1 audio may differ, but the standard is 48 kHz, 16-bit AIFF files, as this is what is used in the most prominent authoring programs. Surround for DVD will be encoded as an AAC file for Dolby or some other codec for a different surround format, such as DTS. Usually the audio person supplies the 48 kHz, 16-bit AIFF files, and the encoding is taken care of at the DVD authoring stage. If you are required to supply encoded files, you will need to get either a program that does the encoding or an add-on for your DAW that allows you to do this encoding within the DAW.

The standard order for 5.1 files is as follows:

Channel 1: Front left
Channel 2: Front right
Channel 3: Center
Channel 4: LFE
Channel 5: Rear left
Channel 6: Rear right

It is critical that the files be in this order for them to encode properly.

Delivery for video games

Formats for delivery of audio for video games may vary, but it is likely that you will be asked to deliver a stereo mix, stems (described below), and possibly a 5.1 surround mix. Because video games require so much music to accompany the many hours of game play, each audio element may get used in different versions at different times. In order to do this, stereo stems are made, taken from the final stereo mix. A *stem* is simply an element taken from the larger mix of the composition; taken all together, the stems recombine to form the original composition and mix. A typical group of stems might be broken down as follows: drums, percussion, bass, guitars, and keyboards. In this case, there would be five stems. More complex compositions may require more stems, such as drums, high percussion, low percussion, bass, rhythm guitars, lead guitars, horn section, piano, keyboards, lead vocal, and harmony vocals—making a total of 11 stems. Once the final mix is done, stems are made by simply muting all other tracks and running a "mix" of each particular stem element. Again, in all of these collaborative projects that combine audio and other elements, you will need to coordinate your work with those working on other parts of the project.

Digital Audio Storage

Hard drives have become the primary medium for audio storage. The key hard-drive configuration options are computer interface, size of drive, speed of drive, drive buffer size, and drive bridge. There are new developments regarding each one of these drive options so frequently that the following information can be used as a guideline, but you may need to do additional research to determine your best options at any given time.

For audio storage, it is best to use the fastest available interface, though of course both your computer and your DAW must support it. The most common interfaces are USB-1, USB-2, firewire 400, and firewire 800. The firewire 800 connection will be the fastest, and should be used when possible. SATA drives, which are replacing the traditional ATA/IDE drives in many new computers, use a new interface protocol called eSATA (external Serial ATA), which is faster still. A USB-1 interface is not fast enough to handle typical recording requirements; it can be used for storage, but not for recording.

Hard-drive storage sizes continue to expand, and to get cheaper and more readily available. It can be problematic for a computer to manage very large drives; the hardware and operating systems don't always keep up with the latest in available drive capacities. However, drives as big as a terabyte (1,000 gigabytes) are becoming common, reasonably priced, and can be managed by most recent model computers. Because audio requires quite a bit of storage space, and because you get bigger drives for comparatively less money, the big drives represent good value for audio storage. A terabyte drive might hold as many as 10 complete, typically sized CD projects or more (depending on how much audio was recorded for each project, of course).

There are portable hard drives (3.5-inch drives) that are powered from your computer (buss powered, meaning that no AC is required) and may connect via USB or firewire. Very small USB flash drives have become common. The flash drives currently come in sizes up to 256 GB (gigabytes), with larger models on the way. These little drives are inexpensive and fit in your pocket—great for transporting data, such as grabbing files of a single song to move from the studio to home. You may be able to effectively record on a firewire portable drive, but it is unlikely that you will be able to record to or play back from a flash drive that uses current technology.

Drive speed is an important factor in allowing for large quantities of data transfer as is required for large audio sessions. Older drives and some of the portable drives spin at 5,200 or 5,400 rpm, and this can create problems with larger files. Drives that spin at 7,200 rpm are much better suited for audio. There are a few drives running at 10,000 rpm, but this is not necessary for even very large audio files. The newer Solid State Drives (SSD) are faster still, but as of this writing only available with relatively smaller storage capacity. It seems likely that SSD drives, without the moving parts of a traditional hard drive, will find their place, especially for remote and portable recording systems.

Drive buffer or cache size is also important, and larger drives require larger caches to function smoothly when handling large amounts of audio. Although drives as large as 1 terabyte will probably provide adequate performance with 16 MB caches, 32 MB is recommended for 1 terabyte and above. The chipsets that handle the hard-drive operations also affect data-transfer speed and reliability, and some have been developed specifically for streaming large quantities of audio and video. The Oxford 911 chipset for FW400 (Firewire 400) connections, the Oxford 912 for FW800, and the Oxford 934 for SATA drives are frequently used by drives that are maximized for handling a lot of data. Multiple hard drives can be set up in RAID enclosures (redundant array of independent disks) that require only one connection to the computer.

Many of the specs described above are changing so frequently as to require new research each time you buy a new drive. There are various packagers

253

of drives that are optimized for media (audio and video), and it is a good idea to use them as resources for the latest in specs and stick to their products, if possible; not all of them charge substantially more just for being "specialized" media drive. DVD-R (recordable DVD discs) can be used for relatively small file storage, and even CD-Rs hold enough data for some backup or transfer functions. The plethora of legacy storage media, from Exabyte tape drives, to zip drives, and back to the variously sized floppy drives, reminds us that storage formats come and go.

Online Glossary Link

A comprehensive glossary of audio terms requires a lot of entries. There is not the space to undertake such a project here, but fortunately there is a very good audio and recording glossary available on the Internet. The online audio store Sweetwater is an excellent source of information about gear, as well as one of many good options for online purchasing, and it has an outstanding glossary provided as a public service. The glossary can be accessed here:

http://www.sweetwater.com/expert-center/glossary/

Index

Note

Italic page numbers indicate photographs, screen shots, or diagrams.

255

269